THE RIGHT KIND OF
REVOLUTION

THE RIGHT KIND OF REVOLUTION

Modernization, Development, and U.S. Foreign Policy from the Cold War to the Present

Michael E. Latham

CORNELL UNIVERSITY PRESS   ITHACA AND LONDON

First published 2011 by Cornell University Press
First printing, Cornell Paperbacks, 2011

Printed in the United States of America

Library of Congress Cataloging-in-Publication Data

Latham, Michael E.
   The right kind of revolution : modernization, development, and U.S. foreign policy from the Cold War to the present / Michael E. Latham.
      p. cm.
   Includes bibliographical references and index.
   ISBN 978-0-8014-4604-7 (cloth : alk. paper)
   ISBN 978-0-8014-7726-3 (pbk. : alk. paper)
   1. United States—Foreign relations—1945–1989.   2. United States—Foreign relations—1989–   I. Title.
   E840.L38   2011
   327.73009'04—dc22   2010029822

Cornell University Press strives to use environmentally responsible suppliers and materials to the fullest extent possible in the publishing of its books. Such materials include vegetable-based, low-VOC inks and acid-free papers that are recycled, totally chlorine-free, or partly composed of nonwood fibers. For further information, visit our website at www.cornellpress.cornell.edu.

Cloth printing   10 9 8 7 6 5 4 3 2 1
Paperback printing   10 9 8 7 6 5 4 3 2

For Jennifer, Maile, and Anya

Contents

Acknowledgments

In writing this book I received assistance from many sources, and it is a great pleasure to express my thanks here. At Cornell University Press, Alison Kalett originally suggested this project and guided it through the initial stages. Michael McGandy provided expert advice as I wrote the manuscript, seeing it through to completion. Ange Romeo-Hall and Marian Rogers played vital roles in the production process. I am grateful to them all.

In addition to the intellectual debts acknowledged in the notes, I have benefited from conversations with many colleagues. Mario del Pero provided me with a chance to present elements of this work at the University of Bologna, and Niu Ke's invitation allowed me to trade ideas with scholars at Beijing University and the Beijing Forum. Anonymous referees helped me frame the book's argument and improve its presentation, and Frank Ninkovich gave the entire manuscript a thorough, insightful reading. Part of chapter 5 was previously published in *Third World Quarterly* 27 (2006), and I thank the journal for permission to incorporate that material here.

Fordham University provided essential resources as well. A Faculty Fellowship allowed me to dedicate several months to writing, and my colleagues in the University Library, the History Department, the Fordham College at Rose Hill Dean's Office, and the Office of Academic Affairs all supported this work. Samanta Brihaspat, Sean Byrnes, Patrick Hege, and Philip Pilmar provided excellent research assistance.

My greatest thanks go to my family. My parents, Nancy and Peter Latham, and my sister, Jules Latham, were sources of encouragement throughout. This book is dedicated with love and gratitude to my wife, Jennifer Briggs Latham, and our daughters, Maile and Anya.

INTRODUCTION

On September 23, 2003, six months after the United States and its coalition partners invaded Iraq, President George W. Bush addressed the United Nations General Assembly. The United States and its allies, he argued, had done more than simply remove Saddam Hussein from power and ensure that his regime would never threaten neighboring states with "weapons of mass destruction." The invasion had also radically altered Iraq's future, and that of an entire region. "The success of a free Iraq," Bush declared, would demonstrate that "freedom, equality, and material progress are possible at the heart of the Middle East. Leaders in the region will face the clearest evidence that free institutions and open societies are the only path to long-term national success and dignity." A "transformed Middle East," he promised, would also "benefit the entire world, by undermining the ideologies that export violence to other lands."[1]

As the president framed it, his administration's initiative was a novel response to a radically new era, the "post-9/11 world." The "war on terrorism," Bush and his advisers explained, required that the United States respond to unprecedented threats. In "failed states" like Afghanistan, they argued, conditions of poverty, insecurity, and unmet hopes provided fertile ground for the growth of radical ideologies, allowing movements like the Taliban to emerge and providing terrorist groups with sanctuary and support. In brutal regimes like Saddam Hussein's Iraq, they warned, the suppression of freedom had given rise to "rogue states" that rejected peaceful diplomacy, defied nonproliferation conventions, and sponsored international terrorism. The United States, however, could now reverse those dangerous trends by promoting larger, structural changes in the world's environment.

The Bush administration's vision of broad transformation, and its ultimate turn toward "nation building," many agreed, marked a striking departure. Prior to the terrorist attacks of September 11, 2001, commentators observed, the administration had avoided speaking in such terms, choosing instead to condemn the Clinton administration's failed interventions in places like Somalia and Haiti. Others pointed out that "neoconservatives" within the administration had gained new authority after the attacks, and argued that it was their specific and exceptional influence that led to this sudden, moralistic emphasis on the promotion of democracy and the redirection of foreign societies. Charged rhetoric declaring the start of "World War III" or even "World War IV" also contributed to the impression of a stark, fundamental turning point.[2]

On a deeper level, however, the Bush administration's arguments were not new at all. Only a little more than a decade after the close of the Cold War, the president and his advisers had actually returned to a very familiar theme, promising that the United States would once more fight a war of potentially infinite duration for absolute ends. By declaring that the United States would define the "path" of the region and create a "transformed Middle East," moreover, George W. Bush invoked an older set of assumptions that had become deeply embedded in the intellectual and political life of the United States much earlier in the twentieth century.

I am most interested in that wider, more enduring trajectory, and the way that the concept of modernization embodied a long-standing conviction that the United States could fundamentally direct and accelerate the historical course of the postcolonial world. At the height of its influence during the Cold War, modernization was an intellectual framework as well as a political objective. It described the transformation that the world's so-called emerging nations were experiencing, and proposed ways to shape and guide that process. Put forward as a model useful for studying the new states appearing as European empires collapsed, theories of modernization stressed several overlapping principles. First, they argued that *traditional* and *modern* societies were fundamentally distinct in nature. In some societies, the forces of culture and religion provided the integrating values and ideals, shaping economic life, political organizations, and human attitudes toward the external environment. In others, however, a great transformation had occurred. In place of received authority, a new emphasis on individual achievement took hold. Where production was once local and limited, capitalist economies geared toward expanded production and future investment now reigned. While the laws of custom dominated traditional politics, in modern societies complex bureaucracies and diverse institutions provided avenues for social mobility and responsible, democratic authority.

Theorists also argued that social, economic, and political changes were fundamentally integrated, such that transformations in one aspect of a society would necessarily trigger others, producing systematic results. Modernization, in this regard, was a comprehensive process driven forward across multiple fronts. As new technologies reshaped traditional economies, new political organizations and values systems emerged as well. The import of modern media, in turn, altered the psychology of traditional men and women, changing the way they perceived their relationship to their fellow citizens and creating opportunities for rapid political and economic transformations. Where common culture and history once preserved them in a stable, long-term equilibrium, the irrepressible force of modernization made traditional societies tenuous and transitory. In historical terms, finally, such changes had a clear direction. Although societies moved at different rates, they ultimately traveled toward the same destination. Despite differences of culture or history, they would eventually converge on common forms. In the mid–twentieth century, leading U.S. social scientists, government officials, and political commentators identified that universal end point with their own society. The United States was, in their terms, the world's "first new nation." Itself the product of an anticolonial revolution, the United States' liberal values, capitalist economy, and pluralist democracy provided an example of what a truly modern society could become.

Concerned with questions of economic growth, industrialization, and rising living standards in addition to fundamental social and political changes, theories of modernization clearly resonated with broader visions of development. What made modernization so compelling to U.S. foreign policymakers, however, was the promise of acceleration, and the perceived potential to link the promotion of development with the achievement of security. As European political power faded and the Cold War's ideological lines hardened, U.S. policymakers came to envision modernization as a way to speed up the course of history. By using development aid, technical assistance, foreign investment, and integrated planning, they hoped to accelerate the passage of traditional societies through a necessary yet destabilizing process in which older values, ideas, and structures gave way to the liberal, capitalist, and democratic ways of life that they recognized most clearly in the United States itself. Because Communists preyed on vulnerable societies in the throes of this fundamental transition, efforts to drive emerging nations down this common historical path would help ensure a safer, more peaceful world.

Modernization, in that regard, functioned as an ideology. Academic and scholarly research on the subject, much of it supported by the U.S. government, made its way into policymaking. Philanthropic foundations and nongovernment organizations also promoted modernization in important ways, often with their own particular agendas. But modernization's influence cannot be explained simply by tracing the movement of experts from universities into Washington agencies and New York offices. Modernization was most powerful because it resonated with cultural understandings. It reiterated an idea deeply held by liberals in the United States in a period of postwar affluence—that their society stood at history's leading edge and that they possessed the power to transform a world struggling in its wake. As historian Nils Gilman noted, Americans imagined modernization as "the right kind of revolution," a process that they could direct and control for the benefit of all concerned. Modernization promised an altruistic solution to some of the Cold War's most vexing problems, suggesting that the United States could promote democracy and alleviate poverty. It would not only contain the dangers of Communist subversion but also dramatically improve the lives of millions of people in Africa, Asia, the Middle East, and Latin America.[3]

Modernization certainly was not the only force shaping U.S. policies directed toward the postcolonial world. Economic and strategic interests, driven by the need to preserve access to vital natural resources, keep markets open, and shore up European allies, were often crucial motives. Fears about possible damage to the credibility of the United States also shaped U.S. policy in influential ways. Nor was modernization always readily accepted and endorsed by U.S. officials. As an ideology, however, modernization provided a compelling explanation of how decolonization affected the world and what the United States might do in response to it.

Since the mid-1990s, historians of U.S. foreign relations have increasingly focused on modernization to explore the way that Cold War policymakers and intellectuals sought to define and accelerate the future of a developing world. Specialized studies have treated modernization's intellectual history, its deployment in specific national cases, and its impact at particular points in time, focusing especially on the late 1950s and early 1960s. What remains missing, however, is an integrated analysis of this scholarship, one that explores the way that modernization was deployed across a wide range of geographic regions, and puts forward an argument about its deeper roots and enduring legacies. This critical synthesis shows that in actual practice modernization rarely went as its architects anticipated. Combining reformist injunctions with the deployment of tremendous force, modernizers often wound up helping to create authoritarian, dictatorial regimes instead of liberal states. Because the universal assumptions of modernization promoted a disregard for the significance of local history and culture, defining them as transitory matters, modernizers also reduced crucial political problems to matters of mere administration and technical expertise. The cultural and ideological appeal of modernization, moreover, often blinded its advocates to evidence of policy failure.

To explore this history, this book presents a combination of chronological and thematic chapters. The chronological sections provide an expanded study of modernization, evaluating the rise, partial collapse, and subsequent reformulation of the concept. The thematic chapters analyze modernization in practice, focusing on attempts by the United States to promote it in diverse geographical settings and exploring parallels among them. As these cases illustrate, even as U.S. policymakers promoted their vision of modernization, foreign actors embraced, modified, and reformulated it to serve their own ends. Modernization, in that regard, was not simply directed by the United States. Those on the "receiving end" of U.S. programs instead contested and negotiated its deployment in important ways.

Although most studies tend to date its emergence in the late 1940s and 1950s, in chapter 1 I argue that thinking in the United States about modernization had older foundations. Theories of modernization were grounded in Enlightenment concepts of social progress, and the United States' imperial experiences in the Philippines and Latin America were important antecedents as well. While development was already the subject of a broad, international discourse in the early twentieth century, the thinking of Woodrow Wilson and Franklin Delano Roosevelt helped create the framework for a distinctly American ideology of modernization to emerge. Their concern with the deeper, structural forces at work in world politics, and their commitment to a broadly internationalist vision linking U.S. security to the global environment, profoundly shaped the way that later policymakers tried to understand and respond to the impact of decolonization in the Cold War period.

Chapter 2 then puts modernization in the context of U.S. Cold War culture. In it I analyze the rise of the global Cold War, the dilemmas that U.S. officials faced in dealing with nationalist, anticolonial revolutions, and the reasons that a theory of modernization became so appealing in the 1950s and early 1960s. After tracing the rise of modernization as an intellectual framework in the fields of sociology, political science, and economics, I explore how and why modernization seemed to provide a solution to pressing foreign-policy problems. I also argue that modernization became most influential because it crystallized a deeper set of cultural understandings.

In chapter 3 I focus on how modernization shaped the relationship between the United States and the first generation of postcolonial states. As cases drawn from India, Egypt, and Ghana demonstrate, even as U.S. policymakers tried to promote modernization and direct its course, foreign actors embraced, modified, and reformulated the ideology to fit their own purposes. Nationalist leaders were eager to transform their own societies, hoping to stimulate economic growth, promote industry, raise agricultural productivity, fight poverty, and improve education. But their diverse visions of development did not easily fit into the more rigid, American template. Where the United States sought to promote a kind of global New Deal and aimed to create capitalist, market-based economies and liberal states, postcolonial leaders proved far more willing to experiment, combining elements of American and Soviet experience in attempts to generate more rapid progress. Deeply committed to policies of nonalignment and determined to preserve their hard-won sovereignty, they also rejected U.S. attempts to link the delivery of U.S. and international foreign assistance to changes in their foreign policies.

U.S. policymakers, social scientists, and nongovernment organizations also envisioned technology as a key catalyst of postcolonial modernization. As I explain in chapter 4, experts were especially worried about the twin problems of rapid population growth and low agricultural productivity. In the postcolonial world, they feared, high birthrates and declining mortality rates would trigger a population explosion that would prevent development by consuming scarce resources. Growing destitution and the threat of famine, moreover, would lead to greater political instability, opening doors to radicalism and subversion. New birth control technologies and genetically modified seeds, however, presented an appealing solution, and modernizers in the United States joined forces with a thriving, transnational network of nongovernment organizations, philanthropic foundations, United Nations agencies, and foreign governments to limit human fertility and increase agricultural productivity. Their efforts, however, frequently produced unintended consequences and deleterious results. Emphasizing the control of populations over the rights of individuals, they promoted coercive policies, deepened inequality, and damaged fragile environments.

In this regard, the story of modernization is an ironic one. U.S. liberals sincerely believed that their efforts would improve the postcolonial world and the lives of those within it. They imagined that modernization would replace the injustices of racism and imperialism, ensuring progress and development for peoples long seen as inherently incapable of advancement. At the same time, however, they were deeply ambivalent about democracy, distrustful of populist politics, and far more comfortable with the idea of elite-led societies. While they often described modernization as a kind of "revolution," they were most interested in promoting revolutions from above, fundamentally altering foreign societies in ways that clearly fit U.S. security goals. As I argue in chapter 5, moreover, their overriding Cold War concerns often led them to pursue policies that had little to do with liberation of any kind. In Guatemala, South Vietnam, and Iran, U.S. officials and policymakers turned to modernization as a means of counterinsurgency and control. In each case they shed their tenuous commitment to democratic values in favor of repressive policies that shored up dictatorial regimes and ultimately helped create the very dangers that they hoped to avoid.

These failures, in turn, contributed to the growing challenge to modernization in the late 1960s and 1970s. As I contend in chapter 6, modernization told a compelling story of American advance and promised that the United States might direct the course of an emerging world. Yet by the end of the 1960s the optimistic foundations of this vision were seriously undermined. The United States' own domestic problems appeared far more intractable than previously assumed, raising questions about whether the United States presented a model worthy of global emulation. The devastation of the failed war in Vietnam, moreover, deepened intellectual and political criticism of modernization's pretensions. While scholars attacked the paradigm's assumptions, experts and practitioners also came to reject it as a framework for development, calling for a new focus on issues of inequality, basic needs, sustainability, the environment, and gender. As development came to be seen as a far more complex and even infinite task, conservative, "neoliberal" arguments ultimately took the field, replacing modernization's vision of a global New Deal with their own, market-centered promise of swift transformation.

The final chapter analyzes the resurgence since the end of the Cold War of a reformulated version of modernization. In contrast to other studies claiming that modernization died in the late 1960s and 1970s, I argue that rumors of its demise have been greatly exaggerated. Although they now focused much more heavily on the magic of markets, U.S. policymakers again confronted crises in Latin America, Asia, Africa, and especially the Middle East by linking the promotion of development with the enhancement of U.S. security. As they did during the Cold War, they also argued that history had a clear, universal direction, and that the United States could accelerate it, dramatically reconstructing supposedly malleable foreign societies in benevolent ways.

Above all, modernization provided a powerful and appealing narrative. It promised that sweeping changes were possible, and that the world would be rapidly transformed. Social scientists of the Cold War period emphasized that a concentrated "big push" of directed investment and foreign aid would allow postcolonial societies to reach the crucial "take-off" point, after which they would enter the period of "self-sustaining growth," ready and able to advance without recourse to external help. From the 1980s onward, neoliberals presented their own panaceas. Just get the state out of the way and let markets do their work, they insisted, and the rising tide of prosperity would lift all boats.

History, however, has not turned out that way. Nearly fifty years ago, in his famous inaugural address, John F. Kennedy made a solemn promise. "To those peoples in the huts and villages of half the globe, struggling to break the bonds of mass misery," he declared, "we pledge our best efforts to help them help themselves, for whatever period is required—not because the Communists may be doing it, not because we seek their votes, but because it is right." That promise went unfulfilled. Contrary to Kennedy's statement, U.S. attempts to link development with the imperatives of security left U.S. policymakers unable to reach an accommodation with nonaligned, nationalist visions of progress. Focused on the goal of accelerating history's course, through the 1960s and into the 1970s leaders in government, philanthropic foundations, and universities deployed technologies with little attention to the socioeconomic and cultural context in which they functioned. Their focus on aggregate measures of growth also led them to disregard questions of individual rights and welfare, leading them to cast a blind eye to coercive applications and regressive effects. Distrustful of democracy, they aligned themselves with authoritarian governments that devastated their own populations.

The neoliberal recasting of modernization that took hold in the 1980s did not fare much better. Post–Cold War interventions in Africa, Central America, and the Caribbean did not suddenly create thriving market-democracies. The drive to remake Iraq resulted in a long, bloody engagement, and while violence there started to level off and decline, it did so only after five years of intense, devastating war. In 2010, the Afghan war remained a quagmire, with little chance of a quick resolution or any major advances in that country's development. The high human and material cost of "nation building" in Iraq and Afghanistan raises serious questions about the ability of the United States to continue trying to reorder the world. More broadly, at the start of the twenty-first century, hunger afflicted the livelihood of approximately 800 million people, over 10 percent of the global population. More than 1 billion, roughly one-sixth of the global total, lived in what the World Bank defined as "extreme poverty," surviving on one dollar per day or less. The deep divide between the world's affluent and poor countries has continued to grow. To make matters worse, older diseases like malaria and measles and newer ones like AIDS have added to the spiraling death toll. Environmental damage has also accelerated, while global climate change threatens to imperil some of the poorest regions of the world.[4]

Modernization remains an enduring American ideology, but it is a poor guide for policy. The global problems of poverty, inequality, and environment demand urgent national and international attention. But they cannot be successfully addressed through a framework that promises easy transformation and ignores the realities of history, culture, and local context. A determined campaign to alleviate global poverty and human suffering may indeed help enhance U.S. security, but programs built on the premises of modernization have often undermined that political objective. A critical examination of the wider history of modernization should help us understand those failures, and stimulate the pursuit of better alternatives.

NOTES

1. George W. Bush, Speech to the United Nations General Assembly, September 23, 2003, American Presidency Project, http://www.presidency.ucsb.edu/ws/index.php?pid=58801&st=&st1=.

2. Thomas Friedman, "World War III," Foreign Affairs, *New York Times,* September 13, 2001; Eliot A. Cohen, "World War IV: Let's Call This Conflict What It Is," *Wall Street Journal,* November 20, 2001.

3. Nils Gilman, *Mandarins of the Future: Modernization Theory in Cold War America* (Baltimore: Johns Hopkins University Press, 2003), 11–12.

4. Michael Hunt, *The American Ascendancy: How the United States Gained and Wielded Global Dominance* (Chapel Hill: University of North Carolina Press, 2007), 316–19.

SETTING THE FOUNDATIONS
Imperial Ideals, Global War, and Decolonization

On January 20, 1949, President Harry S. Truman delivered his inaugural address before a massive crowd of more than 100,000 spectators and a televised audience estimated at 10 million. Standing before the Capitol, he promised that the United States would seize the initiative in the struggle against communism, a "false philosophy" that offered only "deceit and mockery, poverty and tyranny," instead of democratic liberties, social justice, and individual rights. Three of the "four major courses of action" Truman proposed that afternoon—strong support for the United Nations, the continuation of the Marshall Plan, and the creation of NATO—were already well-established components of the U.S. approach to containing the Soviet danger. To the surprise of many commentators, however, the fourth point of Truman's speech turned in another, more striking direction— that of international development. "More than half the people of the world," he emphasized, "are living in conditions approaching misery. Their food is inadequate. They are victims of disease. Their economic life is primitive and stagnant. Their poverty is a threat both to them and to more prosperous areas." But now, "for the first time in history, humanity possesses the knowledge and skill to relieve the suffering of these people." The United States, Truman promised, would "embark on a bold new program for making the benefits of our scientific advances and industrial progress available for the improvement and growth of the underdeveloped areas." In stark contrast to "the old imperialism—exploitation for foreign profit," Truman heralded "development based on the concepts of democratic fair-dealing," a process that would help "the human family achieve the decent, satisfying life that is the right of all people."[1]

In many ways, Truman's "Point Four" proposal marked a pivotal moment. Amid the uncertainty of the early Cold War, as U.S. policymakers anxiously watched decolonization advance across Asia and move toward Africa, Truman officially committed the United States to a massive global project that would ultimately outlive the Cold War itself. He also defined that commitment in ways that would become central elements of a powerful ideological framework. First, by emphasizing the problem of "underdevelopment" among the members of the "human family," the president conveyed the idea that the destitute societies of the non-Western world were not trapped in an inevitable condition of "backwardness" by the particularities of race or culture. They were instead struggling to travel along the very same historical trajectory as the world's more advanced nations. The transmission of investment capital, technical knowledge, and activist values, moreover, could dramatically accelerate their productivity and progress, enabling them to leap the gap toward liberal modernity. Second, by defining poverty as a strategic threat, Truman firmly linked development and security. Just as the Marshall Plan and the reconstruction of Europe had "beaten back despair and defeatism and saved a number of countries from losing their liberty," development would alleviate the desperation in which radicalism flourished. Third, Truman framed U.S. support for development as an inherently anticolonial venture, and an expression of a new set of cooperative, mutually beneficial relationships among nations. As one State Department policy paper argued, the Point Four program would repel communism and replace imperialism. It would strengthen "political democracy" and show that "world development can take place peacefully and with increasing political freedom, as the energies of the masses of the people are released into channels of constructive effort aimed at greater production, greater exchange, and greater consumption." Finally, Truman's proposal suggested that development was ultimately a matter of scientific and technical expertise, a field governed more by the application of universally valid knowledge and technique than by questions of specific historical context or political choice. Though Americans did not yet use the term, Truman's proposal articulated the core elements of what would soon be referred to as modernization.[2]

Truman's ambitious, sweeping vision was not entirely original. The collapse of European empires, the growing strength of anticolonial nationalism, and the greatly amplified global power of the United States did indeed make the early Cold War a crucial period for American thinking about modernization. The concept's underlying assumptions, however, have a more deeply rooted history. Modernization was grounded in older imperial assumptions about the United States' ability to transform a foreign world, the legacies of Wilsonian thinking about the meaning of modernity, and shifting understandings of race, culture,

and the perils of revolutionary change. As an American ideology, modernization fit squarely within the larger history of liberal, internationalist visions of
an open, integrated world in which ideals and values as well as capital and commerce would flow across borders and markets. Its assumptions about the universal validity of U.S. institutions and the malleability of foreign societies were
also tempered by long-standing reservations about the nature of foreign peoples
and the need for their transformation to be carefully channeled and controlled.
Modernization put the United States on the leading edge of the world's history.
It promised a more productive, more just, and more democratic international
order. But it did so in ways that reflected a persistent ambivalence about the
people and societies that were to be transformed.

Imperialism and the Cause of Civilization

The idea that the United States is uniquely ordained to carry out a vital world-
historical role is deeply embedded in expressions of American identity. As
Thomas Paine boldly declared in 1776, the revolutionary commitment to natural rights and republicanism made America exceptional. "Every spot of the old
world is overrun with oppression," he wrote, and "freedom hath been hunted
round the globe." But America would "receive the fugitive, and prepare in time
an asylum for mankind." As the new country grew in territorial and economic
terms, a powerful nationalism emerged to link the expansion of the United States
with historical mission. New York newspaper editor and Democratic Party sup-
porter John O'Sullivan clearly defined that sense of "manifest destiny" in 1839.
"Our national birth," he proclaimed, "was the beginning of a new history, the
formation and progress of an untried political system, which separates us from
the past and connects us with the future only; and so far as regards the entire
development of the natural rights of man, in moral, political, and national life,
we may confidently assume that our country is destined to be the great nation
of futurity."[3]

Expansion across the North American continent, however, rarely involved attempts to ensure the liberation and development of the foreign peoples living
there. By the mid-nineteenth century, Americans had come to define expansion
less as the triumph of universally relevant republican ideals than as evidence of
the inherent superiority of the Anglo-Saxon race. In contrast to Paine's emphasis
on the exceptional characteristics of the "new world" experiment, by the 1850s
the growing popularity of racial determinism led Americans to identify themselves as the latest, most western branch of a transatlantic family. In historian
Reginald Horsman's words, "Americans had long believed they were a chosen

people, but by the mid-nineteenth century they also believed that they were a chosen people with an impeccable ancestry." As scholars emphasized the American rediscovery and recreation of purportedly ancient English liberties, and ethnologists classified the skull measurements of diverse racial "types," Native Americans and Mexicans were increasingly defined as mere obstacles to the execution of a biologically rooted mission. Americans considered the supposed lack of technological and material sophistication of such peoples as confirmation of their ultimate inferiority and doubted their innate capacity to adapt to the dominant society. While some reformers attempted to "civilize" Indians through the resettlement and educational efforts of the 1870s, Americans more commonly stressed the inevitable extinction of racial inferiors in competition with vigorous Anglo-Saxons. By the late nineteenth century, social Darwinist ideas were also invoked to justify wars of extermination as the natural manifestation of a universally progressive trend. At home, the solidification of rigid Jim Crow laws of segregation and sharply restrictive immigration policies also reflected the racial dimensions of republicanism.[4]

The idea of a racially inflected destiny also shaped the United States' acquisition of an overseas empire in 1898. The fundamental causes of U.S. imperialism at the turn of the century remain a source of intense debate, and historians have put forward competing explanations stressing the search for foreign markets, the pursuit of strategic interests, and growing psychosocial anxiety amid the rapid industrialization and political turmoil of the 1890s. Yet Americans also imagined their conquest of the Philippines and intervention in Cuba as part of a broader process in which they were taking on the obligations of a great power to act as a civilizing force in the world. American missionaries, traders, military officers, and administrators often invoked the British Empire as a model. For pro-imperialists like Indiana's Republican senator Albert Beveridge, taking the Philippines was an exalted, noble cause, for the "English-speaking and Teutonic peoples," ordained by God as "the master organizers of the world." Like their English cousins, Americans possessed the "blood of government." Ruling the Filipinos without their consent, moreover, was a simple necessity. "Would not the people of the Philippines," Beveridge asked, "prefer the just, humane, civilizing government of this Republic to the savage, bloody rule of pillage and extortion from which we have rescued them?" For many Americans at the turn of the century, overseas imperialism represented not so much a repudiation of republican values as the embrace of an international responsibility. Up to that point, many pro-imperialists argued, the United States had demonstrated its formidable industrial and commercial prowess but had exerted little influence in defining the wider world's future course. The time had now arrived for the United States to play a leading role in shaping a global civilization.[5]

It was at that moment, as part of the call for a civilizing imperialism in the Philippines, that U.S. officials, intellectuals, and opinion leaders took the first tentative steps toward a comprehensive vision of development. The process began haltingly. President McKinley spoke of a duty to "uplift" the Filipino masses, but he remained far more concerned with gaining a point of entry to the imagined potential of the Chinese market and keeping the islands out of Europe an hands. Most U.S. policymakers also shared the perspective of Secretary of War Elihu Root, who claimed that the Filipinos were "little advanced from pure savagery." As Princeton professor Woodrow Wilson concluded, "it would be wrong to try to give the same government now to the Philippine islands as we enjoy who have been schooled for centuries to the use of our liberties." The official policy of "benevolent assimilation," moreover, was carried out through a horrific counterinsurgency campaign. Between 1899 and 1902, the United States sent seventy thousand troops to suppress the Filipino revolutionaries. Tens of thousands of Filipino soldiers were killed, and probably as many as 700 thousand Filipino civilians died, many due to disease and malnutrition. U.S. commanders launched brutal attacks against Filipino guerrillas and destroyed homes, crops, and livestock. They ordered the torture of suspected insurgents, designated vast areas "free fire zones," and, in one case, ordered that the island of Samar be turned into a "howling wilderness." But, in an argument that would become all too familiar in the twentieth century, imperialists insisted that such lethal violence was necessary to prepare the ground for comprehensive reform. The invocation of American mission also helped overcome anti-imperial objections stressing the incompatibility of empire and democracy, the problem of assimilating racial inferiors, and the "degenerating" effects the Philippine environment might have on white settlers.[6]

In the aftermath of the war, the concept of development began to take firmer hold, bolstered by new arguments about the nature of the Filipinos themselves. In the process of creating a colonial state, U.S. imperialists reformulated their understandings of race and shifted away from the previous emphasis on the absolute debilities of nonwhite subjects. In place of the older language of "race war" and extermination, colonial administrators substituted what historian Paul Kramer referred to as a new, "aggressively optimistic colonialism of 'capacity'" defined by "progressive, future-oriented visions of Filipino evolution, maturation, and tutelary assimilation toward self-government under indefinite U.S. control." Claims of racial difference certainly did not vanish. Indeed, they justified the denial of independence to the Filipinos and resolved the apparent contradiction between imperial rule and republican principle. But the language of tutelage and improvement also suggested that U.S. guidance might promote the gradual, evolutionary passage of the Filipinos along a common, developmental scale. Instead of absolute, racially defined savages, Filipinos now became what colonial governor William Howard Taft referred to as "little brown brothers."[7]

By the first decades of the twentieth century, U.S. colonial administrators in the Philippines made the "development" of the archipelago their central purpose. Major infrastructure and engineering projects built railways, roads, harbors, and sewer systems. Public works were also defined as educational vehicles, and U.S. officials argued that changing the "backward" material environment of the Filipinos would instill a new set of modern values and attitudes. American agricultural projects introduced mechanized equipment, fertilizers, and experiment stations as part of a broader effort to build a thriving economy made up of small landowners producing crops for export. The Philippine Commission launched equally ambitious programs in education, stressing that a comprehensive system of schools would "prove one of the most forceful agencies for elevating the Filipinos, materially, socially, and morally, and preparing them for a large participation in the affairs of government."[8]

American visions of tutelage and development also extended to political training. As early as 1899, during the period of military occupation, colonial officials ordered the creation of municipal governments to be run by Filipinos elected through a system of limited suffrage. General E. S. Otis explained that this policy would allow natives to "demonstrate a fitness for self-administration" and receive an education in democracy. Over time, Filipinos were expected to learn to vote, hold office, draft legislation, and earn increasing amounts of autonomy as they demonstrated the capacity for progressive self-government. While the U.S. Congress still retained final authority, Filipinos did gain greater responsibility. The Organic Act of 1902, defining the Philippines as an "unincorporated territory" of the United States, provided for the election of a national legislative body. The U.S.-dominated Philippine Commission was replaced by an elected Senate in 1916. U.S. officials also trained Filipinos to take over the vast majority of civil service positions; of 13,000 administrative offices in 1921, only 614 were held by Americans.[9]

Most of those plans for sweeping, transformative development failed. Although U.S. administrators imagined creating a prosperous, thriving democracy, in the end they produced little in the way of lasting, structural changes. Because U.S. policymakers pursued a policy of "attraction," seeking profitable trade and stable government through political alliances with educated, landholding Filipino elites, the United States backed a class deeply committed to preserving its own economic and social dominance. Determined that any form of development would have be grounded on a firm basis of law and order, U.S. policymakers also presided over a system that defined democracy in extremely narrow terms. In the first elections for a Philippine assembly in 1907, the franchise was so sharply limited by literacy and tax requirements that only 3 percent of the population was able to vote. In that situation, it was perhaps unsurprising that neither the Filipino legislators nor their U.S. sponsors did much to address the continuing poverty of the islands' small farmers and urban workers.[10]

Much like the modernizers of the Cold War era, American colonial officials also came to understand the process of development in ways that obscured the significance of history and culture. Because they envisioned development as a kind of social engineering and viewed the transformation of Filipino society primarily as a technical matter, Americans tended to view local cultural practices, beliefs, and social relationships as transitory phenomena that would eventually be swept away. U.S. administrators knew little about the seven thousand islands they sought to govern, and when they did think about Philippine history and culture they often did so in ways that denied the Filipinos any real agency. U.S. officials consistently suggested that any Filipino progress was largely due to their "supposed penchant for mimicry." Taft remarked that the Filipinos would "need the training of fifty or a hundred years before they shall even realize what Anglo-Saxon liberty is."[11]

In the Caribbean and Central America, U.S. officials also spoke the language of development. Yet here, in the context of informal empire, their ambitions were often more limited, with a stronger emphasis on the immediate demands of stability and the prevention of revolution. As the post-1898 U.S. intervention in Cuba illustrates, this was partially a result of the much higher degree of U.S. economic interest and investment in the region. While some officials argued in favor of broad socioeconomic and political transformations, prominent figures like General Leonard Wood, commander of the U.S. military occupation of Cuba, took a different view. Because Cubans were "a race that has steadily been going down for a hundred years," the United States needed to "infuse new life, new principles, and new methods of doing things." Yet the idea of instilling democratic values would have to take a back seat to other imperatives. As Wood put it, when "people ask me what we mean by stable government in Cuba, I tell them that when money can be borrowed at a reasonable rate of interest and when capital is willing to invest in the island, a condition of stability will have been reached." In the Cuban case, the pursuit of a favorable climate for investment also led the United States to *oppose* many development projects. U.S.-owned sugar and land companies expanded their control of Cuban enterprises after 1898, and U.S. firms jealously guarded against the intrusion of foreign capital. In 1909, when the Cuban government turned toward a series of state-sponsored development initiatives, U.S. officials were decidedly unenthusiastic. The problem was that many of the plans to dredge Cuban harbors, construct irrigation systems, build railroads, and reclaim swamplands created openings for British investors, enlarged the scope of Cuban government control of the economy, and imposed new costs for American landowners. Unless such "ill-advised, ill-considered and dangerous fiscal measures" were abandoned, U.S. officials warned, it might be necessary for the United States to send troops back to Cuba to ensure the "re-establishment of a government adequate for the protection of life, liberty, and property."[12]

Yet the focus on capitalist opportunity in Latin America could also reinforce ideologies of development. In Haiti, a country under U.S. military occupation from 1915 through 1934, American officers controlled financial institutions. They also used the revenue to hire workers for road-building, sanitation, electri-fication, and water supply projects. Improved transportation and communica-tions systems certainly did create opportunities for additional U.S. investment, but they also were conceived of as part of a progressive effort to transform the Haitians themselves. Under U.S. tutelage, Haitians could be trained in business and management, allowing them to slowly advance. With its vast black popula-tion, officials doubted that Haiti could ever become another United States. But with U.S. assistance it might at least rise to an intermediate position, and become what one prominent missionary referred to as an "American Africa."[13]

Through the practice of "dollar diplomacy," Americans envisioned capitalism as a powerful civilizing vehicle. In 1904, in his famous "corollary" to the Mon-roe Doctrine, Theodore Roosevelt insisted that the United States should take on the role of an "international police power" whenever any Latin American nation conducted its economic affairs in ways that might lead to European intervention. Countries that fell heavily in debt, Roosevelt reasoned, were likely targets for foreign retribution, a process that could endanger U.S. hegemony in the region. Perceived as less costly than formal military occupation or the creation of protec-torates, dollar diplomacy still allowed for the exercise of substantial U.S. control. In exchange for the receipt of privately financed loans, foreign countries were required to accept the imposition of U.S. financial experts, effectively ceding the management of central banking and commercial systems. In the Dominican Re-public, for example, the U.S. government collected revenue and administered customhouses while private bankers worked out methods of refinancing claims by creditors. Similar arrangements were later implemented in Haiti, Nicaragua, and across the Atlantic in Liberia. As historian Emily Rosenberg argued, such measures were also understood as part of a larger developmental project. Mar-kets, money, and credit were freighted with cultural meanings, and Americans retained a "faith that fiscal stabilization and economic expansion would bring social progress."[14]

There was, of course, a profound tension between claims about the pro-motion of "self-government" and the realities of imperial control. Early twentieth-century U.S. attempts to promote development were also coupled with force and repression. U.S. programs to restructure Philippine society followed a devastating war against indigenous nationalists and continued in parallel with an ongoing counterinsurgency campaign. In Latin America, U.S. troops repeatedly landed on the beaches of Cuba, Haiti, the Dominican Republic, and Nicaragua, ensuring that whatever forms "development" took would be carefully controlled and guided in accordance with the wishes of the United States. Before departing, U.S. forces also frequently trained local civil guards and constabularies that promoted ruthless dictatorial rule, helping bring to power the likes of Cuba's Fulgencio Batista, the Dominican Republic's Rafael Trujillo, and Nicaragua's Anastasio Somoza. Thus, by the early 1900s, U.S. practices of imperial development reflected a volatile combination of reformist idealism and lethal coercion. American conceptions of development and modernization would change over time, but that particular pattern, as we shall see, would persist throughout the rest of the century.

Development and the Meaning of Modernity

Development, of course, was not a uniquely American concept, born suddenly in 1898. European thinkers of the Enlightenment and the nineteenth century also sought to formulate models of universal change in which one could identify specific developmental stages and define the crucial mechanisms for advance along a single historical continuum. As Robert Nisbet observed, the idea that "the recent history of the West could be taken as evidence of the direction in which mankind as a whole would move, and, flowing from this, should move," exercised a powerful hold on European social thought. Historical change, scholars like French economist Jean-Baptiste Say (1767–1832) believed, followed an iron-clad, unyielding course. Industrial production, Say reasoned, marked the pattern of social progress, and all those on the periphery would either "become civilized or they will be destroyed. Nothing can hold out against civilization and the powers of industry." Karl Marx's (1818–83) historical dialectic, defining the passage of societies through sequential stages of feudalism, capitalism, and communism, also put forward a universal, ordered representation of history's direction by linking changes in economic structures to changes in social relations. As he noted in *Capital*, a "country that is more developed industrially only shows, to the less developed, the image of its own future." English philosopher and theorist Herbert Spencer (1820–1903) also stressed the evolutionary transition from the diffuse human relationships of "wandering tribes" to the well-defined, "determinate" social order of industrialized life.[15]

In the early decades of the twentieth century non-Western actors also contributed to a wider, global discourse about development. Among Indian nationalists, the subject became a heated topic of debate. Some figures, most famously Mohandas K. Gandhi, rejected the sweeping transformations embedded in Western models of capitalist development. According to Gandhi, imperial exploitation was only part of a larger affliction. "It is my deliberate opinion," he wrote in 1909, "that India is being ground down, not under the English heel, but under that of modern civilization." Railroads "accentuate[d] the evil nature of man" and damaged Indian society by spreading disease and deepening famine. Imports from England's textile mills debilitated Indian handicraft production and destroyed the possibility of genuine personal and spiritual independence. Machinery, Gandhi argued, was the "chief symbol of modern civilization," and "a great sin." Others, however, took a decidedly different view, emphasizing that national independence would require a program of economic, political, and social development involving sharp changes in attitudes and values as well as institutions. As political economist M. G. Ranade insisted in 1892, the technological gap between India and England was so great that any newly independent Indian government would have to promote the growth of infant industries. Traditional religions, condemning the desire for wealth, also deepened popular fatalism. According to Ranade, problems of economic growth were intimately related to cultural and psychological failings: "Our habits of mind are conservative to a fault.... Stagnation and dependence, depression and poverty—these are written in broad characters on the face of the land and the people."[16]

The transformation of culture as a central element of development was emphasized even more directly by Turkey's authoritarian president Mustapha Kemal Ataturk. After the defeat of the Ottoman Empire in World War I, Ataturk built an army, vanquished the occupying Allied forces, and imposed a series of radical programs. The Republic of Turkey, he determined, would have to emulate its former enemies and become "a progressive member of the civilized world." Civilization, in his mind, was also decidedly Western. In addition to establishing state-owned factories and creating a national railroad, he sought to fundamentally reorient Turkish society. After sending the sultan into exile and abolishing the caliphate, Islamic schools, and religious courts, Ataturk constructed a legal code inspired by those of Switzerland and Italy, romanized the alphabet, established compulsory primary education, instituted new civil and voting rights for women, and even launched a sartorial campaign banning the wearing of fezzes. Ataturk was the first to use the word "modernization" to describe a deliberate, integrated process of social transformation and nation building.[17]

In Republican China, Sun Yat-sen turned toward the idea of international development as a means to contain imperial competition, prevent Japanese aggression, and unify a country divided by warlord rule. In his 1921 book, *The International Development of China,* he outlined a monumental ten-point plan for the importation of foreign capital to build railroads, canals, commercial ports, irrigation systems, mines, and iron, steel, and cement factories. Reasoning that the belligerent powers of World War I would soon have to redirect their economies toward peacetime endeavors, Sun argued that "proper development" of China's vast natural resources and immense population would help that country become an "unlimited market." "The world," as he put it, "has been greatly benefited by the development of America as an industrial and a commercial Nation. So a developed China with her four hundred millions of population, will be another New World in the economic sense." Like other nationalists, Sun wrote about development as a process that would have broad social effects. China, he acknowledged, was a "late comer," but "after centuries of sound slumber," he proclaimed, "the Chinese people are at last waking up and realizing that we must get up and follow in the world's progress."[18]

In the early twentieth century, U.S. journalists, philanthropists, scholars, and businessmen also thought they perceived modernizing transformations under way around the world. Inspired by "the thrilling vision of a China purged of its traditionalism," the Rockefeller Foundation established a medical school in Beijing in 1921 and started an ambitious program in rural social planning in the 1930s. The diffusion of expertise and professionalism, foundation executives believed, would promote liberalism in intellectual as well as political life. Through the North China Council on Rural Reconstruction, established in 1936, the foundation supported a broad array of programs in agricultural technology, education, library financing, public health, and even research designed to determine "how...the unsophisticated rural Chinese really think." The goal, as one progress report explained, was to create "a comprehensive experimental program of research, education and application, designed to bridge the gap between a rural medieval society and twentieth century knowledge." Although the Japanese invasion of 1937 ultimately derailed the program, the idea that the United States could channel the course of China's future along liberal lines remained a dearly held American dream.[19]

Many American diplomats and writers were captivated by the drama of Russian development as well. University of Chicago Russian expert Samuel Harper had originally condemned the rise of the Bolshevik regime as a betrayal of Russian liberalism, but by the mid-1920s he praised the Soviet "civic education" system and even lauded the Red Army as creating a "new type of peasant." The Russian masses, he avowed, were no longer passive or ignorant but were instead "articulate, discontented, and hopeful." Many American intellectuals, even those who steadfastly condemned Soviet politics, were still impressed with the sheer ambitions of Soviet social engineering. By the start of the Great Depression, the enthusiasm of many American experts for technocratic solutions, combined with a growing skepticism about the prospects for popular democracy, also led them to accept the severe human costs of crash industrialization and forced collectivization. As the economist Stuart Chase put it, "I am not seriously alarmed by the sufferings of the creditor class, the troubles which the church is bound to encounter, the restrictions on certain kinds of freedom which must result, nor even by the bloodshed of the transitional period. A better economic order is worth a little bloodshed." In 1932 and 1933, Soviet policies of taking food from rural areas to fund industrialization and feed workers and the military caused a massive famine, killing approximately eight million people. Yet the appeal of modernization led many of America's Russian experts to describe that atrocity as a down payment on future progress.[20]

Gradual and complex changes in American understandings of race during this period helped raise expectations about the prospects for rapid modernization in traditional societies. In the early twentieth century, anthropologists, sociologists, and psychologists took important steps away from older forms of scientific racism. Instead of attributing particular behaviors or capabilities to biologically defined, racial types, they increasingly turned toward the concept of culture as an explanation for differences among diverse peoples. As the most prominent anthropologist in the United States, Franz Boas (1858–1942) was especially influential in promoting that turn. Boas successfully discredited the older, racial claims of physical anthropologists and argued that the supposed distance between "primitive" and "civilized" peoples was not nearly as great as commonly believed. Along with his team of prolific and talented students, including Margaret Mead and Ruth Benedict, Boas also argued that autonomous and independent human cultures, well adapted to their particular environments, served to fulfill an immense range of human needs. It made no sense, therefore, to speak of their inferiority or superiority, or to rank them along any kind of linear or evolutionary scale.

Those arguments, however, were often only partially understood and selectively appropriated. Boas had sided with the anti-imperialists in 1898 and, as a German Jewish immigrant, he attacked the use of racial categorizations by the proponents of immigration restrictions targeting Jews, Slavs, and Asians. It would not be until the era of World War II and the U.S. confrontation with Nazi Germany, however, that the assault on scientific racism would begin to have a broader public and political impact. Americans also absorbed only part of the argument that Boas and his colleagues put forward. While theories based on claims of inherent racial difference gradually lost ground among social scientists and intellectuals, the practice of ranking cultures along an evolutionary or linear scale did not. This fact had important implications for American thinking about modernization. Since the inherent limits associated with fixed biology and racial destiny were replaced by an understanding grounded in the malleability of culture, the idea of transforming foreign societies gained greater credibility. In the post–World War II understanding, contact with modernity would not eliminate deficient races, but it would utterly transform deficient cultures.[21]

Thus, from World War I through the 1930s, ideas about development and modernization as a directional, systemic, and comprehensive phenomenon, involving changes in economics, politics, and culture, were in international circulation. It was also during this period that a particularly American variant of that thinking became deeply rooted in U.S. foreign policy, decisively shaped by liberal, internationalist convictions that grew out of the experience of two global wars, the Great Depression, and sustained reflections on the meaning of modernity itself. Two related points would be particularly central to this new perspective. First, U.S. policymakers would come to perceive the world as a seamless whole, fully integrated by new technologies that allowed threats and dangers to rapidly cross the barriers of time and space. U.S. security, they came to believe, depended not merely on the defense of U.S. territory or resources, but also on the creation of a world environment in which American values and institutions would be most widely shared. The protection of U.S. security, therefore, would require not merely military force, but also the promotion of structural solutions shaping and directing the development of foreign economies, societies, and political systems. Second, the experience of global war led Americans to view this imperative with a heightened sense of urgency. Because they came to believe that the threats of dictatorship and totalitarianism placed civilization itself in the balance, the United States could not merely wait for history to run its course, slowly pulling the world in America's wake. Instead, the United States would have to seek ways to dramatically *accelerate* the world's transformation, leading nations in liberal, capitalist directions before hostile ideologies might take hold.

American attempts to interpret the meaning of World War I produced a burst of innovative thought, most notably by Woodrow Wilson, a professional political scientist as well as U.S. president. Like many of his contemporaries, Wilson held the view that the United States had a vital historical destiny. While campaigning in 1912, he asserted: "I believe that God planted in us visions of liberty... [and] that we are... prominently chosen to show the way to the nations of the world." Yet it was Wilson's analysis of the fundamentally novel dangers reflected in the world war and their significance for U.S. security that set him apart. The specter of fully industrialized, total war unfolding on the European continent, a cataclysm that consumed a generation of French, German, and English young men, led him to believe that the existing system of international politics was bankrupt.

War, he concluded, had simply become too lethal to function as a means of diplomacy. Of course, Wilson responded to that problem in part by arguing for a new mechanism that would replace the increasingly destructive competition of nation-states with a system of collective security—which he proposed in the form of the League of Nations.[22]

More directly relevant to the history of American thinking about modernization, however, is Wilson's search for a comprehensive structural solution. Wilson, Frank Ninkovich argued, defined the danger posed by total war and militarized dictatorship in "apocalyptic, world-historical terms." His "new perception of threat," moreover, "made American intervention absolutely necessary if a world environment hospitable to liberalism was to survive." To "make the world safe for democracy," in Wilson's terms, meant ensuring that future wars would not erupt, and a pledge by the world's civilized powers to work in concert against aggression was a major part of that goal. But it also meant putting in place the institutions and processes that would destroy the walls behind which dictatorships were protected. This required promoting the kind of open, interdependent flow of ideas, values, and goods in which liberal, capitalist institutions would ultimately prevail. Wilson's famous Fourteen Points sketched out his sense of how such a world would be created, emphasizing disarmament, free trade, and an end to imperial rivalries.[23]

In the short run, of course, Wilson's proposals came to naught. In place of a cooperative, open, liberal turn, after World War I the United States rejected the League of Nations, the victorious powers imposed punitive reparations payments on defeated Germany, military alliances proliferated, and trade barriers rose. In addition, despite the hopes of nationalists from Egypt to Vietnam, neither Wilson nor the Allies took any concrete steps toward granting rights of self-determination to colonized peoples outside Europe. More than his specific remedies, however, it was Wilson's basic style of thought that mattered most in laying the ideological foundations for future U.S. approaches to modernization. Wilson did not, to be sure, use the term in the way that U.S. policymakers would in the Cold War. But his emphasis on structural factors and his liberal internationalist conviction that U.S. security required reshaping the world's political, economic, and cultural systems were crucial steps toward the vision of development as an urgent global project after 1945.

The American experience in the Great Depression further shaped a modernizing agenda. Within U.S. political culture a strong distrust of state intervention in the economy tightly constrained the potential for sustained, centralized planning, even in the midst of a capitalist crisis. But the regional planning experiment of the Tennessee Valley Authority (TVA) was idealized as a success story that could be transplanted throughout the world. Federal management of a river network in the form of hydroelectric power, irrigation, soil conservation, fertilizer production, and the employment of thousands of workers appealed to many policymakers as a new and vital form of development. According to David Lilienthal, one of the TVA's first directors, the agency illustrated the virtues of "democratic," "grass-roots" development, since it brought scientific management and technology together with the active participation of the citizens affected by its policies. In reality, the truth was more complex, particularly since many TVA decisions were made by administrative elites, and pragmatism tended to eclipse systemic planning in agency operations. Yet the conviction that the TVA represented planning without Soviet-style oppression shaped later beliefs that it could be applied universally. By adopting the TVA model, Lilienthal argued, foreign societies could "skip stages" and move more rapidly down the developmental path. What worked in the United States, he later insisted, could be directly applied in China, India, Colombia, Iran, and South Vietnam.[24]

New Deal fiscal policy shaped later thinking about modernization as well. U.S. economists had stumbled upon fiscal approaches to the Depression before John Maynard Keynes first published his economic doctrine in *The General Theory* (1936). The American experience also appeared to validate the truth of Keynes's central claims. After the recession of 1938 and through the mobilization for World War II, sharp increases in government spending did indeed stimulate aggregate demand, promote consumption, and drive a sagging economy toward full employment. Most crucial to thinking about the nature of development was Keynes's insistence on the categorical difference between the economic principles governing an economy running at full speed and those at work in stagnant cases of underemployed labor and capital. In the midst of the Great Depression, the economy of the United States had fallen into the latter case, in which orthodox, neoclassical economic models did not apply, but the unconventional tactics of deficit spending and fiscal management could. The idea that diverse conditions required diverse forms of economic analysis, in turn, helped stimulate thinking about the plight of "underdeveloped areas." The American experience, even in the midst of a crisis, was not considered identical to the situation facing those impoverished regions, where massive poverty and late industrialization were taken to be decisive differences. But the growing acceptance and popularity of Keynesian thought ultimately generated a sense of confidence that "underdevelopment" could be addressed successfully.[25]

By the late 1930s, the specter of a second global war led to a crucial revival and reformulation of Wilsonian thinking. The Japanese invasion of China and the Nazi quest to dominate Europe deeply worried Franklin Delano Roosevelt. After the failed Munich conference of 1938, the German attack on Poland in 1939, and the fall of France in mid-1940, Roosevelt recognized a profound danger for the United States and the world. Most significantly, however, he did not define the problem in conventional terms of military strength. Instead he emphasized the way that the forces of communications, technology, trade, and warfare had created an increasingly integrated world in which U.S. security demanded a new level of global engagement. "The world," Roosevelt reflected in 1939, "has grown so small and weapons of attack so swift...events of thunderous import have moved with lightning speed." The Japanese march in Asia and the German blitzkrieg in Europe, in his words, represented the "annihilation of time and space." In early 1941 he observed: "The problems which we face are so vast and so interrelated that any attempt even to state them compels one to think in terms of five continents and seven seas." The U.S. response, therefore, could not merely take the form of military mobilization and territorial defense. Like Wilson before him, Roosevelt argued that the United States would have to transform the international environment.[26]

Roosevelt articulated a global vision of modernization as an essential part of that project. In his State of the Union address on January, 6, 1941, he declared that the United States would create "a world founded upon four essential human freedoms." Freedom of speech, freedom of religion, and "freedom from fear" would all be pursued alongside a commitment to "freedom from want—which, translated into world terms, means economic understandings that will secure to every nation a healthy peacetime life for its inhabitants everywhere in the world." By defining U.S. war aims in terms of the triumph of civil and economic rights, Roosevelt built on and far exceeded Wilson's solutions. Where Wilson promised to "make the world safe for democracy," a formulation that suggested creating the conditions in which liberalism could survive, Roosevelt suggested that the United States would seek to restructure the world in accordance with its own fundamental principles. Figures like Henry Luce, the influential publisher of *Time* and *Life,* also gave these ideas a dramatic cast. "America," Luce declared, "cannot be responsible for the behavior of the entire world, but America is responsible, to herself as well as to history, for the world environment in which she lives."[27]

Decolonization and a World in Turmoil

Some of the more pivotal questions about modernizing the "international environment" were raised by the problem of decolonization. The Atlantic Charter, issued by Roosevelt and British prime minister Winston Churchill in August 1941, clearly defined an anticolonial position. In particular, the United States and Britain pledged "to respect the right of all peoples to choose the form of government under which they will live," and declared their "wish to see sovereign rights

and self-government restored to those who have been forcibly deprived of them."
Churchill later tried to water the statement down, insisting that its anticolonial
provisions applied only to lands invaded by the Axis powers. But the document's
promises were clearly framed in global terms, and decolonization fit squarely
within the wider ethos of a war defined as a struggle for democratic freedoms
against fascist oppression.[28]

That ideological framework created an awkward problem as the British,
French, and Americans called on their colonial subjects to fight on behalf of
principles that they themselves did not enjoy. Writing in 1941, Gandhi made the
point with typical clarity: "Both America and Great Britain lack the moral basis
for engaging in this war unless they put their own houses in order.... They have
no right to talk about protecting democracies and protecting civilization and
human freedom, until the canker of white superiority is destroyed in its entirety."
In 1945, Indonesia's Ahmed Sukarno echoed that sentiment, asking whether "liberty and freedom" were "only for certain favored peoples of the world." "Indonesians will never understand," he continued, "why it is...wrong for the Germans
to rule Holland [under wartime occupation] if it is right for the Dutch to rule
Indonesia." With fascism finally defeated and much of Western Europe in ruins,
many nationalist leaders believed that the moment for genuine independence
would soon arrive.[29]

The rising expectations of anticolonial elites that the victorious Allies would
live up to their promises were largely disappointed. In a few cases, decolonization
did take place relatively swiftly. In India, for example, the British moved toward
a policy of negotiated withdrawal. Although Britain had ruthlessly suppressed
the wartime campaign of nationalist demonstrations, officials recognized the
growing strength of the Indian Congress Party and feared that rising ethnic and
religious conflicts were driving the colony toward civil war. In such a situation,
they worried, it would be increasingly difficult to deny Indian independence,
particularly since any delay might increase the danger of widespread violence between the subcontinent's Hindu and Muslim populations. Domestic factors also
contributed to the British decision, as popular demands for an expanded welfare
state at home made it politically difficult to continue pouring scarce resources
into colonial affairs. Faced with that combination of pressures, an exhausted,
war-weary Britain accepted the partition of its former colony and recognized
the independence of India and Pakistan in August 1947. The United States also
granted independence to the Philippines in July 1946, maintaining exclusive
rights to a network of military bases but finally fulfilling a promise made a decade earlier.[30]

In most other cases, however, decolonization stalled in the immediate postwar years. While the British recognized the independence of Burma and Ceylon

in 1948, they did not relinquish control of any of their other colonies in Asia or Africa until the mid-1950s. The Dutch and the French proved even more intransigent. The leaders of the new French Fourth Republic, founded in 1946, keenly remembered their nation's collapse in the face of German power and resented the small role that the Free French had taken in planning for the postwar world. To yield their colonial claims, they believed, was to subject themselves to an even further demotion from great power status, and to cut themselves off from potential resources and markets considered essential for postwar reconstruction. Algeria, with its large, white settler population, was defined as an essential part of France, and the other French colonies in Asia and Africa were still seen by much of the metropolitan public in terms of a vital French mission. The Dutch also dug in their heels, refusing to prepare for or even consider the independence of the Dutch East Indies, despite the effects of wartime devastation there and at home.[31]

The result was a global clash along a North-South axis between recalcitrant or, at best, stubbornly gradualist European colonial powers and a rising generation of committed nationalists. In August 1945, Indonesia's Ahmed Sukarno and Mohammed Hatta declared their country's independence from Dutch rule. With an interim constitution already drafted by the time of the Japanese surrender, they were determined to prevent the return of their former European masters. One month later, Ho Chi Minh famously demanded his country's freedom by invoking the U.S. Declaration of Independence and the French Revolution's Declaration of the Rights of Man. Having "acknowledged the principles of self-determination and equality of nations," he argued, the Allies surely would "not refuse to acknowledge the independence of Viet-Nam." In Algeria, Muslim leader Ferhat Abbas issued a wartime "Manifesto of the Algerian People" insisting on a new state led by the Arab majority without French control. In West Africa, the Gold Coast's Kwame Nkrumah led a campaign of strikes, boycotts, and protests against British rule. "We cannot get what we want by asking, pleading and arguing," Nkrumah declared. "We are in a world of action, not talk."[32]

The conflict between European powers and anticolonial nationalists provoked ambivalent responses from U.S. policymakers. During World War II, Franklin Delano Roosevelt repeatedly expressed the view that colonialism produced international conflict, stimulated revolution, and posed a grave danger to the peace of the postwar world. But there was a substantial gap between the expression of principle and the execution of policy. The U.S. position on the future of Indochina provides a telling illustration of the problem. Roosevelt believed the French had been poor colonizers, and he repeatedly lamented that France had done little to educate or guide the peoples of Vietnam, Cambodia, and Laos toward independence. In July 1943, at an interallied planning meeting on Pacific affairs, President Roosevelt insisted that "Indo-China should not be given back to the French Empire after the war." Yet he also went on to assert that "naturally they could not be given independence immediately but should be taken care of until they are able to govern themselves." For Roosevelt, U.S. policies of colonial development provided a model: "In 1900 the Filipinos were not ready for independence nor could a date be fixed when they would be. Many public works had to be taken care of first. The people had to be educated in local, and finally, national governmental affairs. By 1933, however, we were able to get together with the Filipinos and all agree on a date, namely 1945, when they would be ready for independence. Since this development worked in that case, there is no reason why it should not work in the case of Indo-China." To prepare Indochina for freedom, Roosevelt proposed that it be held as an international trusteeship under the auspices of the new United Nations.[33]

Roosevelt's reference to the Philippines illustrates the underlying assumptions at work. For Roosevelt, equating the Philippines and Indochina made sense, since both were supposedly backward Asian societies requiring further U.S. tutelage to develop in Western ways. The president's statement also captured his confidence in the global validity and applicability of U.S. approaches. According to Roosevelt and much of the State Department, any steps toward independence would also have to unfold over a very long period, as the Vietnamese in the 1940s, much like the Filipinos at the turn of the century, were politically immature. Ultimately, in the face of growing anxieties about the postwar future, even those tentative plans were abandoned. Determined to preserve a strong wartime alliance against Germany and Japan, and worried about the effects of instability in colonial regions, Roosevelt did little to press Western European nations toward granting independence to their colonies. Reversing his earlier position, he also agreed that the French would be allowed to resume control of Indochina after the war.[34]

The start of the Cold War made the problem of imperialism far more pressing as the North-South conflict intersected with a growing East-West divide. Between 1945 and 1949, U.S. policymakers wrestled with the difficulties of reconciling competing imperatives. In order to secure British and French agreement to postwar U.S. security plans, U.S. officials muted their opposition to colonialism. The demands of anti-Soviet solidarity, State Department officers warned, would have to take precedence over the protests of anticolonial nationalists. U.S. policymakers also focused on the problem of rebuilding Western Europe and Japan. Devastated by war, afflicted with severe shortages ranging from foodstuffs to foreign exchange, and deeply in debt to the United States, the Western European nations were seen as increasingly vulnerable to radical appeals. Their reconstruction, along with the creation of a new, prosperous, democratic Japan, would require ensuring continued access to the raw materials, investments, and markets of the colonized world. As Senator Henry Cabot Lodge argued during hearings on the formation of the North Atlantic Treaty Organization (NATO), "we need...these countries to be strong, and they cannot be strong without their colonies."[35]

The Truman administration, therefore, continued the retreat from the principles of self-determination. In 1945, U.S. officials worked to ensure that instead of endorsing immediate independence, the new United Nations Charter merely required colonial powers to take "progressive" steps toward independence "according to the particular circumstances of each territory and its peoples and their varying stages of advancement." In March 1947, the Truman Doctrine also sidestepped the issue. While drawing a sharp, morally charged distinction between a democratic way of life "based upon the will of the majority" and totalitarian systems "based upon the will of a minority forcibly imposed upon the majority," Truman simply ignored the obvious contradictions raised by colonialism.[36]

Yet Truman administration officials also concluded that they could not entirely ignore anticolonial forces. Although they did not anticipate direct Soviet-American military conflict in Europe in the immediate postwar years, they did fear that the Kremlin leadership would opportunistically exploit upheavals in the "peripheral" areas of the world. Nationalist elites, many of them graduates of prestigious Western universities, made articulate, compelling challenges to the ideology of colonialism. Their goals centered not merely on political freedom, but also on ambitions for development itself. Independence, in their terms, required rapid economic growth as well as advances in social services, health care, and education. It also meant sweeping structural change, much of it to be planned through the public sector. To reject wholesale the aspirations of Indians, Indonesians, Vietnamese, Egyptians, Iranians, Algerians, Kenyans, and Gold Coasters, U.S. officials feared, would embitter nationalists and cede the field to Soviet intervention. In this context, the United States began to chart an intermediate course, one in which development would ultimately play an important role. Ideally, U.S. officials hoped, the British, French, and Dutch would take steps toward granting formal independence to their colonies while maintaining close ties through systems of "informal association." The preservation of trade relations would keep essential supplies of rubber, tin, coal, and oil moving from former colonies to fuel European and Japanese reconstruction, and the recognition of official sovereignty would satisfy nationalist demands. Development aid, U.S. officials hoped, would also encourage nationalists to align themselves with the West and against the Communists.[37]

The international organizations founded by the Allies at the end of the war also had strong development components. The Bretton Woods meeting, held in the mountains of New Hampshire in July 1944, created the International Monetary

Fund (IMF) and the World Bank. While the IMF was expected to stabilize exchange rates and promote open, global trade, the World Bank was intended to fund global development projects as well as European reconstruction. By instituting guidelines for foreign aid and stimulating private investment, World Bank experts hoped they could fight poverty, promote steps toward liberal democracy, and reduce the dangers of revolution in destitute regions. As World Bank president Eugene Black put it in a 1952 speech, "world development means nothing less than the illumination of the central idea of freedom." The Food and Agriculture Organization (FAO), created in 1945, and the World Health Organization (WHO), established in 1948, also became central parts of the United Nations development effort. FAO officials dreamed of ending global malnutrition through "a new world order to be achieved through a vast improvement in agricultural production and food distribution and consumption." WHO experts also aimed high, hoping to promote global, standardized medical education, scientific research, data collection, pharmaceutical preparations, and a comprehensive campaign against epidemics, including malaria, tuberculosis, and venereal diseases.[38]

American optimism about the potential for engineering sweeping transformations abroad was raised by the occupation of Japan and the reconstruction of Western Europe. While neither case was framed as a problem of "development," both appeared to prove that U.S. interventions in foreign societies could produce impressive economic growth and lasting reforms. In Japan, the occupation authority set out to redirect national politics, society, and culture. The Americans ordered the defeated government to support the formation of labor unions, enfranchise women, and liberalize its educational system. Convinced that Japan's dominant class of large landholders had bolstered the country's aggressive militarism, U.S. officials implemented an agrarian reform policy that dramatically broadened landownership. They also drafted a new constitution that reduced the emperor's powers to those of a figurehead, proscribed the sovereign right of war, and established a wide range of civil liberties. Some of these reforms were soon abandoned. As economic conditions failed to improve in the late 1940s, regulations applying antitrust principles to Japan's massive industrial conglomerates were dropped. Before long, however, the increased demand created by the Korean War resulted in a massive surge in industrial production and employment, dramatically raising economic growth rates and living standards. Although the process was heavily shaped by Japanese initiatives, by the early 1950s Americans took great pride in helping transform an erstwhile enemy into a thriving center for Asian capitalism.[39]

The Marshall Plan shaped American thinking about the relationship between economic growth and Cold War security demands as well. Like later modernization programs deployed in Asia, Africa, Latin America, and the Middle East, it was based on the firm expectation that expert planning could make the United States' own historical experience a kind of universal template for liberal transformations. Proponents of the Marshall Plan described a replication of the New Deal in Europe as moderate government intervention, once embodied in the TVA or the Rural Electrification Administration, promoted a healthy, productive capitalism allowing the engines of private enterprise to meet broad, public needs. First announced in 1947, the Marshall Plan provided roughly $13 billion through mid-1951, and while some countries benefited more than others, it helped produce a major increase in the Western European gross national product. In Japan and Western Europe, of course, the task was largely one of *reconstruction,* of rebuilding a previously existing industrial base and putting a preexisting, skilled labor force back to work. While seeking to transform the cultures of their former enemies, Americans also observed that the Germans and Japanese were certainly "modern" enough to become dangerous military threats. But many U.S. policymakers eventually came to believe that a combination of expert planning, investment, and technology could produce similar effects in the developing regions of the world.[40]

It was in the context of decolonization and Cold War tension, therefore, that Harry Truman announced the "Point Four" program in January 1949. In practical terms, the "bold, new program" of technical aid and increased foreign investment in the "underdeveloped world" got off to an unimpressive start. The State Department struggled to define the program's scope. Was the goal an increase in "production" and economic growth? Or was President Truman also calling for "economic development in the broadest sense," targeting not only increased living standards but also advances in education and public health? Did the president's reference to "capital investment" extend to direct lending by the U.S. government? Or did it refer solely to private funds? The uncertainty in the State Department was compounded by caution in the White House and strong resistance on Capitol Hill. In contrast to the mammoth scale of the Marshall Plan, Truman requested only $45 million for Point Four, a figure that Congress cut to $27 million when it finally made appropriations in September 1950. Having asked for billions to fund European recovery, Truman was reluctant to press for additional funds, and Republican critics like Ohio senator Robert A. Taft were quick to denounce Point Four as a "global W. P. A." Government spending to fund development, they insisted, was a weak and ineffective substitute for the only real engine of progress, the unregulated, capitalist marketplace. In 1953, appropriations for technical aid projects in health care, education, and agriculture totaled only $155 million.[41]

Yet the Point Four program did mark an important milestone. In particular, Truman's proposal applied a set of assumptions deeply rooted in the American past to the novel, uncertain historical situation of the immediate postwar years. The idea that the United States might catalyze the movement of "less-developed" societies along a universal, historically defined trajectory was central to the early twentieth-century justification of U.S. imperialism in the Philippines and the Caribbean. Wilsonian approaches linking the security of the United States to the structure of the international environment and the quest for an open, liberal world also contributed to the idea of development as a foreign-policy imperative. World War II and the problem of decolonization, finally, helped make development part of the United States' wider global strategy. Worried that imperialism had become a threat to lasting postwar peace, U.S. officials still remained ambivalent about the prospects for self-determination of supposedly inferior peoples. Development, in their eyes, promised a liberal, even altruistic means to meet and manage the ambitions of anticolonial elites. Building infrastructure and promoting investment would keep natural resources and raw materials flowing into vital European markets, while promoting economic growth, better living standards, and improvements in education and health care would satisfy nationalist aspirations and prevent radical alternatives.

It was the inherently ideological nature of the emerging Cold War struggle that ultimately made development and modernization crucial elements of U.S. foreign policy. As Odd Arne Westad argued, "Soviet communism came to be seen as a deadly rival of Americanism because it put itself forward as an alternative modernity; a way poor and downtrodden peoples could challenge their conditions *without* replicating the American model." For U.S. policymakers, sharing the ascendant vision of a seamless, interconnected world, the prospect of a competition between irreconcilable developmental models over the future direction of civilization itself was essential to their understanding of the Soviet challenge. Because the peoples of the "underdeveloped" regions were considered immature, volatile, and unprepared for responsible self-government, the dangers of subversion and the need for the United States to guide their rising expectations appeared all the greater. A few years after Truman announced his Point Four program, revolution in China and war in Korea would transform the Cold War into a global conflict, making the "periphery" one of its front lines. The expansion of the Cold War would also harden the perceived link between international development and U.S. security. In that context, U.S. policymakers would increasingly conclude that their nation's future, and that of the world, depended on rapid, wholesale modernization.[42]

NOTES

1. Harry S. Truman, Inaugural Address, January 20, 1949, Harry S. Truman Library, http://www.trumanlibrary.org/whistlestop/50yr_archive/inagural20jan1949.htm.

2. Memorandum, Dean Acheson to President Truman, March 14, 1949, *Foreign Relations of the United States* [hereafter FRUS] *1949* (Washington, DC: U.S. Government Printing Office), 1: 778; Gilbert Rist, *The History of Development: From Western Origins to Global Faith* (London: Zed, 1997), 70–79.

3. Thomas Paine, *Common Sense* (Mineola, NY: Dover, 1997), 33; Hunt, *American Ascendancy*, 34.

4. Reginald Horsman, *Race and Manifest Destiny: The Origins of American Racial Anglo-Saxonism* (Cambridge, MA: Harvard University Press, 1981).

5. Paul Kramer, *The Blood of Government: Race, Empire, the United States, and the Philippines* (Chapel Hill: University of North Carolina Press, 2006), 1–2; Frank Ninkovich, *The United States and Imperialism* (Malden, MA: Blackwell, 2001), 37, 40–41.

6. Ninkovich, *United States and Imperialism*, 51–52, 56–57.

7. Kramer, *Blood of Government*, 5, 200.

8. Glenn Anthony May, *Social Engineering in the Philippines: The Aims, Execution, and Impact of American Colonial Policy, 1900–1913* (Westport, CT: Greenwood Press, 1980), 77; H. W. Brands, *Bound to Empire: The United States and the Philippines* (New York: Oxford University Press, 1992), 71–72.

9. Julian Go, "The Chains of Empire: State Building and 'Political Education' in Puerto Rico and the Philippines," in *The American Colonial State in the Philippines: Global Perspectives*, ed. Julian Go and Anne L. Foster (Durham, NC: Duke University Press, 2003), 182–84; Ninkovich, *United States and Imperialism*, 59–61.

10. Ninkovich, *United States and Imperialism*, 58–59, 63–66.

11. Michael Adas, *Dominance by Design: Technological Imperatives and America's Civilizing Mission* (Cambridge, MA: Harvard University Press, 2006), 146–47; Vicente L. Rafael, "White Love: Surveillance and Nationalist Resistance in the U.S. Colonization of the Philippines," in *Cultures of United States Imperialism*, ed. Amy Kaplan and Donald Pease (Durham, NC: Duke University Press, 1993), 197–98, 200; Kramer, *Blood of Government*, 200.

12. Peter H. Smith, *Talons of the Eagle: Dynamics of U.S.-Latin American Relations* (New York: Oxford University Press, 1996), 52, 62; Louis A. Pérez, Jr., *Cuba under the Platt Amendment, 1902–1934* (Pittsburgh: University of Pittsburgh Press, 1986), 33, 44, 123–30.

13. Mary A. Renda, *Taking Haiti: Military Occupation and the Culture of U.S. Imperialism, 1915–1940* (Chapel Hill: University of North Carolina Press, 2001), 114, 117–18, 125.

14. Emily S. Rosenberg, *Financial Missionaries to the World: The Politics and Culture of Dollar Diplomacy, 1900–1930* (Durham, NC: Duke University Press, 2003), 6–9, 33, 39, 41–46.

15. Robert A. Nisbet, *Social Change and History: Aspects of the Western Theory of Development* (New York: Oxford University Press, 1969), 190; Rist, *History of Development*, 40–41; Murray J. Leaf, *Man, Mind, and Science: A History of Anthropology* (New York: Columbia University Press, 1979), 77.

16. H. W. Arndt, *Economic Development: The History of an Idea* (Chicago: University of Chicago Press, 1987), 18–19.

17. Céngiz Candar and David Pryce-Jones, "Ataturk's Ambiguous Legacy," *Wilson Quarterly* 24 (Autumn 2000): 88–96; Gilman, *Mandarins of the Future*, 31.

18. Sun Yat-sen, *The International Development of China*, 2nd ed. (Chungking: China Publishing, 1941), 3–10, 231–37.

19. Frank Ninkovich, "The Rockefeller Foundation, China, and Cultural Change," *Journal of American History* 70, no. 4 (1984): 799–820.

20. David C. Engerman, *Modernization from the Other Shore: American Intellectuals and the Romance of Russian Development* (Cambridge, MA: Harvard University Press, 2003), 131, 155, 165, 197.

21. Rosenberg, *Financial Missionaries*, 207; Elazar Barkan, *The Retreat of Scientific Racism: Changing Concepts of Race in Britain and the United States between the World Wars* (Cambridge: Cambridge University Press, 1992); David A. Hollinger, "Cultural Relativism," in *The Cambridge History of Science*, vol. 7, *The Modern Social Sciences*, ed. Theodore Porter and Dorothy Ross (Cambridge: Cambridge University Press, 2003), 708–20.

22. Thomas J. Knock, *To End All Wars: Woodrow Wilson and the Quest for a New World Order* (Princeton, NJ: Princeton University Press, 1992), 11.

23. Frank Ninkovich, *The Wilsonian Century: U.S. Foreign Policy since 1900* (Chicago: University of Chicago Press, 1999), 61, 64.

24. David Ekbladh, "'Mr. TVA': Grass-Roots Development, David Lilienthal, and the Rise and Fall of the Tennessee Valley Authority as a Symbol for U.S. Overseas Development, 1933–1973," *Diplomatic History* 26, no. 3 (2002): 335–74; David Ekbladh, *The Great American Mission: Modernization and the Construction of an American World Order* (Princeton, NJ: Princeton University Press, 2010).

25. Albert O. Hirschman, "How the Keynesian Revolution Was Exported from the United States, and Other Comments," in *The Political Power of Economic Ideas: Keynesianism across Nations*, ed. Peter A. Hall (Princeton, NJ: Princeton University Press, 1989), 358–59.

26. Michael S. Sherry, *In the Shadow of War: The United States since the 1930s* (New Haven, CT: Yale University Press, 1995), 30–33; Hunt, *American Ascendancy*, 119–22.

27. Franklin Delano Roosevelt, State of the Union Address, January 6, 1941, American Presidency Project, http://www.presidency.ucsb.edu/ws/index.php?pid=16092; Ninkovich, *Wilsonian Century*, 132–33; Henry R. Luce, *The American Century* (New York: Farrar and Rinehardt, 1941), 20–24, 32–34; Elizabeth Borgwardt, *A New Deal for the World: America's Vision for Human Rights* (Cambridge, MA: Harvard University Press, 2005), 50–51.

28. David Abernethy, *The Dynamics of Global Dominance: European Overseas Empires, 1415–1980* (New Haven, CT: Yale University Press, 2000), 144.

29. Abernethy, *Dynamics*, 145; John Springhall, *Decolonization since 1945: The Collapse of European Empires* (Houndmills, UK: Palgrave, 2001), 29.

30. Abernethy, *Dynamics*, 149–50; Springhall, *Decolonization*, 67–69.

31. Abernethy, *Dynamics*, 151–53; Springhall, *Decolonization*, 117.

32. Vietnamese Declaration of Independence, as reprinted in Robert J. McMahon, *Major Problems in the History of the Vietnam War*, 3rd ed. (Boston: Houghton Mifflin, 2003), 23; Springhall, *Decolonization*, 114; Hunt, *American Ascendancy*, 193–94.

33. Mark Bradley, "Franklin Roosevelt, Trusteeship, and US Exceptionalism: Reconsidering the American Vision of Postcolonial Vietnam," in *A Companion to the Vietnam War*, ed. Marilyn Young and Robert Buzzanco (Malden, MA: Blackwell, 2002), 131–32.

34. Ibid., 133, 141.

35. William Roger Louis and Ronald Robinson, "The Imperialism of Decolonization," *Journal of Imperial and Commonwealth History* 22, no. 3 (1994): 468.

36. Hunt, *American Ascendancy*, 198–99; Thomas Borstelmann, *The Cold War and the Color Line: American Race Relations in the Global Arena* (Cambridge, MA: Harvard University Press, 2001), 69–70.

37. Louis and Robinson, "Imperialism of Decolonization," 472.

38. Amy L. S. Staples, *The Birth of Development: How the World Bank, Food and Agriculture Organization, and the World Health Organization Changed the World, 1945–1965* (Kent, OH: Kent State University Press, 2006), 33, 38, 85, 137–38.

39. John W. Dower, *Embracing Defeat: Japan in the Wake of World War II* (New York: Norton, 1999), 73–84, 346–404, 525–46.

40. Michael Hogan, *The Marshall Plan: America, Britain, and the Reconstruction of Western Europe, 1947–1952* (Cambridge: Cambridge University Press, 1987), 19; Diane Kunz, *Butter and Guns: America's Cold War Economic Diplomacy* (New York: Free Press, 1997), 35, 48–49, 52, 55.

41. Memorandum regarding the Technical Assistance Working Group, February 9, 1949, *FRUS 1949*, 1: 770; Thomas G. Paterson, "Foreign Aid under Wraps: The Point Four Program," *Wisconsin Magazine of History* 56, no. 2 (1972): 122, 125.

42. Odd Arne Westad, *The Global Cold War: Third World Interventions and the Making of Our Times* (Cambridge: Cambridge University Press, 2005), 17, emphasis in original.

TAKE-OFF
Modernization and Cold War America

In a landmark essay published in the midst of the Korean War, Harold Lasswell reflected on the need for the U.S. government and American social scientists to forge new links in response to the Cold War emergency. "The continuing crisis of national security," he argued, required a new set of "policy sciences" that would be valuable "in the decision-making process itself." "Moscow," he warned, was the "eruptive center of the world revolutionary pattern," and "a major problem of [the] epoch [was] to bring to completion the revolutionary processes of [the] historical period with the smallest human cost." Social scientists, therefore, needed to direct their energies toward providing policy-relevant knowledge and intelligence about "the principal social changes in [the] epoch." They needed to develop models to "specify the institutional pattern *from* which we are moving and the pattern *toward* which we are going."[1]

Modernization theory provided just the sort of historical construct that Lasswell called for. One of the country's most influential political scientists, Lasswell spent his career trying to mobilize scholarly knowledge for the benefit of the state. During the 1930s, worried by rising Soviet and Nazi strength, he drew on psychoanalytic theory to propose ways that U.S. elites might manipulate public opinion to ensure an antiauthoritarian consensus. During World War II, he analyzed foreign propaganda at a project based at the Library of Congress and went on to play a key role in establishing U.S. psychological warfare programs as a consultant to the Office of Strategic Services, the Office of War Information, and the U.S. Army. Many other U.S. social scientists, enlisted in the wartime crusade against fascism, shared Lasswell's conviction that their expertise could meet the needs of national security. The start of a truly global cold war, moreover, made the demand for programmatic, policy-oriented knowledge appear even greater. Though Nazi Germany and imperial Japan were finally defeated, the Soviets had emerged as deadly ideological adversaries. If the United States were to compete with revolutionary appeals it would require a strong sense of the decolonizing world's historical trajectory and a map of global universal change. U.S. policymakers would also need to understand the aspirations and anxieties of postcolonial leaders and peoples and know which social and institutional levers might be used to accelerate the movement of those societies in liberal directions. In the Cold War context, modernization became a theoretical model as well as a political agenda.[2]

Modernization also reflected aspirations deeply embedded in U.S. liberalism. Modernizers were convinced of their ability to mine the United States' own historical experience to find valuable lessons for postcolonial nations. While strongly motivated by anti-Communist convictions, many theorists and policymakers also imagined that they might promote progressive social and economic development. In an ambitious fashion, and with a sense of hopeful optimism that is difficult to recapture today, many of them anticipated that they might radically improve the overall quality of life of some of the poorest regions of the world.

Nationalism and the Global Cold War

In October 1949, Americans watched in dismay as Mao Zedong triumphantly proclaimed the founding of the People's Republic of China. Since the early twentieth century, missionaries, diplomats, businessmen, and journalists had reveled in the prospect of a China that would shed its traditional particularities and embark on the road to liberal, democratic modernity. After 1937, transfixed by the images of a Chinese people suffering under a brutal invasion by imperial Japan, Americans had also rallied to Chiang Kai-shek's Nationalist cause. A converted Methodist married to a Wellesley College-educated wife, Chiang enjoyed a popular acclaim that eclipsed the doubts of U.S. policymakers about his regime's corruption, authoritarianism, and halfhearted efforts in fighting the Japanese. Even as U.S. foreign service officers in the field reported their growing concern about Chiang's loss of public appeal and the striking efficiency of his Communist rivals, politicians and publishers at home continued to describe the United States as China's champion and inspiration. Nebraska's Republican senator Kenneth Wherry captured that sentiment in 1940. "We will lift Shanghai up and up, ever up," he declared, "until it is just like Kansas City." Only a few

years after Tokyo's defeat, however, it became clear that China's transformation would take on a decidedly different character. Mao's declaration in June
1949 that China would "lean to one side" in the Cold War and his decision to
sign a thirty-year treaty of mutual assistance with the Soviet Union in February
1950 made the revolutionary success all the more alarming. Despite the Truman
Doctrine's universalist language about resisting armed subversion, the Communists had triumphed in Asia.[3]

The jarring realization that the world's most populous country had fallen
under Communist control had a tremendous impact on both U.S. foreign policy
and domestic politics. The Truman administration's political adversaries quickly
cast the "loss of China" as a betrayal of Chiang's government and clear evidence
of disloyalty at home. Branding the State Department's leading China experts as
Communist sympathizers and "fellow travelers," Republicans promoted a Red
Scare that dovetailed with a broader ideological campaign against the New Deal
and its liberal legacies. Along with the Soviet detonation of an atomic bomb, also
in 1949, defeat in China amplified popular fears of subversion and fueled the rise
of McCarthyism. In the face of growing pressure, the Truman administration
failed to produce a compelling analysis of the reasons why the Chinese Communists had been able to harness the forces of rural class conflict, anticolonialism, and patriotic nationalism. In the absence of a sustained explanation of the
underlying historical factors, the reductive, conspiratorial claims about a mono-
lithic, "international communist movement" wholly directed and controlled by
Moscow became entrenched in U.S. Cold War politics.

The start of the Korean War in June 1950 reinforced that conclusion. Although that conflict was rooted in a civil war—and newly released Soviet and
Chinese documents make clear that the initiative for the North Korean invasion
came from Kim Il-sung—the Truman administration concluded that the North
Korean attack and the Chinese entry into the war were parts of a wider, comprehensive Kremlin plan to expand the Soviet Union's strategic power and ideological system. Although U.S. officials did not believe Korea itself was strategically
vital, they feared that if Stalin were permitted to prevail there he would continue
to press the advantage, exploiting weaknesses until he dominated the region or
precipitated a third world war.[4]

From that point forward, U.S. policymakers came to define the Cold War in
increasingly global terms. Although they frequently recognized that the most
powerful forces at work in Asia, Africa, Latin America, and the Middle East were
rooted in nationalism, anticolonialism, and indigenous economic and political
conflicts, the Truman and Eisenhower administrations struggled to translate that
understanding into an effective foreign policy. Reluctant to alienate vital European allies and distrustful of anticolonial elites that they considered politically

unreliable, they feared that the upheavals generated by revolutionary nationalism would provide new opportunities for Communist subversion. As the Cold
War turned hot, with flash points ranging from Indochina to Guatemala, policymakers also gave the "periphery" a heightened degree of importance. The State
Department's Paul Nitze and his colleagues expressed that global concern in the
strategic blueprint known as NSC-68: "In the context of the present polarization
of power a defeat of free institutions anywhere is a defeat everywhere. . . . At the
ideological or psychological level, in the struggle for men's minds, the conflict is
worldwide."[5]

As they confronted the specter of revolution and its implications for the global
Cold War during the 1950s, U.S. officials hoped that nationalist movements would
turn in liberal, pro-Western directions. But they remained ready to repress those
that did not. Determined to secure strategically significant regions, protect vital
economic resources, repel Soviet opportunism, and ensure the United States' Cold
War credibility, the Truman and Eisenhower administrations moved forcefully.
Because they viewed many postcolonial leaders as politically immature and unprepared for self-determination, they exercised little restraint in trying to undermine
governments that, in their assessment, opened doors to Communist subversion.
In Vietnam, when war broke out between the Vietminh and the French in 1946,
a transnational campaign of like-minded French, British, and U.S. officials began
to push the United States toward intervention. In 1950, the United States finally
committed itself to France's military campaign to recover its Indochinese colonies, and over four years the United States poured a massive $3 billion into the
war effort, bankrolling more than 80 percent of its material costs in 1954. When
Iranian prime minister Mohammad Mosaddeq challenged a long-standing British
monopoly on Iranian oil production and declined to suppress his country's well-
organized Communist Party, the CIA and British intelligence mounted a coup
against him in 1953. The Eisenhower administration followed a similar course a
year later in Guatemala. After Jacobo Arbenz Guzmán started a sweeping agrarian
reform program, refused to expel the handful of Communist officeholders from
the government, and dared to accept an arms shipment from Czechoslovakia, the
United States organized a military coup to force him from power. In Indonesia,
finally, after Ahmed Sukarno accepted Soviet economic aid, dissolved the country's political parties, and denounced parliamentary authority in the name of a
"guided democracy," U.S. officials intervened again. Fearing that country might
slide toward Communist control, in 1957 the Eisenhower administration launched
an ill-conceived and ultimately unsuccessful plan to destroy the government by
supporting a rebellion of army dissidents.[6]

Those interventions represent a consistent pattern in which, as historian
Robert McMahon points out, U.S. policymakers "grievously misunderstood and

underestimated" the force of postcolonial nationalism and tied the United States "to the status quo in areas undergoing fundamental social, political, and economic upheaval." From the mid-1950s through the end of the decade, however, U.S. officials also began to recognize that nationalist movements were only gaining in strength and power, and that policies designed with the sole objective of blocking them entirely presented serious risks of their own. As Eisenhower wrote to Winston Churchill in 1954, "there is abroad in the world a fierce and growing spirit of nationalism. Should we try to dam it up completely, it would, like a mighty river, burst through the barriers and create havoc. But again, like a river, if we are intelligent enough to make constructive use of this force, then the result, far from being disastrous, could redound greatly to our advantage, particularly in our struggle against the Kremlin's power."[7]

By the early 1960s, that perspective would gradually lead to another approach centered on concepts of development and modernization. If the United States were going to prevail in the global Cold War, many commentators and policymakers came to believe, it would have to demonstrate that a liberal, capitalist social order could meet the aspirations of postcolonial leaders for economic growth, strong state structures, and human progress at least as effectively as Marxist alternatives. This new vision never renounced coercive force; in fact it often defined it as a valuable modernizing tool. It was also uncertain at best regarding questions of democracy. Yet its proponents ultimately held that the United States would have to win the Cold War at the structural level, producing the economic, political, cultural, and psychological transformations necessary to create a world in which revolution would no longer have any appeal.

The factors that shaped this additional trend in American thinking were varied and complex. In many ways, however, the intractable problems created by the Cold War dilemma of balancing support for European allies against growing anticolonial demands helped promote a reassessment. This was particularly the case in North Africa and the Middle East. Since World War II, the United States had followed a careful "middle-of-the-road" policy regarding Algeria, publicly expressing support for French control over the colony while privately encouraging gradual steps toward reform. After the Algerian War began in 1954, however, U.S. policymakers became increasingly concerned as the French fought to retain possession of a land in which approximately one million settlers of European descent lived among eight million Muslim Arabs and Berbers. As terrorist violence escalated on both sides and the Front de Libération Nationale (FLN) put up a tough resistance, the Eisenhower administration gradually determined that U.S. support for French repression might have disastrous consequences. The United States backed France in Indochina, but by the middle of the 1950s Secretary of State John Foster Dulles concluded that French colonial policies suffered from a profound "short-sightedness and lack of realism." The ability of the FLN and its allies to use radio, film, and the public forum of the United Nations to define their struggle as one for self-determination against colonialism and white supremacy also helped raise the international costs of U.S. support. In February 1958, after France bombarded a Tunisian village in an attempt to destroy an FLN sanctuary, killing scores of unarmed civilians and arousing international condemnation, the Eisenhower administration dramatically curtailed its support for the war. U.S. policymakers perceived little evidence of direct Communist involvement in Algeria, but they worried that French intransigence would push the nationalists into the Soviet embrace. Rather than continuing to support an anticolonial campaign, Washington decided that it made more sense to try and force Paris toward a peaceful solution, even if the only way to do that was to risk the Franco-American relationship by pressing for Algerian independence.[8]

The United States' experience in dealing with the radical pan-Arab nationalism of Egypt's Gamal Abdel Nasser produced a similar set of conclusions. In 1956, after Nasser nationalized the Suez Canal, and France, Britain, and Israel attacked Egypt in response, Dulles worried that the United States could no longer stand on the perilous line between European colonizers and nationalist ambitions: "In view of the overwhelming Asian and African pressure upon us we could not walk this tightrope much longer." "Win or lose," he warned, "we will share the fate of Britain and France. . . . [And] the British and French would not win." Arab nationalism, Dulles explained to a visiting European diplomat in 1958, was "a turbulent stream," and the "United States did not have the slightest intention of trying to stem it." The best one could do was to "erect dikes to contain it." "Later on," Dulles suggested, "when the turbulence of the stream has moderated, we would hope to work with it."[9]

U.S. officials, historian Matthew Connelly observes, frequently defined nationalist movements as "a force of nature, often using the imagery of a flood, a tide, or a wave." Since such forces could not simply be stopped or repelled, their course would have to be channeled, managed, and directed. The search for a means to do that took on new importance after nearly thirty postcolonial leaders met in Bandung, Indonesia, for the first Asian-African conference in 1955. As figures like Nehru, Nasser, and Sukarno condemned imperialism and declared their neutrality in the Cold War, Eisenhower lamented the fact that the United States had not yet found a way to "utilize this spirit of nationalism in its own interest." The problem, Eisenhower and his advisers reflected, was to separate the United States from imperialism and present a far more appealing vision.[10]

A newly ambitious Soviet policy also alarmed Washington. Following Stalin's death in 1953, Soviet strategists became more interested in the process of decolonization. Stalin's characterization of elite nationalist leaders as mere "stooges of imperialism," Nikita Khrushchev argued, was deeply flawed. Postcolonial states, even resolutely nationalist ones, could become integral parts of a progressive coalition. Socialism, Soviet planners now suggested, might also move forward along various paths, even without a vanguard party or a prolonged armed struggle. In postcolonial and nonaligned states, they argued, working-class and proletarian forces could lead bourgeois nationalists into alliances that would drive anti-imperial revolutions in anticapitalist directions. Soviet strategists also expected that their country's impressive record of economic growth and consistent pattern of opposition to colonial rule would appeal to nationalist elites embittered by their struggles with imperial powers. Accordingly, they began an active program to promote links between Soviet power and postcolonial ambitions for development and security. In the late 1950s, the Soviets sent large amounts of economic and military aid to India, Egypt, and Indonesia and soon supported Algeria's FLN as well. Russian leaders toured Asia, Africa, and the Middle East, deployed teams of technicians, funded infrastructure projects, and sharply increased Soviet foreign assistance. The Soviet economic model, based on strong, centralized planning, also had tremendous appeal for nationalist leaders eager to pursue rapid development under their firm authority.[11]

Determined to compete with Soviet overtures and hoping to guide nationalist ambitions in pro-Western directions, U.S. policymakers began to give additional weight to programs centered on concepts of development and, in more dramatic terms, "nation building." When the fiscally conservative Eisenhower first took office, he expected that liberalized trade and expanded private investment ("trade not aid") would help generate sufficient growth to raise living standards and dampen radical appeals. By 1957, however, Eisenhower had concluded that "the spirit of nationalism, coupled with a deep hunger for some betterment in physical conditions and living standards, creates a critical situation in the underdeveloped areas of the world." In the spring of that year, he called on Congress to create a large Development Loan Fund to make public, long-term loans to Asian, African, Middle Eastern, and Latin American countries. In October 1960, following the shock of the Cuban Revolution, the Eisenhower administration also supported the creation of a multilateral Inter-American Development Bank and promised to provide nearly half of its initial $1 billion in capital. Fearful that Cuban radicalism would spread throughout the rest of Latin America, the administration then committed an additional $500 million to a regional Social Progress Trust Fund to pay for health care, land reform, and housing projects.[12]

The shift in Eisenhower's approach was limited by several factors. Conservatives in Congress, committed to market principles and objecting that such aid would displace private ventures, cut his requested appropriations. Eisenhower himself also considered development assistance as only a small part of a much larger policy still based on a fundamentally market-driven international political economy. Foreign aid, he and his advisers concluded, would be deployed primarily to deal with immediate security emergencies. Their primary objective, moreover, was economic growth, not the broad social, cultural, and psychological transformations envisioned in far more sweeping concepts of modernization.[13]

This more ambitious idea of modernizing and fundamentally transforming the decolonizing world, however, was already gaining ground in U.S. foreign policy. As he campaigned for the presidency, John F. Kennedy constantly argued for a bolder approach. As early as 1957, Kennedy had criticized the Eisenhower administration's support for French colonialism in Algeria. By 1960, he also charged that the administration's reliance on nuclear weaponry to deter the Soviets had failed to respond to the global problems of nationalism and development. A full third of the world, Kennedy argued, was "rocked by the pangs of poverty, hunger, and envy." He went on to describe the threatening immediacy of the world situation: "More energy is released by the awakening of these new nations than by the fission of the atom itself. Meanwhile, Communist influence has penetrated farther into Asia, stood astride the Middle East, and now festers some ninety miles off the coast of Florida." While the State Department remained hobbled by pin-striped diplomats lacking language skills, Kennedy warned, "out of Moscow and Peiping and Czechoslovakia and Eastern Germany are hundreds of men and women, scientists, physicists, teachers, engineers, doctors, nurses . . . prepared to spend their lives abroad in the service of world communism." Kennedy himself came of political age at the outset of the Cold War, entering Congress only months before the announcement of the Truman Doctrine. He and his advisers accepted the Cold War's fundamental ideological assumptions and were deeply committed to confronting Soviet expansionism. Yet they also believed that a far more assertive policy—bringing to bear the full resources and expertise of the United States to guide and direct the aspirations of people in Latin America, Asia, Africa, and the Middle East—was needed to turn the tide.[14]

As we saw in chapter 1, American ideas about development and modernization as a means of preserving U.S. national security were grounded in older, liberal internationalist assumptions. Truman's Point Four program had put the issue on the official agenda, and by the late 1950s it gained far greater emphasis. Struck by the rise of a "nonaligned movement" of newly independent states and by the proliferation of revolutionary aspirations for self-determination and socioeconomic progress, U.S. policymakers came to understand the global Cold War as a contest between two diametrically opposed visions of the world's future. Liberal, capitalist democracy, they believed, represented the natural end point of social progress, and the United States stood at the leading edge of history. To combat the threat of communism, however, the historical trajectory of the "emerging" regions of the world would have to be decisively accelerated. By the 1960s, through foreign aid, development planning, and the transformation of infrastructure, politics, and psychologies, the United States would attempt to produce a comprehensive change. While U.S. officials continued and even increased their reliance on covert and overt force, they would begin to promote a second, closely related, yet far more ambitious, policy track. They would seek to alter the very environmental conditions in which they believed that radicalism grew and attempt to control the course of nationalist aspirations. They would wage the Cold War through modernization.

The Rise of Modernization Theory

As a social scientific theory, modernization represented an interdisciplinary attempt to define a universal model of global change. Modernization theorists such as Talcott Parsons, Gabriel Almond, Lucian Pye, and Walt Rostow sought to unite diverse branches of social analysis in a comprehensive effort to define the essential stages through which all societies traveled from traditional to modern conditions. They also claimed to do so in a rigorously scientific fashion, even when they attempted to provide knowledge that they expected would be of great utility to U.S. policymakers seeking to comprehend a world in tremendous flux. Modernization theory, in this regard, always had a strong normative component. In Harold Lasswell's terms, it was an ideal "policy science," geared toward the identification and solution of strategic problems.[15]

A theory of modernization first required a useful theory of society itself, and it was the great ambition of sociologist Talcott Parsons to provide one. As he argued in his massive theoretical work, *The Structure of Social Action* (1937), the common assumptions of classical, nineteenth-century liberalism failed to provide an accurate understanding of the way that human agency in all societies was shaped by a functioning social structure. Where classical liberalism stressed utilitarian, profit-maximizing behavior and treated society merely as an aggregate of naturally self-serving individuals, Parsons rejected that approach as reductive and deterministic. Human beings, he contended, were not merely the victims of innate drives and environmental forces. They were instead profoundly shaped by the values and cultural norms transmitted through institutions.[16]

When first published, Parsons's work was widely reviewed but received little sustained scholarly attention. After World War II and the start of the Cold War, however, it quickly gained recognition. Parsons's emphasis on the pivotal role of human values in preserving consensual social equilibrium also took on new political meaning amid the affluence of 1950s America. A defender of the New Deal,

Parsons argued that in the United States individuals participated actively in social life, and it was their common adherence to ethical values and social principles, especially those of freedom and justice, that allowed for the preservation of a stable, fundamentally democratic order capable of alleviating poverty and reducing the dangers of social turmoil. In Nazi Germany, by contrast, the results had been profoundly different. As Parsons argued in an essay originally written in 1942 and first published in 1949, because German society was not integrated around a similar set of humane, liberal ideals, it was ultimately thrown into chaos and destructive violence during the interwar period. In combination with the harsh economic consequences of the Treaty of Versailles, Parsons maintained, rapid, destabilizing change in the form of industrialization, urbanization, and increasing occupational mobility had unleashed widespread insecurity, "free-floating aggression," and a "susceptibility of emotionalized propaganda appeals." As he diagnosed Germany's illness, Parsons identified a wide range of social pathologies. Elite classes of landed gentry and military officers, he explained, viewed bourgeois culture and freedoms with disdain. Prussian "conservatism" enlarged the sphere of the state to the detriment of an independent-minded civil service and legal profession. German gender roles, moreover, reflected an overwhelming emphasis on masculine superiority and a strong "romantic idealization of solidary groups of young men—sometimes with at least an undercurrent of homosexuality." As a result, amid the transformations of the 1930s, Germany failed to continue in "the main line of the evolution of Western society, the progressive approach to the rationalization of 'liberal-democratic' patterns and values." Instead, the Nazis mobilized "the extremely deep-seated romantic tendencies of German society" in the name of a movement driven by brutal forms of social control and violent aggression. Though he did not yet use the term, Parsons effectively defined National Socialism as a case of modernization gone wrong.[17]

Parsons's political commitment to the preservation of a liberal, consensual social order and his intellectual desire to provide a universal description of the structures that integrated all societies profoundly shaped his postwar work. As the chair of Harvard's enormously influential Department of Social Relations, established in 1946, he sought to combine the insights of sociology, social and cultural anthropology, and social psychology. In collaboration with scholars like the University of Chicago's Edward Shils, Parsons also worked to develop a general theory for the social sciences as a whole. Parsons and his colleagues claimed that societies were best considered as "functioning systems" in which the range of roles in each person's personality could be correlated with the different structures of society. When social structures met individual needs and reflected the common ideals and values of the culture, then society would rest at a perfect, consensual equilibrium, just as it appeared to do in the United States. When thrown out of balance, as in the German case, disjunction, disorder, and violence would result.[18]

Although Parsons was still more focused on the problem of defining the essential elements for the preservation of liberal social harmony, he also began to develop a model of social change. Drawing on the work of anthropologists like Ruth Benedict, Parsons and Shils argued that diverse human societies tended to cluster around specific, integrated sets of attributes, a phenomenon they described in terms of "pattern variables." In some social systems, individual actions were shaped by a sense of ascribed status, particularist values, an orientation toward oneself, diffuse and uncertain social roles, and an "affective" psychological inability to defer gratification. In others, however, values emphasizing achieved status, universal standards, an orientation toward one's responsibility to a wider group, clear, specific social roles, and deferred gratification through self-discipline carried the day. Their construction of two, dichotomous social orders also implied a sense of historical direction. Though Parsons and Shils did not yet define it as such, readers correctly assumed that the two had framed "traditional" and "rational" (or "modern") as historical conditions, and that "development" involved the successful transition from the former to the latter. Within a few years, Parsons himself made the point directly. Inspired by Max Weber's emphasis on the role of culture in shaping social evolution, Parsons drew direct contrasts between the "Judeo-Christian" inheritance, which he termed "highly activistic in relation to the external environment," and the civilizations of China and India, which had "quite a different character." The impact of transformative Western ideals, he reflected, was "the most crucial factor at present in the widespread attempts at industrial development in the 'underdeveloped' societies."[19]

Parsons's emphasis on the crucial role of human values and psychology in providing for social equilibrium as well as social change had an enormous effect, promoting many further studies of modernization. The concept also gained far broader circulation, most famously in MIT sociologist Daniel Lerner's hugely popular book, *The Passing of Traditional Society: Modernizing the Middle East* (1958). In his preface to the 1964 edition, Lerner insisted that modernization was a genuinely universal phenomenon: "The same basic model reappears in virtually all modernizing societies on all continents of the world, regardless of variations in race, color, or creed." After analyzing 1,600 interviews conducted by the United States Information Service in Iran, Lebanon, Syria, Egypt, Jordan, and Turkey, Lerner concluded that the Middle East was undergoing a transformation similar to the one that the West had previously passed through. The key catalyst, moreover, was the psychological component of "empathy." As in the West, increases in physical and social mobility had generated a new spirit of "rationality" and engagement. As young men moved from rural areas into cities, mass communications and media in the form of radio, film, and television exposed them to an "infinite vicarious universe," through which they came to identify themselves as part of a broader, participatory society and developed new aspirations. Modernization, Lerner determined, infused the Middle East with "a 'rationalist and positivist spirit' against which, scholars seem agreed, 'Islam is absolutely defenseless.'" Yet, like Parsons, Lerner also warned of the perils of the transitional process. Middle Eastern elites, he observed, "have little patience with the historical *pace* of Western development" and "want to do it their 'own way.'" Because they were drawn toward "new routes and risky by-passes," it would be crucial for the West to guide volatile Middle Eastern societies along the correct route to modernity. Otherwise, the persistent "psychocultural gap" between rising popular expectations and backward conditions could ultimately develop "an explosive charge."[20]

The sense of modernization as a unifying, integrative framework and the growing concern of social scientists with the potential instabilities produced by the "transitional" process also had a direct effect on U.S. political science. This was especially the case in the field of comparative politics, where Princeton's Gabriel Almond and MIT's Lucian Pye played pivotal roles. Like Parsons in sociology, Almond and Pye established modernization as an integrating theoretical model and argued that it would place their discipline's research on a more scientific basis. Like Parsons as well, they also shared a firm conviction that social research could and should serve political ends.[21]

Working in tandem, Almond and Pye placed the study of comparative politics on a foundation supported by analyses linking psychology, development, and modernization. Harold Lasswell, a former teacher of both men, strongly influenced their thinking. An expert on propaganda, which he defined as "the management of collective attitudes by the manipulation of significant symbols," in the late 1920s Lasswell had become keenly interested in psychoanalytic theory. Political behavior, he came to believe, was frequently the manifestation of inner anxieties and turmoil. Radical political dissent, he suggested, could also be understood in terms of psychological deviance as much as a result of ideological or socioeconomic forces. In *World Politics and Personal Insecurity* (1935), Lasswell argued that the dangers of lethal global violence made it incumbent on elite political leaders to mobilize political symbols in order to control eruptions of collective, psychologically driven turmoil. "Wars and revolutions," he maintained, "are avenues of discharge for collective insecurities and stand in competition with every alternative means of dissipating mass tension. . . . The special province of political psychiatrists who seek to develop and to practice the politics of prevention is devising ingenious expedients capable of discharging accumulated anxieties as harmlessly as possible." In 1954, Almond applied that framework in

The Appeals of Communism, an analysis that proposed to determine why men in the West joined Communist parties. While acknowledging that Italian and French workers might become Communists because the party was the only force promoting the interests of their socioeconomic class, Almond argued that middle classes in Britain and the United States did so largely out of psychological alienation. Communist recruits in those countries, he pointed out, were often resentful, isolated deviants who longed for the sense of meaning that the party could provide. They knew little of the Communist Party's "esoteric" doctrine but joined out of "impulses to deviate, to reject parental and religious patterns, to do something exciting, romantic, bohemian, antagonistic."[22]

Two years later, Pye put the theoretical claims of Lasswell and Almond to work in the "developing" world. In *Guerrilla Communism in Malaya* (1956), Pye focused specifically on the destabilizing "transitional" process that sociologists like Parsons and Lerner had also identified. The rebellion against British colonial rule in Malaya, he contended, provided a clear illustration of a wider, universal phenomenon. As postwar Malaya was increasingly exposed to the impact of Western technology, institutions, mass communications, and ideals, according to Pye, "People's Liberation Communism" came to appeal most to those who were caught in the personal uncertainty generated by the jarring social transition from tradition to modernity. Malayan radicals, he noted, were losing touch with the world of their parents but had not yet found a means to comprehend and respond to their uncertain futures. The Communist Party, therefore, was attractive not because of anticolonial, ideological principles, or even because it promised a redistribution of power or resources. Instead, the Communists gained members because the party provided a structure through which displaced individuals believed they could "find a closer relationship between effort and reward than anything they have known in either the static old society or the unstable, unpredictable new one." "Rootless" men joined the Communist Party, in other words, because they wanted to be modern.[23]

Almond and Pye also found the idea of modernization theoretically useful in defining their field's research agenda. Impressed by the rapid transformations produced by the collapse of European empire and the emergence of a host of "new states," in 1953 the prestigious Social Science Research Council (SSRC) established a new Comparative Politics Committee. Although SSRC President Edward Pendelton Herring had hoped that the committee would produce a "conceptual scheme which would lead to a higher comparability of data" and help guide fieldwork, its members were initially unsure how to proceed. In 1955, committee members George Kahin, Guy Pauker, and Pye observed that "most of the non-Western political systems have many features in common," including the experience of colonial rule and a clear, conscious desire to move "from a definite past to an idealized future." Like other social scientists, they also warned of potential turbulence, suggesting that "the possibility of unorganized and generally inarticulate segments of society suddenly finding expression contributes to the potentially explosive nature of politics in some non-Western countries." Despite those common elements, they ultimately concluded that regional variations and cultural differences were significant barriers to an overarching theory. The "resilient forces of tradition," moreover, were "capable of rejecting and modifying many Western patterns."[24]

Once the committee turned toward sociological concepts of modernization, however, those theoretical obstacles seemed far less daunting. As Almond reported to the SSRC in 1956, committee members had initially worried that "the present state of the field did not justify a global comparative effort." Since "no common body of scholarship deals with comparative politics," and the field was divided into "specialists on Europe, Africa, the Middle East, Southeast Asia, and East Asia," he explained, it was difficult to imagine arriving at a "genuinely comparative theory of social systems." Almond did suggest, however, that "the classification of types of value orientation" and "Talcott Parsons's concept of 'pattern variables'" could provide a means of "distinguishing the cultures and ideologies of the different political systems." If researchers were to "stress *function* and the interrelationships between political, cultural, and social processes," it would be much easier to build a common framework.[25]

Before long, that approach emerged triumphant, shaping the field's scholarship for the rest of the decade. By assuming that all political systems fulfilled common, universal functions, scholars could then identify, compare, and order the structures in different societies that fulfilled those functions and take important steps toward defining an overarching model of "political modernization." In 1960, in the first of a series of books sponsored by the SSRC, Almond proclaimed that this approach to comparative politics marked nothing less than the "intimation of a major step forward in the nature of political science as science." It would enable scholars to "break through the barriers of culture and language and show that what may seem strange at first sight is strange by virtue of its costume or name, but not by nature of its functions." As Almond's coeditor James Coleman agreed, the comparison of the political structures of traditional and modern societies would enable researchers to identify the universal patterns of development, marked by urbanization, improved literacy, increases in per capita income, geographic and social mobility, industrialization, mass communication, and broad participation. It would prove Daniel Lerner's claim that "modernization as a process has a distinctive quality of its own, that the various elements in this process 'do not occur in haphazard and unrelated fashion,' and that they have gone together so regularly because 'in some historical sense they *had* to go together.'"[26]

The concept of modernization also transformed the field of development economics, although its scholarly impact there was of a very different character. Sociologists and political scientists gravitated toward modernization because it seemed to provide a unifying, foundational theory, but most economists believed that they already had one. The fundamental laws governing supply, demand, production, and consumption, they assumed, applied to all economies, everywhere. The problem, they thought, was not to frame an integrating, universal theory, but instead to determine whether the developing world was in fact so *different* from the modern one that the orthodox principles did not apply there. In the first years after World War II economists also wrestled with the question of defining "development" itself. Most agreed that raising living standards was an urgent objective, but even that topic generated a broad range of questions pertaining to employment, health care, education, housing, nutrition, and industrialization. Eventually economists sidestepped that problem by narrowing their focus to economic growth. The new concept of "gross national product" (GNP), first deployed as a standard of measurement only in the 1940s, reflected that turn. Rather than confronting enormously complex questions about the causes of poverty or the persistence of inequality, economists would instead use statistical assessments of aggregate national production as the key benchmarks of progress. GNP growth, in their terms, became the essential index of development.[27]

Initially, many economists also expected that the same Keynesian methods that had helped industrialized countries recover from the Great Depression might be deployed in Asia, Africa, Latin America, and the Middle East. Wartime mobilization and the impact of the Marshall Plan generated a sense of optimism, and since development was conceived of in terms of raising the overall level of economic equilibrium between supply and demand, many hoped that Keynes's approach to short-term problems of stabilization could be modified to address problems of long-term growth. As economists like R. F. Harrod and Evsey Domar argued, increases in capital investment would stimulate higher levels of production, raising overall levels of economic activity and reducing unemployment. Once growth started, moreover, it would accelerate, since part of the profit from each increase in output would be reinvested. At higher income levels, the marginal propensity to save would also be higher, holding out the promise that beyond a certain critical threshold growth would ultimately become self-sustaining. The central problem, therefore, was simply to determine the level of capital investment and savings required to reach the desired output and growth levels.[28]

By the early 1950s, however, the expected improvements had not arrived, leading many development economists to the conclusion that rural underemployment, "late-coming industrialization," and a host of other, "non-economic" factors made conditions in much of the postcolonial world so distinct that their growth would require more original approaches. Key figures like W. Arthur Lewis and Gunnar Myrdal also began to put forward "structural" explanations, arguing that in poor, agricultural regions ordinary market principles did not fit well. Because communications were lacking and entrepreneurship largely absent, supply and demand were inelastic, and the price mechanism did not work. Custom and culture, it also appeared, frequently made peasants less than fully rational actors. "Progress," Lewis observed in 1951, "occurs only when people believe that man can, by conscious effort, master nature. . . . Even when people know that a greater abundance of goods and services is possible, they may not consider it worth the effort. Lack of interest in material things may be due to the prevalence of an other-worldly philosophy which discourages material wants."[29]

It was this vision of a developing world afflicted by a complex, systemic combination of economic, social, cultural, and psychological variables that ultimately led significant numbers of development economists to consider the goal of growth in terms of a broader process of modernization. Among the most important figures leading the field in that direction was MIT economist Paul Rosenstein-Rodan. Because of the tenacious economic and social problems to be overcome, he argued that any successful development strategy would have to involve an initial "big push" of massive foreign investment coupled with comprehensive state planning and social engineering. As he put it in 1957, "there is a minimum level of resources that must be devoted to . . . a development program if it is to have any chance of success. Launching a country into self-sustaining growth is a little like trying to get an airplane off the ground. There is a critical ground speed which must be passed before the craft can become airborne." Reaching that "critical ground speed," moreover, was not a purely economic problem. The University of Chicago's Bert Hoselitz, founder and editor of the influential journal *Economic Development and Cultural Change*, made this point emphatically by stating that measuring progress merely in terms of "the growth of per capita real output" was insufficient. As he put it, "if different stages of economic development are associated with different systems, each exhibiting a particular social structure and culture, we must look for further criteria by which to separate economically 'advanced' and 'underdeveloped' countries." Only then would it be possible to build a framework that might expand "the boundaries of our general theoretical knowledge" and provide a "guide for present policy."[30]

It was that perspective that Walt Whitman Rostow articulated most clearly and dramatically, for professional and public audiences alike, in his famous book, *The Stages of Economic Growth: A Non-Communist Manifesto* (1960). In 1951, Rostow accepted an appointment at MIT's Center for International Studies, where he was soon joined by Pye, Lerner, and Rosenstein-Rodan. Interested in the long-term patterns of economic growth and determined to provide a countertheory to Marxism, Rostow built on and expanded previous definitions of economic development. While still discussing macroeconomic questions centering on the promotion of investment to increase per capita income, he also proposed that societies were "interacting organisms" and insisted that "the worlds of politics, social organization, and culture" were key factors in the scope of economic history.[31]

Most strikingly, Rostow defined a linear, universal trajectory of social and economic change, moving through five successive stages, ranging from the "traditional society" through a pivotal "take-off" and on to a final "age of mass consumption." As he saw it, traditional societies were debilitated by more than a lack of the technology needed to raise agricultural output levels and generate surplus capital for investment. They also suffered from "pre-Newtonian attitudes towards the physical world" and a "long-run fatalism" that sharply limited their horizons. In time, however, such societies might develop new production functions in agriculture and industry and begin to build "an effective centralized national state," enabling them to enter the next stage, the "preconditions for take-off." Such progress, Rostow noted, was frequently the result of the "external intrusion" of more advanced societies, which "set in motion ideas and sentiments which initiated the process by which a modern alternative to the traditional society was constructed out of the old culture." In the crucial "take-off" stage, "old blocks and resistances to steady growth" were finally vanquished. It was here, Rostow explained, that pivotal economic transformations made growth "self-sustaining." As savings increased as a percentage of national income, an entrepreneurial class appeared, and commercialization accelerated. Next, during the "drive to maturity," investment rates continued to increase and the economy diversified into more industrial and technological sectors, reaching into international trade as well. Finally, at the end of the historical scale, societies entered the "age of high mass-consumption," a period characterized by the production of more consumer goods, a wide array of services, sharply increased per capita income, urbanization, and the formation of a welfare state.[32]

Rostow also argued that while the world's historical patterns were uniform, and every society did pass through the same five stages, not all did so at the same speed. Referring to Louis Hartz's classic *The Liberal Tradition in America* (1955), Rostow reflected that American society was "born free." Blessed with the presence of nonconformist groups, abundant land, and natural resources, the U.S. government put forward vital incentives for economic growth. Most importantly, its people "never became so deeply caught up in the structures, politics and values of traditional society; and, therefore, the process of their transition to modern growth was mainly economic and technical." Yet there was hope for even the most backward of societies, especially if they received the aid and assistance of the more advanced world in overcoming the historical barriers to progress. In the past, Rostow noted, colonialism had often produced unintended yet beneficial effects by stimulating a "reactive nationalism." "Men holding effective authority or influence," Rostow pointed out, "have been willing to uproot traditional societies not, primarily, to make more money but because the traditional society failed—or threatened to fail—to protect them from humiliation by foreigners." Imperialists did not always "optimize the development of the preconditions for take-off," but "they could not avoid bringing about transformation[s] . . . which moved the colonial society along the transitional path." Now, in a new geopolitical age, the developed nations might replace imperialism with more powerful and deliberate forms of assistance. By transferring new technologies and a massively increasing foreign aid, they could drive an impoverished, materially and culturally deficient world forward.[33]

The ambition and optimism of modernization, however, were tempered by a sense of growing political emergency. Although they worked across different disciplines, most theorists believed that the world was ultimately bound to converge on common, modern forms. As MIT political scientist Robert Wood argued in a speech written for the Voice of America, to "foresee the course of modernization," the citizens of new states merely needed to "investigate the conditions of life in today's so-called 'advanced' societies and then project an immediate future." Yet most theorists also recognized that the Soviet Union, with its high economic growth rates, massive industrial complex, increasing urbanization, and technological sophistication was itself a formidably "modern" rival. The essential problem, therefore, was to make it clear that the Soviets offered a false, perverted path, and that only in the "free world" could development follow a genuinely natural, humane course. The task, in other words, was to present the U.S. version of the "end of history" as the more appealing target, and to prove, in Rostow's terms, that the best engine of fundamental historical change was compound interest, not class struggle.[34]

The Policy Imperative

In 1963, Edward Shils attempted to explain the relationship between the production of social theory and the shaping of public policy. Professional scholars studying the postcolonial world, he argued, were practicing a "disciplined extension of experience." He explained further: "The categories we employ are the same as the ones we employ in our studies of our own societies, and they postulate the fundamental affinities of all human beings." By promoting a greater recognition of a common humanity, the work of social scientists would, in turn, inform a more "constructive policy." Shils and his colleagues, however, did not "intend to attain these moral effects through preaching, exhortation, or manipulation." They sought to produce them through "systemic research, conducted under the auspices of the best traditions of contemporary social science." In Shils's formulation, social scientists studied the developing world out of a sense of profound human "affinity," driven by the poignant realization that their own familiar past mirrored a foreign world's present, and that they had a moral obligation to assist "traditional" peoples as they struggled along the same historical trajectory. Their research, however, was rigorously dispassionate and objective. Modernization, as Shils and other scholars defined it, was not a social construction. It was a fact, and whatever impact it produced in the world of policy was due solely to its fundamental validity.[35]

Such arguments, drawing a clear line between the production of knowledge and its application, were no doubt appealing to scholars who sought to reconcile their claims of scientific objectivity with their hopes of political influence. Under close inspection, however, such assertions quickly break down. While modernization theory certainly did reflect the liberal hopes, scholarly aspirations, and intellectual curiosities of its proponents, it was also intimately associated with government institutions and philanthropic foundations seeking to understand and transform the Cold War world.

As early as 1945, Brigadier General John Magrader of the Office of Strategic Services told a Senate hearing that "in all of the intelligence that enters into the waging of war soundly and the waging of peace soundly, it is the social scientists who make a huge contribution." While never approaching the amounts channeled into universities for physical science research and weapons development, federal support for social science played a significant role in several key fields. Defense Department contracts put economists to work on complex problems in logistics, game theory, and nuclear strategy. Psychologists secured funding by analyzing revolutionary movements, designing counterinsurgency programs, and evaluating propaganda techniques. The military, intelligence, and diplomatic agencies of the U.S. government provided substantial support for U.S. communications research, amounting to approximately $1 billion per year in the early 1950s. Edward Shils himself was an important spokesperson for the Congress on Cultural Freedom, an organization of anti-Communist intellectuals covertly sponsored by the CIA that, among other things, organized international conferences promoting concepts of modernization before audiences of Asian, African, and Latin American scholars, journalists, and politicians. Major philanthropic foundations, particularly the Ford and Rockefeller foundations, also provided strong support for academic research regarding problems of population control, health care, agricultural technology, and communications in the "developing world."[36]

The history of MIT's Center for International Studies provides a vivid illustration of the extent to which Cold War security concerns were embedded in the establishment and functioning of a leading center of modernization theory. In 1950, the State Department approached MIT for technical assistance on a program designed to counter Soviet jamming of Voice of America radio broadcasts into the USSR. MIT accepted the assignment and recommended that the project, now named TROY, also conduct research more broadly into the nature of political warfare itself, including potential target audiences in Russia, Europe, and China and the specific messages to be conveyed. That proposal eventually led to the establishment of a permanent institute to examine what MIT president James Killian called the "long-term problems of international policy which confront decision-makers in government and private life." While the State Department was interested in the project, it lacked the funds to back it. The CIA, however, had the resources and in 1962 provided $600,000 to create the Center for International Studies (CIS). MIT economist Max Millikan, the Center's first director, also came to the job immediately following a year as the CIA's second in command. By the end of the decade, MIT was the home of several leading proponents of modernization, including economists Walt Rostow, Max Millikan, and Paul Rosenstein-Rodan; political scientists Lucian Pye and Donald Blackmer; and sociologist Daniel Lerner. Through the 1950s CIS also engaged in two primary types of research: analyses of the Soviet Union and China and studies of the process of modernization in the postcolonial world. The CIA funded much of the work on Communist societies, while other government and philanthropic sources, particularly the Ford and Rockefeller foundations, supported the development studies.[37]

CIS faculty and administrators were aware of the questions that such relationships posed for an ostensibly academic institution, dedicated to the production of objective knowledge. Rostow later recalled that the university provost, Julius Stratton, had told Millikan and himself that they could "go forward with our enterprise on the understanding that we would maintain rigorous intellectual standards and, of course, complete intellectual independence from the government." Rostow also insisted that the CIA "at no time tried to influence our analysis or conclusions," and Blackmer agreed that while CIS did conduct a few studies directly at the request of the CIA, most decisions about which projects would be pursued "were entirely in [CIS's] hands."[38]

Yet the problem of "complete intellectual independence" was more complex than those statements suggest, and the matter involved far more than questions of funding: modernization theorists at CIS and many other institutions frequently defined their purpose in *explicitly* political terms and wrote directly for policy-making audiences. To borrow Shils's language, they engaged in a great deal of "preaching" and "exhortation," insisting that their work had immediate policy applications. As Blackmer recalls, the "principal justification" for the existence of CIS was the "international crisis." The questions that CIS scholars sought to answer, therefore, were often driven at least as much by the perceived needs of the state as by the internal debates and dynamics of scholarly inquiry.[39]

The MIT group took to their mission with enthusiasm. In the spring of 1954, Millikan and Rostow organized a meeting with CIA director Allen Dulles and representatives from the White House as well as the State, Treasury, and Commerce departments to consider how U.S. development programs might challenge Soviet overtures to postcolonial states. Millikan and Rostow also produced a memorandum that circulated through the Eisenhower administration making the case for modernization as a crucial Cold War strategy. Victory over communism, they claimed, would be achieved through a fundamental *structural* change in the world environment itself, driving the postcolonial regions through the difficult, destabilizing transitional process and into the higher developmental stages in which Marxist revolution would lose all appeal. "In the short run," Millikan and Rostow argued, "communism must be contained militarily. In the long run we must rely on the development, in partnership with others, of an environment in which societies which directly or indirectly menace ours will not evolve."[40]

In 1957, with the collaboration of Rosenstein-Rodan, the two also published an expanded, declassified version of their work as *A Proposal: Key to an Effective Foreign Policy.* "For centuries," they explained, "the bulk of the world's population has been politically inert . . . essentially fixed in the mold of low-productivity rural life centered in isolated villages." But now transformations brought on by mass communication, urbanization, and decolonization were "rapidly exposing previously apathetic peoples to the possibility of change." At the height of the Cold War, therefore, it was imperative that the United States use its great "potential for steering the world's newly aroused human energies in constructive rather than destructive directions." The key would be to encourage postcolonial states to frame comprehensive national development plans, including provisions for commercial enterprise, agricultural growth, social services, and education. Using rates of overall investment and per capita income growth, U.S. policymakers would then determine the "absorptive capacity" of developing nations and provide the correct level of support from a "long term capital fund" of $10 billion to $12 billion. Development programs, moreover, would do more than catalyze economic change. Because modernization was a systemic, integrated process, it would sweep all before it. Rising living standards would give citizens the sense of progress and social mobility on which democratic institutions could be fostered, and new values would promote entrepreneurial initiative and popular participation in liberal civic life. Faced with such a challenge, the appeal of Marxist revolution would pale in comparison.[41]

Those arguments impressed John F. Kennedy. His senate office remained in regular contact with CIS economists, and after winning the presidential election of 1960 he appointed Rostow and Millikan to his new task force on foreign economic policy. Convinced that the decolonizing world represented a crucial battlefield in the global Cold War, Kennedy and his advisers fully expected that planning, development, and foreign assistance could become key elements in a broad strategy designed to steer nationalist forces toward liberal capitalism. In a major speech to Congress in March 1961, Kennedy also proclaimed a new "Decade of Development." "We live in a very special moment in history," he declared. "The whole southern half of the world—Latin America, Africa, the Middle East and Asia are caught up in the adventures of asserting their independence and modernizing their old ways of life." Now, as Moscow and Beijing sought to subvert that process for their own ends, it was imperative that the United States make a "historical demonstration that in the twentieth century, as in the nineteenth—in the southern half of the globe as in the north—economic growth and political democracy can develop hand in hand." To promote that goal, Kennedy established the Agency for International Development (AID) with authority over technical aid, development projects, lending programs, and military assistance, called for multiyear funding authorizations, and recommended special attention to countries on the verge of a "take-off into self-sustaining growth."[42]

The involvement of social scientists in Kennedy administration policymaking toward the postcolonial world was extensive. Determined to put their stamp on Washington's bureaucracy, they also gained significant political authority. Rostow became a deputy national security adviser, and then the chair of the State Department's Policy Planning Council. A collection of Harvard economists also took on significant roles: John Kenneth Galbraith became the ambassador to India, Lincoln Gordon served on the Latin American task force before becoming ambassador to Brazil, David Bell went from the Bureau of the Budget to become the administrator of AID, and Edward Mason served as chair of an AID advisory committee that included Millikan and Pye. Stanford economist Eugene Staley served as a consultant on Vietnam policy, and University of Michigan professor Samuel Hayes helped plan the Peace Corps.[43]

Yet important as these individuals were, the influence of modernization theory was not derived solely or even primarily from the personal impact of specific social scientists. In many cases, the theory of modernization also provided less a specific, detailed set of policy instructions than a particular way of thinking about the postcolonial world. Modernization became powerful in Cold War America because it crystallized a much deeper set of assumptions that were already held in common by a wide range of policymakers, scholars, journalists, and opinion leaders. In contrast to the more defensive phrasing of "containment," it emphasized the far more ambitious, liberal internationalist goal of transforming the structural environment itself. The United States, its advocates insisted, would not simply react to Soviet or Chinese aggression in the crucial arena of decolonization. The United States would compete with the Communists on the plane of universal change. By accelerating the passage of "emerging" nations through the crucial transitional window, the United States would run the common historical race faster and better and take an important step toward Cold War victory.

The Culture of Cold War Liberalism

Modernization was in many ways a product of U.S. liberalism. As admirers of the New Deal, veterans of the wartime struggle against fascism, and proponents of the Marshall Plan, its advocates believed strongly in the capacity of the progressive, democratic state to solve social problems at home and abroad. Capitalism, combined with moderate amounts of planning, they believed, could alleviate poverty, increase literacy, reduce human suffering, and fight against the Communist challenge at the same time. Like Arthur Schlesinger, Jr., modernizers also defined their work as part of an essential defense of democracy, the preservation of a "vital center" standing between the dangers of totalitarianism on the left or the right. Yet if modernization reflected the confidence and convictions of Cold War liberalism, it also revealed much of its uncertainty. While the ideology of modernization encouraged Americans to define a benevolent, even redemptive national mission, it framed democracy in a remarkably narrow way. While it defined the United States as an essential source of guidance for those seeking to build thriving new states and societies, it also rested on an undercurrent of anxiety that its particular form of modernity would face fundamental, perhaps even insuperable challenges in the global struggle against communism.[44]

The idea of the United States standing at the end point of a universal scale of social progress was grounded in a very complacent view of American society. It also resonated strongly with "consensus" histories of the American past. While emphasizing that democracy thrived in the United States because of the country's natural abundance, David Potter suggested in *People of Plenty* (1954) that promoting economic growth abroad would help fulfill a vital precondition for democratic success. As he put it, although the United States' wealth set it apart, "we are qualified to show other countries the path that may lead them to a plenty like our own." Others were even more enthusiastic, defining the United States' history as a template for the "new states" of the postcolonial world. As Max Lerner argued in his massive book, *America as a Civilization* (1957), the United States could "offer the example of a successful colonial revolution against imperialism; it could offer the continuing effort to keep many ethnic strains living together in peace in a complex society; it could offer, finally, the image of the independent farmer and of the career still largely open to talent." William Nisbet Chambers concurred, describing the United States' past as compelling evidence of the universal value of "moderate and pragmatic" approaches to political change, the value of economic development as a "foundation for democracy," and the way that a party system could "contain the forces of pluralism" and establish the "pattern for a responsible opposition." Drawing on Parsons's emphasis on the institutionalization of social values, Seymour Martin Lipset also celebrated the United States as the world's "first new nation." The commitment to the "key values" of equality and achievement, and the crucial distinction between "the source of sovereignty and the agents of authority," allowed the founding generation to create a democratic system that "has broken sharply with the traditional sources of legitimacy." Now, Lipset argued, the United States' example would inspire the "new nations emerging today on the world scene," because, he explained, "the values which they must use to legitimate their political structure, and which thus become part of their political institutions, are also revolutionary."[45]

In such formulations, of course, the American past was painted in harmonious, pacific, and egalitarian hues. The history of American slavery, the wars of Native American removal, the patterns of imperial expansion, the struggles of organized labor, and the persistent inequalities along the lines of race, gender, and class were slighted in favor of an emphasis on the long-term continuity of essentially liberal, integrating, national values. As John Higham lamented in 1962, the emphasis on consensus produced a history "in which conflict is muted, in which the classic issues of social justice are underplayed, in which the elements of spontaneity, effervescence, and violence in American life get little sympathy or attention." In contrast to Soviet totalitarianism and absolutism, American intellectuals emphasized their nation's pluralistic history and viewed their own society in remarkably complacent terms. Democracy itself was also defined in a particularly narrow way, and popular politics were viewed with disdain and distrust. Richard Hofstadter argued in his classic 1955 book, *The Age of Reform*, that the Populists of the 1890s were an irrational, conspiratorial, paranoid bunch, atavistically tied to agrarian culture and unable to adapt to the transformative forces of industrialized modernity. McCarthyism's popular appeal and the subsequent rise of a resurgent conservative movement were also interpreted by many midcentury intellectuals in a similar fashion. Daniel Bell observed: "Social groups that are dispossessed inevitably seek targets on whom they can vent their resentments, targets whose power can serve to explain their dispossession. In this respect, the radical right of the early 1960s is in no way different from the Populists of the 1890s."[46]

The tendency to write off political protest and mass politics of the left or the right as the expression of "status anxiety" or the projection of psychological deviance enabled consensus thinkers to enshrine a moderate, elite-led system as the essence of American success. That perspective also resonated with the way that modernizers thought about the postcolonial world. Influenced by Lasswell's vision of political behavior as the manifestation of inner insecurities, political scientists like Pye and Almond suggested that the survival of democratic systems required a clear consensus among leaders, the containment of radical dissent, and a minimal level of popular political participation, ideally one limited to an electoral choice of candidates from within a narrow ideological range. Less optimistic than many of their economist colleagues that economic growth and improvements in living standards would inevitably and naturally lead to liberal political systems, they favored elite theories of democracy. As Almond explained, "negative emotions and hysterias unleashed by the disruptive changes and the new nationalisms of the non-Western world" could make the United States the target of "violent moods and expressions of hate." Skilled elites, therefore, would have to control the destabilizing transition. Concern about the dangers of dissent and the need to maintain order placed a premium on procedural instead of substantive definitions of democracy. It also led thinkers like Pye to edge toward bureaucratic authoritarian approaches, suggesting that the military forces of the "newly emergent countries" could catalyze a "rational outlook" and "champion responsible change and national development." Although Pye did argue that the creation of modern nation-states would require "the growth of responsible and representative politicians," the idea that a modernizing military might just as well become the core of an oppressive dictatorship did not seem to draw his attention. The fact that concepts of modernization were built on narrow conceptions of democracy helps explain the ease with which their proponents later used them to support and legitimate systems of repression.[47]

Among popular audiences, however, a more upbeat strain of modernization held sway, an image that allowed Americans to envision themselves as the benevolent guides for a world eager to learn the lessons that only they could teach. In the pages of *Reader's Digest* and the *Saturday Review,* novels like Eugene Burdick and William Lederer's *The Ugly American* (1958), and the musical spectacles epitomized by Richard Rodgers's and Oscar Hammerstein's *The King and I* (1951), writers and artists framed a tolerant, inclusive, and sentimental world role for the United States and its citizens. In contrast to the reactive, militarized language of containment, they put forward a liberal, internationalist ideal of integration and education. Whether reading about the arrival of the first contingent of Peace Corps volunteers in Ghana, listening to the radio as Catholic "jungle doctor" Tom Dooley recounted his healing work in Laos, or watching an Americanized Anna Leonowens teach a Thai king's children on the Broadway stage, Americans celebrated their nation's altruistic efforts to reach across the lines of race and culture. The United States, they understood, was not merely fending off the Communist threat. It was also promoting modernity by forging bonds of affection and understanding.[48]

Among its most ardent proponents, modernization was also defined as an essential national mission. In his 1953 inaugural address, President Eisenhower argued that the fight against communism was "no argument between slightly differing philosophies." Rather, "freedom is pitted against slavery; lightness against the dark." Victory, moreover, would require Americans to "give testimony in the sight of the world to our faith." Though modernization was a secular ideology, its advocates often described its significance as a statement of moral belief put forward in the context of apocalyptic struggle. "There may not be much civilization left to save," Rostow warned at the close of his most famous book, "unless we of the democratic north face and deal with the challenge implicit in the stages-of-growth, as they now stand in the world, at the full stretch of our moral commitment, our energy, and our resources." One participant at an MIT-sponsored conference put it as follows: "We must offer a framework within which the nations of Asia and Africa can develop economically as free societies. We must take our part in creating the new world which is evolving out of the upheaval in Asia and Africa. We must be missionaries."[49]

American modernizers were confident in the prospects for scientific and technical advance, and they viewed postcolonial societies as fundamentally malleable. As liberals, they believed that they could solve long-standing social and economic problems and achieve fundamental structural changes, transcending the legacy of imperialism and allowing all peoples, regardless of race or religion, to enjoy the promise of higher living standards. American modernizers also imagined that history was ultimately on their side, and that the world was converging on a set of universally valid common principles, moving steadily toward an end point most clearly reflected in their understandings of American society itself. Quoting his namesake, the poet Walt Whitman, Rostow expressed his conviction "That in the Divine Ship, the World, breasting Time and Space, / All peoples of the globe together sail, sail the same voyage, / Are bound to the same destination." In the postcolonial world, however, Rostow and his colleagues would find their ideals challenged, reinterpreted, and reformulated. While they defined a common future and proposed to accelerate it, they would soon discover that the contest over the meaning of modernity was just beginning.[50]

NOTES

1. Harold D. Lasswell, "The Policy Orientation," in *The Policy Sciences*, ed. Daniel Lerner and Harold D. Lasswell (Stanford, CA: Stanford University Press, 1951), 3, 11, emphasis in original.

2. Ido Oren, *Our Enemies and US: America's Rivalries and the Making of Political Science* (Ithaca, NY: Cornell University Press, 2003), 11, 137–39.

3. Eric F. Goldman, *The Crucial Decade: America, 1945–1955* (Westport, CT: Greenwood Press, 1956), 116–17.

4. Chen Jian, *Mao's China and the Cold War* (Chapel Hill: University of North Carolina Press, 2001), 54; Warren I. Cohen, *America in the Age of Soviet Power, 1945–1991* (Cambridge: Cambridge University Press, 1993), 67.

5. Ernest R. May, ed., *American Cold War Strategy: Interpreting NSC-68* (New York: Bedford Books, 1993), 28–29, 31.

6. Mark Atwood Lawrence, *Assuming the Burden: Europe and the American Commitment to War in Vietnam* (Berkeley: University of California Press, 2005), 277.

7. Robert J. McMahon, "Eisenhower and Third World Nationalism: A Critique of the Revisionists," *Political Science Quarterly* 101, no. 3 (1986): 457; Matthew Connelly, "Taking Off the Cold War Lens: Visions of North-South Conflict during the Algerian War for Independence," *American Historical Review* 105, no. 3 (2000): 755.

8. Irwin Wall, *France, the United States, and the Algerian War* (Berkeley: University of California Press, 2001), 23–24, 100.

9. Matthew Connelly, *A Diplomatic Revolution: Algeria's Fight for Independence and the Origins of the Post–Cold War Era* (Oxford: Oxford University Press, 2002), 126; Salim Yaqub, *Containing Arab Nationalism: The Eisenhower Doctrine and the Middle East* (Chapel Hill: University of North Carolina Press, 2004), 241–42.

10. Connelly, "Taking Off the Cold War Lens," 755; Jason C. Parker, "Small Victory, Missed Chance: The Eisenhower Administration, the Bandung Conference, and the Turning of the Cold War," in *The Eisenhower Administration, the Third World, and the Globalization of the Cold War*, ed. Kathryn C. Statler and Andrew L. Johns (Lanham, MD: Rowman and Littlefield, 2006), 160.

11. Roy Allison, *The Soviet Union and the Strategy of Non-Alignment in the Third World* (Cambridge: Cambridge University Press, 1988).

12. Burton I. Kaufman, *Trade and Aid: Eisenhower's Foreign Economic Policy, 1953–1961* (Baltimore: Johns Hopkins University Press, 1982), 103; Michael Adamson, "'The Most Important Single Aspect of Our Foreign Policy?': The Eisenhower Administration, Foreign Aid, and the Third World," in Statler and Johns, *Eisenhower Administration*, 59–61.

13. Adamson, "Most Important Single Aspect," 61–66.

14. John F. Kennedy, Democratic Convention Speech, July 15, 1960, in *"Let the World Go Forth": The Speeches, Statements, and Writings of John F. Kennedy, 1947–1963*, ed. Theodore C. Sorensen (New York: Laurel, 1988), 98–99; Kennedy, Campaign Speech, November 2, 1960, in Sorensen, *"Let the World Go Forth,"* 119.

15. Gilman, *Mandarins of the Future*, 72–202; Michael E. Latham, *Modernization as Ideology: American Social Science and "Nation Building" in the Kennedy Era* (Chapel Hill: University of North Carolina Press, 2000), 30–46.

16. Howard Brick, *Transcending Capitalism: Visions of a New Society in Modern American Thought* (Ithaca, NY: Cornell University Press, 2006), 127–28; Jeffrey Alexander, *Twenty Lectures: Sociological Theory since World War II* (New York: Columbia University Press, 1987), 22–28.

17. Talcott Parsons, "Democracy and Social Structure in Pre-Nazi Germany," in *Essays in Sociological Theory*, ed. Talcott Parsons (New York: Free Press, 1964), 104–23; Uta Gerhardt, *Talcott Parsons: An Intellectual Biography* (Cambridge: Cambridge University Press, 2002), 58–128.

18. Talcott Parsons and Edward Shils, eds., *Towards a General Theory of Action* (Cambridge, MA: Harvard University Press, 1951), 3–29.

19. Ibid., 90; Gilman, *Mandarins of the Future*, 87; Talcott Parsons, *Structure and Process in Modern Societies* (New York: Free Press, 1960), 138–39, 163.

20. Daniel Lerner, *The Passing of Traditional Society: Modernizing the Middle East* (New York: Free Press, 1964), ix, 45–53, 409–11, emphasis in original.

21. Oren, *Our Enemies and US*, 140, 145; Gilman, *Mandarins of the Future*, 167; Latham, *Modernization as Ideology*, 58, 167.

22. Harold D. Lasswell, *World Politics and Personal Insecurity* (New York: McGraw-Hill, 1935), 19–20; Oren, *Our Enemies and US*, 137–38; Gilman, *Mandarins of the Future*, 165–68; Gabriel Almond, *The Appeals of Communism* (Princeton, NJ: Princeton University Press, 1954), 231–32.

23. Lucian Pye, *Guerrilla Communism in Malaya: Its Social and Political Meaning* (Princeton, NJ: Princeton University Press, 1956), 7–8, 138.

24. Gilman, *Mandarins of the Future*, 121; George McT. Kahin, Guy J. Pauker, and Lucian W. Pye, "Comparative Politics of Non-Western Countries," *American Political Science Review* 49 (December 1955): 1022–23, 1026, 1041.

25. Gabriel A. Almond, "The Seminar on Comparative Politics, June 1956," *Social Science Research Council Items* 10, no. 4 (1956): 46–47, emphasis in original.

26. Lucian W. Pye, "Political Modernization and Research on the Process of Political Socialization," *Social Science Research Council Items* 13, no. 3 (1959): 26; Gabriel A. Almond, "A Functional Approach to Comparative Politics," in *The Politics of Developing Areas*, ed. Gabriel A. Almond and James S. Coleman (Princeton, NJ: Princeton University Press, 1960), 4, 10; James S. Coleman, "The Political Systems of Developing Areas," in Almond and Coleman, *Politics of Developing Areas*, 532, 536, emphasis in original.

27. Albert O. Hirschman, "The Rise and Decline of Development Economics," in *The Theory and Practice of Economic Development: Essays in Honor of Sir W. Arthur Lewis*, ed. Mark Gersovitz et al. (London: Allen and Unwin, 1982), 374; H. W. Arndt, *Economic Development: The History of an Idea* (Chicago: University of Chicago Press, 1987), 51; David C. Engerman, "American Knowledge and Global Power," *Diplomatic History* 31, no. 4 (2007): 617–18; Timothy Mitchell, *Rule of Experts: Egypt, Techno-Politics, Modernity* (Berkeley: University of California Press, 2002).

28. Gerald M. Meier, "The Formative Period," in *Pioneers in Development*, ed. Gerald M. Meier and Dudley Seers (New York: Oxford University Press, 1984), 14–15; Bjorn Hettne, *Development Theory and the Three Worlds* (Essex, England: Longman, 1990), 48–51.

29. Ian M. D. Little, *Economic Development: Theory, Policy, and International Relations* (New York: Basic Books, 1982), 19–21; Arndt, *Economic Development*, 53.

30. Paul N. Rosenstein-Rodan, "Natura Facit Saltum: Analysis of the Disequilibrium Growth Process," in Meier and Seers, *Pioneers of Development*, 210–11; Bert F. Hoselitz, *Sociological Aspects of Economic Growth* (New York: Free Press, 1960), 25–26, 29.

31. Kimber Charles Pearce, *Rostow, Kennedy, and the Rhetoric of Foreign Aid* (East Lansing: Michigan State University Press, 2001), 11–13; W. W. Rostow, *The Stages of Economic Growth: A Non-Communist Manifesto* (Cambridge: Cambridge University Press, 1960), 2.

32. Rostow, *Stages of Economic Growth*, 4–16.

33. Ibid., 17, 26–27.

34. Robert C. Wood, "The Future of Modernization," in *Modernization: The Dynamics of Growth*, ed. Myron Weiner (New York: Basic Books, 1966), 41.

35. Edward Shils, "On the Comparative Study of the New States," in *Old Societies and New States: The Quest for Modernity in Africa and Asia*, ed. Clifford Geertz (New York: Free Press, 1963), 8.

36. Christopher Simpson, *Science of Coercion: Communication Research and Psychological Warfare, 1945–1960* (New York: Oxford University Press, 1994), 9, 32; Roger L. Geiger, *Research and Relevant Knowledge: American Research Universities since World War II* (New York: Oxford University Press, 1993), 50–52; Sigmund Diamond, *Compromised Campus: The Collaboration of Universities with the Intelligence Community, 1945–1955* (New York: Oxford University Press, 1992), 50–95; Irene L. Gendzier, *Managing Political Change: Social Scientists and the Third World* (Boulder, CO: Westview, 1985), 87–96.

37. James R. Killian, Jr., *The Education of a College President* (Cambridge, MA: MIT Press, 1985), 68; Allan A. Needell, "'Truth Is Our Weapon': Project TROY, Political Warfare, and Government-Academic Relations in the National Security State," *Diplomatic History* 17 (Summer 1993): 399–420; Donald L. M. Blackmer, *The MIT Center for International Studies: The Founding Years, 1951–1969* (Cambridge, MA: MIT Center for International Studies, 2002), 12, 20–21, 67–68, 225.

38. W. W. Rostow, "Development: The Political Economy of the Marshallian Long Period," in Meier and Seers, *Pioneers of Development*, 240–41; Blackmer, *MIT Center*, 29.

39. Blackmer, *MIT Center*, 69–70.

40. Memorandum, Max F. Millikan and W. W. Rostow to Allen Dulles, May 21, 1954, in *Universities and Empire: Money and Politics in the Social Sciences during the Cold War*, ed. Christopher Simpson (New York: Free Press, 1998), 41, 44.

41. Max F. Millikan and W. W. Rostow, *A Proposal: Key to an Effective Foreign Policy* (New York: Harper and Brothers, 1957), 3–4, 8, 24, 38–39, 49–50, 127.

42. Blackmer, *MIT Center*, 105–6; Kennedy, "Special Message to the Congress on Foreign Aid," March 22, 1961, *Public Papers*, 1: 203, 205–6.

43. Latham, *Modernization as Ideology*, 58.

44. Arthur M. Schlesinger, Jr., *The Vital Center* (Boston: Houghton Mifflin, 1949), vii-x.

45. Gilman, *Mandarins of the Future*, 12, 63–68; David M. Potter, *People of Plenty: Economic Abundance and the American Character* (Chicago: University of Chicago Press, 1954), 134; Max Lerner, *America as a Civilization: Life and Thought in the United States Today* (New York: Simon and Schuster, 1957), 894; William Nisbet Chambers, *Political Parties in a New Nation: The American Experience, 1776–1809* (New York: Oxford University Press, 1963), 13; Seymour Martin Lipset, *The First New Nation: The United States in Historical and Comparative Perspective* (New York: Basic Books, 1963), 2–3, 10–11.

46. John Higham, "Beyond Consensus: The Historian as Moral Critic," *American Historical Review* 67, no. 3 (1962): 616; Edward A. Purcell, Jr., *The Crisis of Democratic Theory: Scientific Naturalism and the Problem of Value* (Lexington: University Press of Kentucky, 1973), 235–66; Richard Hofstadter, *The Age of Reform: From Bryan to FDR* (New York: Knopf, 1955), 59; Daniel Bell, ed., *The Radical Right: The New American Right* (Garden City, NY: Doubleday, 1963), 3; Michael Rogin, *The Intellectuals and McCarthy: The Radical Specter* (Cambridge, MA: MIT Press, 1967); David S. Brown, *Richard Hofstadter: An Intellectual Biography* (Chicago: University of Chicago Press, 2006), 99–160.

47. Gabriel Almond, *The American People and Foreign Policy* (New York: Praeger, 1960), xxviii; Lucian Pye, *Aspects of Political Development* (Boston: Little, Brown, 1966), 176, 187; Gendzier, *Managing Political Change*, 1–21; Howard Brick, *Age of Contradiction: American Thought and Culture in the 1960s* (New York: Twayne, 1998), 18–20; Gilman, *Mandarins of the Future*, 49–54.

48. Christina Klein, *Cold War Orientalism: Asia in the Middlebrow Imagination, 1945–1961* (Berkeley: University of California Press, 2003), 64–65; James T. Fisher, *Dr. America: The Lives of Thomas A. Dooley, 1927–1961* (Amherst: University of Massachusetts Press, 1997).

49. Seth Jacobs, *America's Miracle Man in Vietnam: Ngo Dinh Diem, Religion, Race, and U.S. Intervention in Southeast Asia, 1950–1957* (Durham, NC: Duke University Press, 2004), 67; Rostow, *Stages of Economic Growth*, 167; Gilman, *Mandarins of the Future*, 69.

50. Millikan and Rostow, *Proposal*, 151.

NATIONALIST ENCOUNTERS

Nehru's India, Nasser's Egypt, and
Nkrumah's Ghana

In 1958, one year after his country gained independence from Great Britain, Ghanaian prime minister Kwame Nkrumah traveled to the United States. In addition to meeting with President Eisenhower and senior U.S. officials, Nkrumah delivered a major address at the prestigious Council on Foreign Relations in New York. As the leader of the first sub-Saharan African country to secure its freedom from imperial control, Nkrumah urged the United States to take a stronger stand in favor of decolonization. He also argued that to achieve genuine self-determination Ghana and its neighbors would have to pursue a course of dramatically accelerated development. "The hopes and ambitions of the African people," he declared, "have been planted and brought to maturity by the impact of Western civilization. . . . Now comes our response. We cannot tell our peoples that material benefits and growth and modern progress are not for them. If we do, they will throw us out and seek other leaders who promise more. And they will abandon us, too, if we do not in reasonable measure respond to their hopes. Therefore we have no choice. Africa has no choice. We have to modernize."

Nkrumah's sense of ambition and urgency was widely shared by a growing cohort of postcolonial elites around the world. For figures like Nkrumah, India's Jawaharlal Nehru, and Egypt's Gamal Abdel Nasser, development was not merely a goal. It was an imperative. Independence, they all agreed, brought new opportunities and new demands. As Nkrumah put it, political freedom created the "atmosphere for a real effort of national regeneration," but it did not "supply all the economic and social tools." After finally breaking the shackles that locked their countries into subservience to Europe, postcolonial leaders now sought to transform their societies. They wanted to achieve economic growth, promote industry, stimulate agricultural productivity, fight poverty, deliver health care, and improve education. They also believed that the legitimacy of their governments and their own political survival depended on meeting those goals. "The leaders are now expected," Nkrumah explained, "to work miracles....If independence is the first aim, development comes straight on its heels, and no leader—in Asia or Africa—can escape the pressure." To succeed, he insisted, the postcolonial world would need a great deal of external help.[1]

Many U.S. policymakers, social scientists, and opinion leaders responded to those appeals with enthusiasm. The leaders of the "emerging nations," they believed, were defining their goals in ways that clearly resonated with U.S. expectations. The idea of helping to fight global poverty and promote postcolonial freedom fired the ambitions of progressive-minded liberals. Modernization, they expected, could now go forward rapidly. In collaboration with a rising generation of nationalist leaders, an infusion of Western capital and technical knowledge could drive the new states of the world from the backward conditions of traditional society into a prosperous, thriving modernity. After years of ambivalence and suspicion regarding the prospects for anticolonial nationalism, the United States might finally seize the moment to align itself with the needs, hopes, and desires of a newly awakened yet deeply impoverished world.

At the height of the Cold War, working alongside postcolonial leaders on a great modernizing project also seemed a strategic necessity. During the 1950s, Moscow's "economic offensive" in Asia, Africa, and the Middle East had alarmed U.S. observers, and Nikita Khrushchev's 1961 pledge to support global "wars of national liberation" heightened U.S. fears that the USSR would seek to exploit conditions of poverty and instability in the developing regions. "Nobody," the Soviet leader declared, "appreciates and understands the aspirations of the peoples now smashing the fetters of colonialism better than the working people of the socialist countries and the Communists of the whole world." By the early 1960s, U.S. policymakers believed that the future of the decolonizing world hung in the balance. A massive effort to guide postcolonial change, they hoped, might ensure that liberal, capitalist solutions prevailed.[2]

During the late 1950s and early 1960s, India, Egypt, and Ghana were important sites for U.S. engagement. While the United States promoted modernizing policies in a broad range of geographic locations, Nehru, Nasser, and Nkrumah were key regional leaders in South Asia, the Middle East, and sub-Saharan Africa, respectively. U.S. officials expected that ensuring modernization in India, Egypt, and Ghana would dramatically demonstrate the U.S. commitment to postcolonial development. Far more importantly, they also hoped to channel the nonaligned and nationalist aspirations in these countries in more clearly pro-Western directions.

Those ambitions were largely frustrated. Despite the great economic resources and technical expertise that the United States and Western international lending bodies offered, Nehru, Nasser, and Nkrumah remained firmly committed to nonalignment as a policy and a philosophy. They rejected the system of military and economic alliances that the United States sought to construct, strongly criticized U.S. interventions in the Cold War flash points of Vietnam, Cuba, and Congo, and continued to play the superpowers off against each other. By insisting that imperialism represented a greater danger to the postcolonial world than communism, they also challenged the ideological vision of the United States. Although U.S. development assistance for India, Egypt, and Ghana may have helped prevent closer ties between those countries and the Soviet Union, their governments remained wary of making any concessions that would infringe on their newfound sovereignty, regional ambitions, and nationalist agendas.

Moreover, as U.S. social scientists and Kennedy administration officials would discover, modernization itself was deeply contested ground. At one level, postcolonial leaders like Nehru, Nasser, and Nkrumah shared some core assumptions with U.S. officials and experts about the process of modernization. Like U.S. policymakers, they believed that a "big push" of investment and sharply increased levels of domestic savings would be necessary for their economies to break out of stagnation and "take-off" into self-sustaining growth. They also shared the U.S. assumptions that modernization required technological advances to raise productivity, the diversification of exports, the education of a trained workforce, and integrated, national development planning. On another level, however, their diverse visions of development did not fit easily into the more rigid U.S. conceptions of modernization. U.S. social scientists and officials understood modernization as an integrated process in which step-by-step advances in capitalist structures, psychological transformations, and political reforms would reinforce each other. Postcolonial elites, however, proved far more willing to "skip stages," experiment, and combine elements of American and Soviet experience. Where U.S. advisers promoted the construction of market-based economies and liberal states along the lines of the New Deal in the United States, postcolonial leaders often turned in more avowedly socialist directions. While glad to receive U.S. aid, they often found Soviet models of development appealing. Instead of limiting the role of the state to the formation of development plans and the promotion of foreign and domestic investment, they frequently stressed the crucial role of a strong central government in controlling a large public sector. In contrast to U.S. recommendations for carefully "balanced growth" in agriculture and manufacturing, they aimed for more rapid progress through comprehensive industrialization. Where U.S. leaders and analysts tended to speak of modernization as inevitable, natural, and uniform, in India, Egypt, and Ghana it became the subject of intense political contestation and negotiation.

India, the United States, and Development Planning

On April 12, 1948, Indian prime minister Nehru visited the eastern Indian state of Orissa to inaugurate the construction of the massive Hirakud Dam. India's first river valley project after independence and ultimately the longest major earthen dam in the world, it was designed to provide flood control, irrigation, and vast amounts of hydroelectric power to support industrial enterprises in the surrounding region. In a letter written a few days later, Nehru recalled his tremendous excitement on that occasion. "All this," he reflected, "is a fascinating vision of the future which fills one with enthusiasm. As I threw in some concrete which was to form the base...a sense of adventure seized me and I forgot for a while the many troubles that beset us."[3]

Since the 1930s, Nehru and his Congress Party colleagues had understood centrally planned development as an essential part of their nationalist campaign. British imperial policy, they argued, had exploited the peasantry and destroyed Indian manufacturing. Genuine independence, therefore, would require a comprehensive, scientific restructuring of social and economic life. In 1938, Nehru became chair of the Congress Party's National Planning Committee, a body assigned the task of drafting a development policy for the day when the British would finally withdraw. Their ambitious targets for gains in nutrition, health care, housing, agriculture, and industry were all, in Nehru's words, aimed at the objective of "national self-sufficiency." While export-driven agriculture would be redirected to feed India's own population, new factories would provide employment for surplus workers in the countryside, produce goods for domestic markets, and help the country avoid the "whirlpool of economic imperialism." Planning by disinterested experts, Nehru believed, would transcend the "squabbles and conflicts of politics" for the "benefit of the common man, raising his standards greatly, giving him opportunities of growth, and releasing an enormous amount of latent talent and capacity."[4]

Industrialization played an especially large role in the thinking of Nehru and his associates. In contrast to the Gandhian emphasis on cottage industry and local handicrafts, they maintained that the route to Indian independence and prosperity lay in the production of steel, iron, machine tools, chemicals, and electric power. Figures like Congress Party president Subhas Chandra Bose argued that the Soviet focus on heavy industry and an expanded state role at the "command-ing heights" of the economy provided an example for India. Late industrializing states, Bose and Nehru insisted, required a level of state intervention that had been unnecessary earlier. Bose warned in 1938 that there was "no escape from the industrial revolution." "We can at best determine," he observed, "whether this revolution that is industrialisation will be a comparatively gradual one, as in Great Britain, or a forced march as in Soviet Russia. *I am afraid that it has to be a forced march in this country.*"[5]

After India gained its independence in 1947, those ideas returned to the fore-front. At that point, 85 percent of the country's population lived in rural areas, and the agricultural sector was desperately poor. Grain consumption amounted to only about nine ounces per person per day, nearly a quarter of the population owned no land at all, illiteracy stood at 84 percent, lethal diseases like smallpox, malaria, and cholera were common, and the country's mortality rate was among the world's highest. India's First Five-Year Plan, launched in 1951, sought to re-spond to these crises. Partly made up of projects inherited from the colonial era, it was largely focused on the need to increase agricultural production and deliver social services in order to feed and care for the country's rapidly growing and predominantly rural population. By 1954, however, India's leadership turned toward a much more ambitious vision of rapid, comprehensive, state-led devel-opment. With Nehru's firm backing, the Cambridge-trained physicist and stat-istician Prasanta Chandra Mahalanobis began to draft a new plan with two core objectives. As Mahalanobis explained to the Indian Planning Commission, the new approach would seek "a rapid growth of the national economy by increasing the scope and importance of the public sector and in this way to advance to a so-cialistic pattern of society." It would also "develop basic heavy industries for the manufacture of producer goods to strengthen the foundation of economic inde-pendence." Launched in 1956, India's Second Five-Year Plan was a bold venture. Total spending was projected at $14.7 billion, more than double that of the first plan. Resources for agricultural production and social services were also sharply reduced in favor of much greater public investment in capital goods production and industrialization to replace the need for imports.[6]

U.S. policymakers and social scientists watched India's development efforts with great interest. As a newly independent state and the world's largest democ-racy, India stood out as a crucial arena in the Cold War struggle for the post-colonial world. As early as 1949 the State Department and the Joint Chiefs of Staff argued that the United States should promote "economic development in South Asia . . . to provide the foundations for more stable and democratic govern-ments" and "contribute to economic recovery in the Far East and throughout the world." In 1954, the Eisenhower administration decided to establish a military alliance with Pakistan, India's regional rival, in hopes that arming that country would deter any possible Soviet incursion in the region. But U.S. officials soon began to emphasize the modernization of India as a crucial strategic goal in its own right. In 1954 the Soviet Union's pledge to build and finance India's massive Bhilai steel mill worried Washington. A year later, Khrushchev offered increased development aid, expanded bilateral trade, and aircraft sales. Concerned that the Soviets might now direct the course of Indian economic planning, CIA chief Allen Dulles warned that Moscow's economic initiatives threatened "political penetration in disguise."[7]

By the end of the decade, an Indian economic crisis and growing strategic fears led to a greatly expanded U.S. commitment. Indian planners had expected that the country's food requirements would double over ten years due to rapid population growth, but in their quest for a new industrial drive they had provided insufficient funding to increase agricultural productivity. The problem of deploying technical inputs like fertilizer, mechanized irrigation, and farm machinery to millions of small peasant plots made it hard to increase the yield of Indian farmland, and the opposition of landed elites undermined agrarian reform policies that could have put more acres under cultivation. As shortages appeared in Indian cities, and food prices began to climb, the prospect of famine grew. The costs of capital equipment, needed for India's industrial projects, also began to rise. By 1957, India's agricultural woes were compounded by a massive deficit in the foreign exchange holdings needed to pay for vital imports.[8]

The prospect of an Indian economic collapse worried U.S. policymakers on several levels. Instability and growing poverty, they feared, might open the door for radicalism to gain ground in India. In desperation, the Indian government might move closer to Moscow in search of badly needed development funds. A collapse of democratic India might also have global psychological ramifications. "No thoughtful citizen can fail to see our stake in the survival of the free government of India," Senator John F. Kennedy warned in 1958. "India," Kennedy declared, "stands as the only effective competitor to China for the faith and following of the millions of uncommitted and restless peoples." The Eisenhower administration agreed. With the president's strong backing, the total level of U.S. aid to India climbed from $92.8 million in 1956 to $364.8 million in 1957. In 1958, the United States also worked with the World Bank to organize an international consortium of aid donors for India, pooling increased U.S. funds with contributions from Britain, Germany, Canada, and Japan.[9]

The increased U.S. aid to India aroused significant U.S. domestic dissent. Nehru's resolute policy of nonalignment, his refusal to join military alliances or allow foreign military bases in India, and his commitment to "peaceful coexistence" with all nations challenged U.S. arguments about the moral imperative of fighting communism. Nehru's criticism of the "neocolonial" dangers inherent in global capitalism, his frequently expressed admiration for Soviet economic accomplishments, and his attacks on U.S. intervention in Vietnam and Cuba also alienated influential U.S. officials and opinion leaders. His apparent lack of gratitude for U.S. help, finally, made him appear arrogant, unrealistic, and self-righteous. The veteran diplomat and journalist William C. Bullitt's rendering of Nehru as "an exquisite and ineffectual dragonfly flashing his iridescent wings above a swamp" captured the impression of many U.S. officials. In the U.S. Congress, aid for India also met fierce resistance. When U.S. ambassador to India Chester Bowles appeared before the Senate, Texas Democrat Tom Connally rejected his arguments for aid by declaring: "You know good and well that the more money we give them the more they want." Since Nehru was "not friendly to the United States," Connally told reporters, he did not deserve U.S. help. Iowa's Republican senator Bourke B. Hickenlooper argued that financing Indian development was like "taking a squirt gun and trying to put out a warehouse fire," while Senate majority leader William Knowland of California warned Eisenhower that "it would be bad if the impression got around that we reward neutralism." Styles Bridges, a New Hampshire Republican sitting on the powerful Senate Appropriations Committee, attacked Nehru for looking east as well as west. The Indian leader, he argued, was "playing both ends against the middle."[10]

Conservatives attacked U.S. policy, but the belief that the United States should help modernize India was strongly held in academia, philanthropic foundations, and the government. During the late 1950s and early 1960s, many U.S. social scientists, particularly economists and anthropologists, viewed India as a kind of laboratory, a great experimental site for the study and promotion of modernization. Their work, moreover, reflected a wide variety of different means and approaches. Some figures, like the architect and urban planner Albert Mayer, plunged into community development. In the northern state of Uttar Pradesh, Mayer launched a "pilot project" in which Indian "village-level workers" were trained to demonstrate new technologies and promote self-help initiatives in the countryside. Rapidly expanded into a major Indian government program with support from U.S. Point Four funds and Ford Foundation grants, Mayer's project aimed to produce psychological transformations as well as economic ones. The goal, Mayer explained, was to gain "entry into the people's minds, into their feelings, into their own expectations and needs." Only then would peasants pass through the "initial stages of awakening" to embrace a new "systematic planning and organization, village outlook, [and the] practice of effective human relations, self-reliance and resourcefulness, and teamwork." Unlike many American modernizers, Mayer did not view tradition and modernity as opposing historical poles. Modern practices, he argued, could be promoted within older forms of local community and in harmony with traditional religious and cultural practices. The objective, however, remained historical acceleration. "The most immediate, pressing, and pervasive problem of the underdeveloped countries," Mayer contended, was "to catch up with centuries of arrears, and to do it much more rapidly than the Western countries." To the question "Why so much faster?" Mayer responded: "Because theirs is a race with chaos."[11]

The hope to produce a rapid, modernizing "take-off" also led to a close and ultimately troubled collaboration among the Indian government, U.S. officials, and the MIT Center for International Studies (CIS). As explained in chapter 2, CIS stood at the nexus between social research and government policymaking. Among the foremost proponents of modernization theory, the CIS experts were also deeply interested in India and the process of economic planning there. Their experience revealed that while Indian and U.S. social scientists and government officials shared a common desire to raise economic growth rates and living standards, they disagreed profoundly over which means would best achieve that end. As much as Indian and U.S. experts defined development as an objective and scientific process, their collaboration did not survive the growing political strain that emerged between U.S. Cold War ideology and Indian commitments to independence and nonalignment.

From 1954 through 1964, CIS received a series of grants from the Ford Foundation and became deeply engaged in India's planning effort. When India's Second Five-Year Plan ran into difficulty, CIS staff lobbied hard for greater U.S. development assistance by sending reports to Congress, supporting Senator Kennedy's calls for an international aid effort, and meeting with Eisenhower administration officials. But CIS wanted to do more than study and report on Indian development. The MIT group also wanted to participate in shaping its ultimate direction. With the support of Pitamber Pant, Nehru's planning secretary, CIS economists developed a working relationship with the Indian Planning Commission and the Indian Statistical Institute. They also gained full access to the Indian government's data regarding the nation's economy, productivity, and population. Two CIS researchers, Louis Lafeber and Richard Eckhaus, then began a critical analysis of India's Third Five-Year Plan, which had started in 1961. Like the Second Five-Year Plan, it too put a strong emphasis on rapid industrialization, devoting roughly twice as much of its total outlays to industry and electricity as to agriculture. Using a new, computer-based economic model, Lafeber and Eckhaus soon concluded that this plan, like the previous one, was likely to produce further economic turmoil.[12]

Lafeber and Eckhaus considered their work part of a careful, social scientific project. In the minds of many U.S. economists, long-term development required "balanced growth." A "big push" of investment was necessary to drive an economy into high gear, but funds had to be allocated across domestic manufacturing and agricultural sectors so that growth in each area would be reinforced by the creation of complementary markets in others. As farm productivity rose, peasants would enjoy higher incomes enabling them to purchase newly produced manufactured goods. Factory workers based in urban areas, meanwhile, would become the consumers of new agricultural bounty. While many analysts agreed that the weak private sector of developing economies made centralized, state planning a temporary necessity, they also viewed government ownership of industry as inefficient at best and trending toward Soviet-style oppression at worst. As Rostow argued in a 1955 article titled "Marx Was a City Boy," the Stalinist and Maoist programs of crash industrialization were coupled with the brutal collectivization of peasant agriculture. Yet even totalitarian controls across the countryside proved unable to produce sufficient food to feed the Soviet and Chinese populations. Investment in agriculture, however, could help reinforce gradual industrialization in a democratic system based on popular consent.[13]

Nehru, Mahalanobis, and many Indian economists saw the matter in very different terms. Without rapid industrial expansion, Indian planners argued, the ceiling for overall economic growth would remain low. The application of new technology to government administered steel, iron, and machine tool plants, however, could trigger gains in productivity and generate revenue for reinvestment. A large public sector, particularly in heavy industry, they expected, would create jobs, promote India's commitment to self-sufficiency, and catalyze a sweeping advance. In contrast to Rostow and his colleagues, many Indian planners were also enthusiastic about the history of Soviet economic performance. "It is now accepted," Mahalanobis declared, "that economic planning in the USSR...has led to a far more rapid rate of industrialization than had been achieved in Western Europe and the United States in the past."[14]

In claiming that India's plan overemphasized industry, therefore, the MIT researchers made more than an economic judgment. When Lafeber and Eckhaus presented their research to the Indian planning officials, they knew they were challenging India's ideological stand. Although one Indian expert jokingly suggested that the CIS economists should be put under house arrest, Lafeber still hoped that it might be possible to "muddle through" the controversy, "particularly if nothing happens which could turn the question into a *cause célèbre*." Before long, however, serious problems did arise. B. K. Nehru, the Indian ambassador to the United States and a cousin of the prime minister, learned about the CIS model, conferred with economists Max Millikan and Paul Rosenstein-Rodan at MIT, and recommended to the Planning Commission that they allow CIS to analyze a draft of the next development plan "for the purpose of reconsidering the targets." While B. K. Nehru was apparently willing to consider revising the

Indian approach, his colleagues were not, and they deeply resented what they considered to be an attempt by CIS to subvert the planning process.[15]

When the links between MIT's Center for International Studies and the U.S. government were exposed, moreover, Indians perceived a covert U.S. attempt to subvert their nation's independent developmental course. After Eckhaus and Millikan briefed U.S. ambassador Chester Bowles about the model's results, Bowles contacted Planning Commission officials and pressed for a new approach that would emphasize agriculture and consumer goods more strongly. A grant from the U.S. Agency for International Development, it also turned out, had funded the creation of the CIS model, hardening the Indian impression that while the U.S. economists claimed to be objective scholars, they were in fact agents of U.S. foreign policy. Finally, in December 1964, an Indian newspaper publicized the long-standing connection between MIT's Center for International Studies and the U.S. Central Intelligence Agency. Earlier that year a book published in the United States had revealed that Millikan had previously worked for the CIA and that the agency had supported CIS's studies of Soviet society. Indian journalists now argued that CIS was "an extended arm of the CIA research division, even if under a more respectable garb." CIS's India project, they insisted, was nothing more than "a deliberate attempt ... to sabotage the country's long-term development programme" by challenging "the major postulates of Indian planning." In the aftermath, Indian officials severed their connections with CIS staff and terminated the relationship between the Planning Commission and CIS. While the specific charges leveled against CIS's India project were exaggerated, the CIS relationship to the U.S. government certainly undermined the economists' claims to apolitical expertise.[16]

The controversy also marked a turning point in the U.S.-Indian relationship. Although the Kennedy administration continued to call for development assistance to India, and total U.S. aid climbed to a peak of $465 million in 1962, relations between the two countries remained tense and uneasy. Nehru's continued criticism of U.S. military aid to Pakistan, resistance to U.S. attempts to mediate the Indo-Pakistani dispute over Kashmir, and protests over U.S. intervention in Vietnam disappointed Kennedy's hopes for closer ties. As critics claimed that "socialist" development projects violated essential U.S. commitments to free enterprise and individual liberty, U.S. economic aid to India fell by more than 50 percent over the next five years. After Nehru's death in May 1964, U.S.-Indian relations continued to decline. In 1966, after Indian prime minister Indira Gandhi publicly criticized the U.S. bombing of North Vietnam, Lyndon Johnson suspended U.S. food shipments to India, despite Indian food shortages and a severe drought. In 1971, when war broke out between India and Pakistan over the creation of Bangladesh, formerly East Pakistan, the Nixon administration condemned Indian support for the Bengali revolt and canceled virtually all U.S. economic assistance. Although India still received aid through the World Bank and the International Monetary Fund, the U.S. attempt to direct the country's modernization through bilateral aid effectively ended.[17]

At the height of the Cold War, the U.S. vision of modernization ultimately proved incompatible with the Indian approach to development. For U.S. cold warriors, modernization was integrally linked to a strategy of global containment. It was intended to steer the development, economies, and policies of postcolonial nations in clearly pro-Western directions. The Indian government, however, strongly resisted those efforts. Determined to protect his country's political independence, Nehru reacted with hostility to U.S. attempts to redirect India's developmental course. Many U.S. observers also misread Nehru's fundamental goals. For Nehru and his colleagues, industrialization and increased state control over the economy were vehicles for the promotion of nonaligned self-sufficiency, not steps down the path toward communism. Soviet economic models were attractive as routes to rapid industrialization, not as blueprints for the construction of a totalitarian state. Nehru's ambivalence about liberal capitalism and apparent ingratitude for U.S. aid, moreover, reflected a determination to prevent control of his nation's economy by foreign donors and investors, not a turn toward Moscow. Though both Americans and Indians spoke of the need to accelerate national progress on the road toward development, they had fundamentally different methods and destinations in mind.

Nasser, Kennedy, and Egyptian Modernization

In 1953, one year after he led a group of "Free Officers" to seize power, Nasser declared that British imperialism had thrust Egypt into a turbulent historical stream: "Torrents of ideas and opinions burst upon us which we were, at that stage of our evolution, incapable of assimilating. Our spirits were still in the Thirteenth Century though the symptoms of the Nineteenth and Twentieth Centuries infiltrated in their various aspects. Our minds were trying to catch up with the advancing caravan of humanity." According to Nasser, independence would require accelerated progress in both human and material terms. In order to complete its historical transition, Egypt would need to pass through "two revolutions." The first, already under way, involved realizing the "right for self-government" and the removal of foreign occupying forces. The second, still to come, would be "social" in nature, a prolonged struggle for "justice for all countrymen." A few years later, Nasser expanded on that agenda. British monopolies, high taxes, foreign privileges, and the concentration of land ownership among elites had stunted Egyptian development. Overcoming imperialism now demanded "national reconstruction," including central planning, industrialization, agrarian reform, and education. Only then would it be possible to "restore human dignity in Egypt."[18]

Though he did not use the term, central elements of Nasser's rhetoric resonated clearly with U.S. concepts of modernization. As they sought to understand the nature of change in the Middle East, many U.S. scholars and policymakers envisioned a process in which ancient societies, dominated by "traditional" culture, were upended and destabilized by the force of Western imperialism. Like Nasser, they understood Egypt as a nation in the midst of a dramatic and pivotal drive toward modernity. The acceleration and ultimate direction of that process, they also concluded, was of utmost importance to the United States.

Some U.S. commentators viewed Egypt's prospects with a skeptical eye. In *The Passing of Traditional Society* (1958), his popular account of Middle Eastern modernization, sociologist Daniel Lerner described Egypt as a land of jarring contrasts and limited prospects. The narrow, "green strip of fertile Nile valley," he wrote, was surrounded by "vast deserts that roll endlessly away beyond the horizons." High birthrates and limited cropland drove poor peasants into crowded urban areas. In Egypt's cities, Lerner lamented, "camels stall Cadillacs as the human mass afoot dominates the roads and regulates the tempo." "By raising expectations among Egyptians," Nasser himself also risked explosive resentment. "Higher hopes," Lerner warned, required "higher payoff," and Egypt's prospects for rapid, concrete advances remained dim. As modernization stalled, and elites confronted the gap between promise and performance, Lerner predicted that they would try to turn public resentment away from themselves and toward the West.[19]

Others took a more sympathetic stance. Among them was former State Department analyst and Princeton political scientist Manfred Halpern. In his influential book, *The Politics of Social Change in the Middle East and North Africa* (1963), Halpern emphasized the rise of a progressive middle class. "The traditional Middle Eastern elite of kings, landowners, and bourgeoisie," he argued, was losing its authority to a new "class of men inspired by non-traditional knowledge … clustered around a core of salaried civilian and military politicians, organizers, administrators, and experts." Placing Nasser within that emerging cohort, Halpern praised the Egyptian leader's sincere attempt to replace the "hollow" and "corrupt forms of the past" with "a disciplined, enthusiastic political organization able to come to grips with the problems of social change and willing to account for its actions to the Egyptian constituency." Halpern did not downplay Egypt's economic and social problems. Like many Middle Eastern societies, Egypt belonged to the "domain of Alice's Red Queen, where everyone will have to run very fast if he is merely to stand still." But Halpern also maintained that modernization was the best alternative to "the politics of despair that leads to communism, neo-Islamic totalitarianism, or ultra-nationalism." The real challenge for the United States, Halpern advised, was "to recognize the full scope of the revolutions now transforming the Middle East and to help nationalists cope successfully with rapid change."[20]

Like many liberal policymakers, Kennedy and his advisers shared the more optimistic perspective that Halpern expressed. They also believed that the Eisenhower administration had pursued a failed strategy in responding to Arab nationalism and in dealing with Egypt in particular. Washington policymakers had originally perceived Nasser's government as a force that might provide greater stability than the fragile monarchy it had overthrown. But Nasser's opposition to U.S.-backed regional military alliances, continued hostility toward Israel, recognition of the People's Republic of China, and repeated insistence that imperialism represented a greater danger for the Middle East than communism all alarmed Dulles and Eisenhower. After Egypt accepted a shipment of arms from Czechoslovakia in 1955, the United States canceled its offer to finance the construction of the Aswan High Dam, a project that Nasser believed was crucial to Egypt's development efforts. That step, in turn, contributed to Nasser's decision to nationalize the Suez Canal, a move that precipitated the Suez Crisis and the invasion of Egypt by Britain, France, and Israel in 1956. Although the United States forced its allies to withdraw from Egypt, the crisis enabled the Soviets to cast themselves as the defenders of Egyptian sovereignty. After Egypt and Syria announced the formation of the United Arab Republic (UAR) in 1958, U.S. analysts remained uncertain of Nasser's ultimate goals in the region. The Eisenhower administration's deployment of 14,000 U.S. Marines to Lebanon in an attempt to keep Nasser's conservative, pro-Western rival, Camille Chamoun, in power, finally, alienated Arab public opinion and deepened Egyptian hostility to the United States.[21]

At that point, the prospects for U.S.-Egyptian reconciliation appeared dim. Nasser's pan-Arabic convictions, in particular, worried Washington. While the United States sought to line up a coalition of resolutely anti-Communist Arab states, aimed to preserve Western access to Middle Eastern oil, and hoped to protect its ally Israel, Nasser challenged all of those objectives. All Arabs, he argued, were part of a single people with a shared historical destiny, and it was imperative for them to formulate a common policy against the dangerous threats of Western imperialism and Zionism. To attain real independence and social justice, Arab states would also need to transform their societies and promote development. In particular, they would need to reject the corrupt monarchical regimes put in place by imperialists, redistribute wealth and political power, and nationalize resources, including oil reserves. Finally, they would have to maintain a "positive neutrality" in the Cold War's ideological struggle, refusing alliance with either superpower. Equally disconcerting to U.S. officials was Nasser's conviction that Egypt's nationalist revolution should provide an essential model and source of support for anticolonial radicals throughout the Arab world.[22]

In late 1958, however, the Eisenhower administration started to change course. Nasser's opposition to a Soviet-backed revolutionary regime in Iraq, his crackdown against the Communist Party in Egypt and Syria, and his tremendous popularity in the region led influential Washington officials to recommend an accommodation with him. Although they still worried about Nasser's pan-Arabism and his hostility toward the conservative, pro-Western states of Jordan, Lebanon, and Saudi Arabia, U.S. experts now began to see the Egyptian leader as a potential barrier to the dangers of Communist incursion. As the National Security Council concluded in November of 1958, to keep the Soviets out of the region and preserve Western access to its oil, the United States would have to "work more closely with Arab nationalism" and "deal with Nasser as head of the UAR on specific problems and issues, area-wide as well as local, affecting the UAR's legitimate interests." As Soviet-Egyptian relations cooled, and a frustrated Nikita Khrushchev called Nasser a "hot-headed young man who has taken on a lot more than he can manage," the United States provided Egypt with development assistance in the form of surplus food sales, export guarantees, and support for a loan of $56 million from the World Bank.[23]

Kennedy administration strategists believed that these steps were long overdue. They also believed that forthright U.S. support for Egyptian modernization could reorient Nasser's priorities and ultimately help create a major political and structural change throughout the Middle East. As John F. Kennedy himself contended in 1959, the Eisenhower administration's intolerance for nonalignment and its tendency to deal with the region "almost exclusively in the context of the East-West struggle" had led it to ignore the real significance of nationalism and economic development. The crucial question, Kennedy insisted, was "not whether we should recognize the force of Arab nationalism, but how we can help to channel it along constructive lines." Promoting Egypt's modernization, Kennedy reasoned, would help close the door to Soviet subversion and encourage Nasser to focus his enormous energies and ambitions in internal directions. It could lead him to downgrade his campaign against Israel and suspend his ongoing conflict with his Arab rivals in favor of meeting the demands for rapid social and economic progress at home. A program of Western-sponsored modernization in Egypt, the Kennedy administration hoped, would also set an example for the rest of the Arab world.[24]

NATIONALIST ENCOUNTERS   79

The conditions for such an initiative also appeared favorable. In September 1961, the Syrian government fell to a coup and seceded from the United Arab Republic, an event that U.S. analysts expected would dampen Nasser's regional ambitions and increase his concern about Egypt's own political stability. Kennedy agreed with that assessment, and in mid-October he approved a National Security Council directive to "create opportunities for bettering U.S.-Egyptian relations via development assistance." Over the course of the year, Egyptian ambassador to the United States Mustapha Kamel also raised U.S. hopes by declaring that his country was now ready to put the Arab-Israeli conflict "in the refrigerator." In meetings with Deputy National Security Advisor Walt Rostow in November, Kamel specifically linked the conflict between Egypt and Israel to questions of development, suggesting that "the possibilities for a more basic settlement would gradually emerge as domestic progress was made by all parties."[25]

Encouraged by those overtures, Kennedy responded favorably to Nasser's request for a new U.S. commitment to Egyptian development. In the late 1950s, the Eisenhower administration had offered deliveries of surplus U.S. food to Egypt on a short-term basis. Nasser now asked for a large, long-term, multiyear commitment through the U.S. Public Law 480 (PL-480) program, which allowed for the delivery of surplus grain at very low costs. Such a step, Kamel argued, would assist Egyptian economic development planning by allowing the government to divert its scarce foreign exchange holdings from food imports to industrial investments. In response, Kennedy recommended a three-year, $500 million package of PL-480 aid, and U.S. officials began discussing the creation of an international development aid consortium for Egypt as well. Some U.S. officials, including AID director William Gaud, protested those moves, arguing that long-term commitments gave away vital U.S. leverage over Egyptian behavior. But Kennedy and his closest advisers were determined to push forward, hoping to make Nasser "turn a little inward" and be "more interested in Egyptian development and less interested in fomenting revolutions." As Kennedy's roving ambassador Chester Bowles put it, the goal was to lead Nasser "to forsake the microphone for the bulldozer" and "assume a key role in bringing the Middle East peacefully into our modern world."[26]

Egypt was also pursuing an ambitious development agenda. Starting in 1952, land reform laws and a state campaign against "feudalism" had addressed staggering inequalities in the countryside. Limits on the size of private landholdings, subsidies for consumer goods, and lowered land rental values had helped to rectify a situation in which the majority of the rural population owned no property while a tiny elite of less than 6 percent of all landowners held more than 64 percent of Egypt's land area. The creation of a system of mandatory, state-run cooperatives, through which peasants received agricultural credit, purchased tools, and made payments on the land they obtained from the government, also provided Nasser with a base of rural support and raised revenue for investment. In the industrial sector, the government created a bank to lend investment capital and provided funding for electricity, infrastructure, and oil projects. After the Suez Crisis in 1956, the state also began to expand its authority by nationalizing foreign oil, tobacco, pharmaceutical, banking, insurance, and concrete firms, all of which were eventually placed in the public sector under a new Economic Development Organization. In 1960, Egypt put forward its First Five-Year Plan, and a year later the country's new "Socialist Laws" increased state control over finance, transportation, and commerce. Progressive tax policies, an increased minimum wage, and greater spending on health care, meanwhile, reinforced a commitment to improved social welfare.[27]

Although many Western observers criticized the statist approach and doubted that it could have long-term success, the Kennedy administration remained committed to providing assistance. In March 1962 Kennedy sent Harvard economist and development expert Edward S. Mason to evaluate Egypt's plans. Mason reported back that Egypt's goal of an 8 percent annual growth rate in real national income was too ambitious. The country's low investment levels and expensive social programs would make that target impossible to hit. Mason warned as well that Egypt's lack of foreign exchange might require it to cut back on imports of capital equipment, slowing industrial production, and that a partial crop failure had temporarily stalled the economy. Yet Mason also argued that a solid 5 percent growth rate was indeed possible, particularly with PL-480 aid from the United States. Strongly recommending U.S. aid, Mason predicted that it would promote Egyptian development and prevent Nasser from turning to the Soviets.[28]

The Kennedy administration took that advice. In addition to confirming the PL-480 deliveries, U.S. policymakers met with Egyptian officials to discuss the possibility of much greater U.S. and multilateral support through the International Monetary Fund and the World Bank. By the summer of 1962, U.S. officials viewed their relationship with Egypt in nearly euphoric terms. As one State Department assessment put it, a "new stage" in U.S.-Egyptian relations had started. The Egyptian desire to join "the rather exclusive development consortium club" gave the United States an unprecedented opportunity "to reduce [the] suspicions, phobias, complexes and frustrations" that had previously driven Egypt in anti-Western and pro-Soviet directions. The appeal of U.S.-sponsored development had led Egypt to resist Soviet interference in its internal affairs, keep "the Palestine problem 'in the icebox,'" drop its support for the Cuban Revolution, improve relations with Europe, and pursue a "much more balanced" form of nonalignment. Over the long term, such a policy could produce the "modernization of the [Egyptian] economy and society; and eventually progress toward democracy." It could also foster a "willingness to live and let live with Israel" and ultimately lead Egypt into "firmer membership in the Free World."[29]

Those illusions, however, were soon shattered. U.S. policymakers expected that, in the face of modernization, Egypt's domestic and foreign policies would be essentially malleable. Their reduction of Nasser's anti-Western and pan-Arabic policies to psychological "suspicions, phobias, complexes and frustrations" also fostered the idea that his policies were transitory manifestations of a childlike immaturity that would disappear as Egypt moved into a higher developmental stage.

Enthralled with their own concept of modernization, U.S. policymakers misread the depth of Nasser's ideological commitments. That fact became clearer when a civil war suddenly erupted in Yemen, a country that bordered Saudi Arabia and the British protectorate of Aden on the southwest corner of the Arabian Peninsula. In September 1962, a group of army officers led by Colonel Abdullah al-Sallal overthrew the government following the death of the country's ruler, Imam Ahmad Hamid al-Din. Inspired by Nasser's commitment to fight against the twin dangers of Western imperialism and entrenched conservative elites, Sallal declared the creation of the Yemen Arab Republic, promised comprehensive development, and demanded that Britain withdraw from Aden. In response, the late imam's son, Mohammed al-Badr, organized a royalist guerrilla force in an attempt to restore the monarchy under his rule.[30]

The Yemeni civil war quickly widened into a regional struggle. Worried that a revolution in Yemen might inspire a Nasserist uprising within their own militaries, the conservative Saudi Arabian and Jordanian monarchies began to finance and arm al-Badr's forces. Nasser, however, moved quickly to recognize Sallal and the Yemen Arab Republic. Syria's secession from the UAR had thwarted Nasser's regional ambitions, but a revolutionary state in Yemen could increase Egypt's influence on the Arabian Peninsula and bolster Nasser's prestige throughout the Arab world. When Sallal asked for help, therefore, Nasser took the dramatic step of sending in the Egyptian army. Covert Soviet air transport facilitated the deployment, and by November 1962 at least 10,000 Egyptian combat troops were fighting alongside Sallal's soldiers, the first contingent of a force that would ultimately number 70,000 men.[31]

The prospect of a widened inter-Arab conflict deeply troubled the Kennedy administration. By promoting Egyptian modernization, Kennedy and his advisers hoped to turn Nasser's focus inward and curb his revolutionary goals. It now appeared, however, that Nasser was unwilling to forsake his broader political agenda. Reluctant to abandon a strategy he had so eagerly embraced, and worried that U.S. opposition to the Yemeni revolution would push Egypt closer to the Soviet Union, in December 1962 Kennedy decided to recognize Sallal's regime.

Hoping to contain the growing conflict, the United States also tried to broker a mutual disengagement of Egypt and Saudi Arabia from the Yemeni war. The Saudi government, however, refused to stop aiding the royalist forces and pushed back by demanding that Aramco, the U.S. oil consortium based in Dhahran, give up two-thirds of its huge concession and pay sharply higher taxes. Britain, Jordan, and Israel also criticized the U.S. decision, arguing that Nasser had violated a misplaced U.S. trust.[32]

Under pressure, the Kennedy administration finally began to reverse course. In early January 1963 State Department Middle East experts argued that the United States still had "enough strings in our diplomatic bow to blunt or divert any UAR thrust" that would endanger U.S. interests in the Middle East. But Nasser's escalation of the crisis by increasing the deployment of Egyptian troops, using poison gas against Yemeni royalist forces, and launching air strikes against Saudi Arabian border towns suggested otherwise. In mid-January, Kennedy personally warned Nasser that his policies were endangering the U.S.-Egyptian relationship. Nasser's response, however, was noncommittal. Angered by Egyptian intransigence and worried about possible damage to U.S. oil interests, President Kennedy finally decided to turn toward Saudi Arabia. In exchange for a Saudi agreement to stop its support of the Yemeni royalists, Kennedy sent a U.S. Air Force squadron and a team of military advisers to Dhahran. Although the aircraft remained under U.S. control, the step marked a clear commitment to the defense of Nasser's enemy.[33]

The United States' relationship with Egypt soon collapsed altogether. As Egypt's engagement in the Yemeni civil war spiraled upward, defense spending drew precious resources away from the economic development programs on which the Kennedy administration had based its hopes. In November 1963, two weeks before Kennedy's death, the U. S. Congress also repudiated the administration's strategy. By a vote of 65 to 13, the Senate cut off all U.S. development assistance to Egypt by passing an amendment prohibiting U.S. aid for any country that was "engaging in or preparing for aggressive military efforts" against the United States or any of its allies. Over the next year, Nasser responded by welcoming hundreds of millions of dollars in Soviet military aid, pressing the Libyan government to expel British and U.S. forces, and pledging to fight the U.S.-backed regime in Congo. In December 1964 Nasser gave full vent to his anger, warning that neither the carrot of U.S. aid nor the stick of U.S. sanctions would ever lead him to "sell Egyptian independence." "Those who do not accept our behavior," he declared, "can go drink from the sea."[34]

While the Egypt-Israeli conflict remained temporarily "in the icebox," Nasser proved unwilling to abandon his goal of promoting radical change throughout the Middle East. His willingness to intervene in Yemen, moreover, brought him into direct conflict with the conservative monarchies that the United States depended on for access to vital Western oil supplies. U.S.-Egyptian relations also continued to deteriorate. Lyndon Johnson viewed Nasser as bent on dominating the Arab world, and in 1964 the State Department warned that he was committed to the "export of revolution" in Libya, Jordan, and Saudi Arabia. Nasser's pledge to train Palestine Liberation Organization guerrillas, his decision to assist radicals in Congo, and his permission for the Vietnamese National Liberation Front to open an office in Egypt further alienated Washington. After protestors burned the U.S. Information Agency library in Cairo, and Nasser refused to apologize, Johnson also terminated the PL-480 agreement that Kennedy had established. By 1967, moreover, war between Egypt and Israel further limited the chance for reconciliation.[35]

Reflecting on Kennedy's approach to Egypt a decade later, Rostow described Nasser as one of the era's "Romantic Revolutionaries" and lamented his "inability to focus [his] efforts on economic and social development." That perspective failed to recognize the deeper problem at hand. Nasser was sincerely committed to Egyptian development, but he did not view it solely in internal, domestic terms. Egypt's revolution, he believed, was ultimately inseparable from the wider, regional campaign against the forces of reaction and imperialism that continued to dominate the Middle East. In this light, Kennedy's former U.S. ambassador to Egypt, John Badeau, came closer to the mark. In 1968 Badeau observed: "[For Nasser] the struggle in Yemen was viewed in terms of its effect on the modernizing of the Arab world, the success of the revolutionary regime and system, and the credibility of a U.A.R. commitment to a sister revolutionary state." In the early 1960s a common interest in improved economic growth and social welfare brought the United States and Egypt closer together, but Nasser's own objectives were not nearly as malleable as the Kennedy administration expected. As Badeau eventually realized, Nasser's radical vision of development was also fundamentally incompatible with the kind of modernization that the United States wanted to promote.[36]

Ghana, the United States, and the Volta Project

On March 4, 1957, Ghana became the first sub-Saharan African state to gain independence. Like Nehru and Nasser, Ghanaian prime minister Nkrumah argued that British imperialism had severely damaged the prospects for his country to advance in the realms of education, agriculture, and industry. Freedom from foreign control was surely a cause for celebration, he explained in his autobiography, but it was only the first step on a much longer road. "The economic independence that should follow and maintain political independence," he emphasized, would require nothing less than a "total mobilisation" of every resource available. "What other countries have taken three hundred years or more to achieve," Nkrumah declared, "a once dependent territory must try to accomplish in a generation if it is to survive. Unless it is, as it were, 'jet-propelled,' it will lag behind and thus risk everything for which it has fought."[37]

Nkrumah's call for rapidly accelerated development was a familiar one among postcolonial elites in the late 1950s and early 1960s. His criticism of unfettered capitalism, preference for "socialistic" solutions, commitment to nonalignment, and anti-imperial convictions had much in common with the views of leaders of countries as diverse as Indonesia, India, Algeria, and Egypt. Ghana's independence, Nkrumah also argued, was "part of a general world historical pattern," and it was his country's duty to promote decolonization abroad. "Our task is not done and our own safety is not assured," he warned, "until the last vestiges of colonialism have been swept from Africa."[38]

Though averse to socialist solutions, and wary of Nkrumah's anticolonial, pan-African ideals, U.S. policymakers also believed that Ghana's independence marked an important historical moment. Sub-Saharan Africa, considered an economic and political backwater, had long remained a very low strategic priority for U.S. officials. By the late 1950s, however, Cold War anxieties led U.S. policymakers to view the region's anticolonial movements with much greater interest. Continued European influence, they believed, was necessary to preserve stability and prevent subversion, and their racial views often made them doubt that black Africans were capable of real self-government. But Ghana's independence presented U.S. policymakers with an accomplished fact and an important challenge. John Foster Dulles characterized Ghana's achievement as one of the "most significant events of contemporary Africa." The continent's other "emergent peoples," he advised, would "follow with particular attention the degree of interest and sympathy which the United States accords these developments." The Eisenhower administration, Vice President Nixon agreed, should "follow most closely the evolution of this state, realizing that its success or failure is going to have a profound impact on the future of this part of Africa."[39]

By the late 1950s, U.S. policymakers began to turn toward a policy of development assistance. Ghana, U.S. analysts argued, was moving through a crucial transition, and U.S. aid could have a powerful impact. As one White House briefing paper put it in 1958, "Ghana's policies and institutions are still in a formative state, and their future character can be affected substantially by the attitude and actions of the United States." Helping Ghana establish "an adequate framework of government dedicated to democratic principles and capable of maintaining political stability and progress in improving the productivity and living standards of the people," another aid assessment argued, would counter Communist attacks and "provide a concrete demonstration of the benefits of association with the West."[40]

Nkrumah also eagerly sought U.S. assistance, particularly for the Volta River project. In a letter to Eisenhower written in November 1957, he emphasized his aim to secure "the political and economic development of [his] country." Ghana, Nkrumah explained, was too heavily dependent on the export of cocoa, its primary crop. As prices for that commodity fluctuated on a volatile world market, the economy went through unpredictable cycles of boom and bust that made long-term development planning impossible. Major structural change, he acknowledged, took time, but the Volta River project held out the potential for "a really big immediate economic advance." Hydroelectric power generated by damming the Volta, Nkrumah believed, would promote diversification and allow for the creation of many new industries. A smelter powered by electricity from the river, meanwhile, would enable Ghana to process its vast deposits of bauxite into aluminum, providing another valuable export. In language that recapitulated the core assumptions of modernization theory, Nkrumah asked the United States to provide the essential "stimulus and drive" needed to catalyze economic development and "strengthen the political independence" of Ghana.[41]

In many ways, the ideal of rapid development provided a framework through which Ghana and the United States found a mutual interest. While Ghana needed U.S. development funds, the United States hoped to shape Ghana's political and economic trajectory, demonstrate its commitment to new African states, and counter Communist appeals. In the summer of 1958, Nkrumah accepted Eisenhower's invitation to visit the United States, and both parties took conciliatory positions. Nkrumah disavowed any interest in communism and, one year after the conflict over school desegregation in Little Rock, Arkansas, even suggested that the issue of U.S. racial discrimination had "often been exaggerated deliberately by those who hoped to bring the [United States] into disrepute." U.S. officials, in turn, ignored Ghana's new "preventive detention law," which allowed for the incarceration of political opponents for up to five years without legal due process. Ghanaian democracy, in any event, was not really a pressing U.S. concern. One State Department analysis noted, paternalistically: "[In a] country where passion, superstition, and rumor play such a large part in political activities, it is most difficult for a new Government faced with the problem of modernization of a backward state to allow complete freedom of action to dissident elements." While promising to study the Volta project, the Eisenhower administration provided Ghana with technical assistance for agricultural development and geophysical surveying and delivered modest amounts of food aid. Over the next two years, Washington also tolerated Nkrumah's decisions to purchase Soviet aircraft, negotiate with the USSR for industrial aid, and allow China to open an embassy.[42]

The civil war in Congo, however, presented a far more contentious problem. In June 1960 Congo gained its independence from Belgium, and within weeks the country plunged into violence. The southern province of Katanga, rich in strategic minerals, seceded with support from Belgian troops and mining interests. Congolese prime minister Patrice Lumumba then requested that the United Nations intervene to end the rebellion. The UN authorized a peacekeeping mission and requested that the Belgians withdraw, but much to Lumumba's dismay it took no action regarding Katanga's secession. Fearing the breakup of the country, Lumumba then accepted Soviet military aid in his attempt to put down the separatists.

U.S. and Ghanaian officials viewed the Congo conflict in starkly contrasting terms. For its part, the Eisenhower administration was convinced that Lumumba was likely to align himself, and his country's uranium reserves, with the Soviets. The United States had tried unsuccessfully to block Lumumba's election, and CIA director Allen Dulles considered him "a Castro or worse." As the war intensified in the fall of 1960, Washington also launched plans to assassinate Lumumba, and then watched with relief as Congolese soldiers under the pro-American general Joseph Mobutu captured Lumumba and transferred him to Katangan forces who finally tortured and murdered him.[43]

Nkrumah, however, considered Lumumba an anticolonial ally and a pan-Africanist protégé. Along with the representatives of thirty-five other liberation movements, the Congolese leader had attended the 1958 All-African People's Conference in Accra, and the two men had remained in close contact. When the fighting in Congo began, Nkrumah raced to help Lumumba by deploying more than two thousand Ghanaian troops to serve in the UN forces. When the UN declined to stop the rebellion and took no action against Belgium, Nkrumah was outraged by the failure to confront what he considered clear evidence of imperial aggression. In September 1960, in an hour-long speech at the UN General Assembly, Nkrumah condemned Belgium for promoting "a system of calculated political castration in the hope that it would be completely impossible for African nationalists to fight for emancipation." He also pointed toward the Congo as clear evidence of the persistence of Western imperialism, rejected Katanga's secession, and recommended that the UN withdraw in favor of an all-African force. In response, an adamant U.S. secretary of state Christian Herter publicly accused Nkrumah of "very definitely leaning toward the Soviet bloc." What Nkrumah considered the defense of African unity, nationalism, and nonaligned sovereignty, U.S. officials viewed as complicity with Soviet expansionism.[44]

Despite the breach in relations with the United States, Nkrumah still hoped that it might be possible to secure Western support for the Volta project. In 1959, a consortium of private firms, including Kaiser Industries, Reynolds Metals Company, Olin Mathieson, the Aluminum Company of America, and the Aluminum Limited Company of Canada, agreed to take on the construction and engineering tasks. By August 1960 Nkrumah had also lined up loan commitments of $20 million from the United States, $14 million from Britain, and $40 million from the World Bank. After the rift over Congo, however, the project's prospects looked dim, and when Nkrumah requested an appointment to discuss the Volta plans with Eisenhower in late September the U.S. president refused to meet with him.[45]

Worried that a U.S. decision to withdraw would jeopardize the entire undertaking, Nkrumah hoped it might be possible to mend fences with the incoming Kennedy administration. During the 1960 election campaign Kennedy had criticized the long-standing pattern of U.S. indifference to Africa. "Although Africa is the poorest and least productive area on earth," Kennedy lamented, "we have done little to provide the development capital which is essential to a growing economy." Only a "bold and imaginative new program for the development of Africa," he argued, would fend off communism and put the United States on the side of the continent's nationalists. But the Volta project faced fierce political opposition in the United States. Critics in Congress and the business world condemned Nkrumah as a left-leaning, pro-Soviet radical. To support him, they insisted, would only bolster anti-Americanism in Africa. The CIA also launched a hostile campaign of its own, ridiculing Nkrumah as an immature, shortsighted "showboy, and a vain opportunist...a politician to whom the roars of the crowd and the praise of the sycophant are as necessary as the air he breathes."[46]

Kennedy, however, decided to support the Volta project. Although Nkrumah continued to attack U.S. policy in Congo, accusing Washington of supporting "puppet regimes" and collaborating in Lumumba's murder, Kennedy believed that to withdraw support would damage U.S. credibility among Africa's new states. It would also, he feared, open the door to Soviet intervention by repeating the mistake the Eisenhower administration had made when it canceled funding for Egypt's Aswan Dam. More importantly, Kennedy and many of his advisers also believed that the fundamental premises of modernization still applied. Promoting rapid economic development in Ghana, they expected, would alleviate the poverty and desperation in which radicalism was most likely to take root and grow. It would also help drive Ghana through the destabilizing transitional period and lead that country in more liberal, capitalist, pro-Western directions. As Walt Rostow recalled, in Ghana the Kennedy administration ultimately decided that "long-run rather than short-run U.S. political interests should guide aid allocations."[47]

In June 1961, Kennedy personally notified Nkrumah that the United States would provide its share of the Volta project funding. Over the next few months Nkrumah angered Washington officials once more by taking a long tour of Communist states, sending Ghanaian troops to the USSR for training, calling for UN recognition of China, and advocating Western acceptance of a permanently divided Germany. Worried about the political fallout of Nkrumah's actions, Kennedy tried to pressure him in the fall of 1961 by leaking a story to the press that the United States was reconsidering its support for the Volta project, and sending emissaries to Accra to demand a public commitment to nonalignment. After Nkrumah professed his "sincere neutralism" and willingness to accept "all forms" of economic development, Kennedy went forward. Although some close advisers, including Attorney General Robert Kennedy, argued against it, Secretary of State Dean Rusk defended the idea of "attempting to turn Nkrumah on a reasonable course." In December 1961, the president finally approved a $37 million loan to Ghana and an additional $96 million loan and $54 million investment guarantee to the aluminum companies working on the project.[48]

The U.S. attempt to influence the direction of Ghanaian development soon failed. In 1959, Ghana had initiated a five-year plan largely designed by the economist and future Nobel laureate W. Arthur Lewis. An influential critic of command economies and an advocate of blending market forces with moderate planning to raise living standards and promote long-term growth, Lewis called for Ghana to seek a sharp increase in foreign investment from public as well as private sources. The plan also advocated a limited government role in industrialization, emphasized the need to build commercial infrastructure, and devoted substantial resources to the Volta project. Supported by foreign capital and designed in collaboration with private foreign business, the Volta project was expected to produce electricity, improve irrigation, and help create the foundation on which industrialization might eventually be pursued.[49]

In late 1961, however, Nkrumah made a sharp turn to the left. Departing from the liberal, capitalist approach, his government scrapped Lewis's plan in favor of a new seven-year "Programme for Work and Happiness." Inspired by Nkrumah's study of Soviet development policy and shaped largely by the Hungarian economist Joszef Bognor, the new program explicitly embraced central planning, state management of the economy, and "scientific socialism." The state-run Ghana National Trading Corporation became the dominant importer of consumer goods, and the government moved quickly to set up a vast array of state-owned enterprises ranging from steel mills to distilleries, tire companies, pharmaceutical firms, and bakeries. Nkrumah's government also created state farms relying on machinery imported from Eastern Europe, denied private entrepreneurs the commercial licenses necessary to stay in business, and mandated that foreign firms reinvest 60 percent of their net profits in Ghana. "[The] domestic policy of my government," Nkrumah boldly declared, "is the complete ownership of the economy by the state."[50]

Washington policymakers were deeply dismayed by this turn of events. Nkrumah had driven his nation's economy down a road most clearly identified with Soviet models. Suspecting that Ghana functioned as an intermediary in arms traffic between Communist states and Congolese radicals, U.S. officials also worried that Ghana would become a haven for left-wing subversives across Africa. By 1964, U.S.-Ghanaian relations were rapidly deteriorating. As Ghana's economy suffered from falling cocoa prices, bureaucratic inefficiency, declining productivity, and rampant corruption, U.S. newspapers and politicians lamented that Ghana had "gone Communist." Although the Volta project went forward on terms very favorable to the U.S. and Canadian aluminum companies, foreign investment in 1964 amounted to only one-tenth of what Ghana's seven-year plan called for. By 1965, the United States also took active steps against Nkrumah's government. Hoping that the growing economic crisis would weaken him and lead to his downfall, the United States refused to provide any additional foreign aid. The CIA also kept in close contact with forces plotting against Nkrumah, and the Johnson administration watched with satisfaction when he was overthrown by a military coup in February 1966.[51]

Worlds Apart

For Nehru, Nasser, and Nkrumah, the idea of rapid development was strongly appealing. It would give their governments political legitimacy, meet the needs of their populations, and redress the damage done by imperial rule. The concept of accelerated development also provided them with a vocabulary that was attractive to U.S. policymakers, and it was an effective language through which to request the funds and technical assistance that they needed. But their understanding of the methods and goals of development, defined in a nationalist, postcolonial context, did not easily fit within the far more rigid U.S. framework of modernization. While Nehru, Nasser, and Nkrumah agreed with U.S. policymakers on the value of national development planning to promote economic growth and raise living standards, serious conflicts ultimately emerged over both the *forms* and the *purposes* of development. Where these postcolonial leaders most desired a leading government role in the economy and a rapid industrial drive, U.S. officials preferred a greater attention to market forces, capitalist incentives, and "balanced growth." Where Nehru, Nasser, and Nkrumah aimed to solidify their domestic political control, achieve full economic independence, and provide the foundation for a genuinely nonaligned stand in the world, U.S. policymakers sought to guide the future trajectory of their countries in ways that would repel communism and demonstrate Western superiority in the Cold War's ideological struggle. In the late 1950s and early 1960s the dream of economic growth and accelerated progress enabled the United States to find common interests with India, Egypt, and Ghana. By the mid-1960s, however, the growing divide between postcolonial understandings of development and U.S. commitments to modernization also helped drive them apart.

As postcolonial leaders continued to criticize U.S. Cold War policies, accepted aid from Communist nations, and pursued diverse approaches to development, Washington officials perceived them as manipulative, ungrateful, and unreliable. Impatient with stubborn nationalists and ambivalent about popular democracy, U.S. policymakers promoted more repressive forms of modernization in countries like Guatemala, South Vietnam, and Iran. Modernization, in that regard, lent itself to policies of ruthless coercion as well as international cooperation.

Worried that modernization might be derailed, U.S. officials and experts also sought more powerful tools to intervene directly in foreign societies. Technological solutions, they hoped, would transcend political barriers and allow them to address the deeply rooted structural problems that might generate revolutionary threats. Among the most pressing and fundamental of these, they believed, were the effects generated by human reproduction itself.

NOTES

1. Kwame Nkrumah, "African Prospect," *Foreign Affairs* 37, no. 1 (1958): 51, 53.

2. Nikita Khrushchev, Speech of January 6, 1961, in *The Cold War: A History in Documents and Eyewitness Accounts,* ed. Jussi Hanhimäki and Odd Arne Westad (Oxford: Oxford University Press, 2003), 358, 360.

3. Jawaharlal Nehru, Letter to Province Premiers, April 15, 1948, in *The Essential Writings of Jawaharlal Nehru,* ed. S. Gopal and Uma Iyengar (Oxford: Oxford University Press, 2003), 2: 66.

4. Jawaharlal Nehru, *The Discovery of India* (New York: John Day, 1946), 402–3, 405.

5. Gyan Prakash, *Another Reason: Science and the Imagination of Modern India* (Princeton, NJ: Princeton University Press, 1999), 194–95, emphasis in original; Ramachandra Guha, *India after Gandhi: The History of the World's Largest Democracy* (New York: Ecco, 2007), 212–13.

6. Dennis Merrill, *Bread and the Ballot: The United States and India's Economic Development, 1947–1963* (Chapel Hill: University of North Carolina Press, 1990), 14, 125–26; Guha, *India after Gandhi,* 216; Judith Brown, *Nehru: A Political Life* (New Haven, CT: Yale University Press, 2003), 241.

7. "Appraisal of U.S. National Interests in South Asia," April 19, 1949, *FRUS 1949,* 6: 9; Robert J. McMahon, *The Cold War on the Periphery: The United States, India, and Pakistan* (New York: Columbia University Press, 1994), 6, 218–20.

8. Francine R. Frankel, *India's Political Economy, 1947–1977: The Gradual Revolution* (Princeton, NJ: Princeton University Press, 1978), 118–20; Merrill, *Bread and the Ballot,* 126; Brown, *Nehru,* 301–2.

9. Kennedy, Speech of March 25, 1958, in Sorensen, *"Let the Word Go Forth,"* 339; McMahon, *Cold War,* 258–59.

10. Andrew J. Rotter, *Comrades at Odds: The United States and India, 1947–1964* (Ithaca, NY: Cornell University Press, 2000), 21; McMahon, *Cold War,* 111, 114–15, 222–23.

11. Nicole Sackley, "Passage to Modernity: American Social Scientists, India, and the Pursuit of Development, 1945–1961" (PhD diss., Princeton University, 2004), 55–56; Albert Mayer et al., *Pilot Project, India: The Story of Rural Development at Etawah, Uttar Pradesh* (Berkeley: University of California Press, 1958), 18, 136, 159, 336–37.

12. Blackmer, *MIT Center,* 88–89, 180; Brown, *Nehru,* 304–6.

13. Sackley, "Passage to Modernity," 234–35; W. W. Rostow, "Marx was a City Boy, or Why Communism May Fail," *Harper's Magazine* 210 (February 1955): 25–30.

14. David C. Engerman, "The Romance of Economic Development and New Histories of the Cold War," *Diplomatic History* 28, no. 1 (2004): 33.

15. Blackmer, *MIT Center,* 181–82.

16. Blackmer, *MIT Center,* 183–88; George Rosen, *Western Economists and Eastern Societies: Agents of Change in South Asia, 1950–1970* (Baltimore: Johns Hopkins University Press, 1985), 132–39; David C. Engerman, "West Meets East: The Center for International Studies and Indian Economic Development," in *Staging Growth: Modernization, Development, and the Global Cold War,* ed. Nils Gilman, David Engerman, Mark Haefele, and Michael Latham (Amherst: University of Massachusetts Press, 2003), 213–14.

17. Merrill, *Bread and the Ballot,* 4, 200, 207–9.

18. Gamal Abdel Nasser, *The Philosophy of the Revolution,* trans. Dar Al-Maaref (Buffalo: Economica Books, 1959), 51; Nasser, "The Egyptian Revolution," *Foreign Affairs* 33, no. 2 (1955): 199–211.

19. Lerner, *Passing of Traditional Society,* 214, 216–17, 240, 248.

20. Manfred Halpern, *The Politics of Social Change in the Middle East and North Africa* (Princeton, NJ: Princeton University Press, 1963), 51–52, 357, 361, 420.

21. Burton I. Kaufman, *The Arab Middle East and the United States: Inter-Arab Rivalry and Superpower Diplomacy* (New York: Twayne, 1996), 18–28; Douglas Little, "From Even-Handed to Empty Handed: Seeking Order in the Middle East," in *Kennedy's Quest for Victory: American Foreign Policy, 1961–1963,* ed. Thomas G. Paterson (New York: Oxford University Press, 1989), 158.

22. Yaqub, *Containing Arab Nationalism,* 31–34; Avraham Sela, "Abd al-Nasser's Regional Politics: A Reassessment," in *Rethinking Nasserism: Revolution and Historical Memory in Modern Egypt,* ed. Elie Podeh and Onn Winckler (Gainesville: University Press of Florida, 2004), 181–82.

23. Malik Mufti, "The United States and Nasserist Pan-Arabism," in *The Middle East and the United States: A Historical and Political Reassessment,* ed. David W. Lesch (Boulder, CO: Westview, 2007), 147–50.

24. John F. Kennedy, *The Strategy of Peace* (New York: Harper and Brothers, 1960), 107–8; Douglas Little, "The New Frontier on the Nile: JFK, Nasser, and Arab Nationalism," *Journal of American History* 75, no. 2 (1988): 501–4.

25. Mufti, "United States and Nasserist Pan-Arabism," 152; Little, "New Frontier," 507; W. W. Rostow, *The Diffusion of Power: An Essay in Recent History* (New York: Macmillan, 1972), 196–97.

26. Little, "New Frontier," 507, 509–10; William J. Burns, *Economic Aid and American Policy toward Egypt, 1955–1981* (Albany: State University of New York Press, 1985), 126.

27. Mourad Magdi Wahba, *The Role of the State in the Egyptian Economy, 1945–1981* (Reading, UK: Ithaca Press, 1994), 48–94; M. Riad El-Ghonemy, "An Assessment of Egypt's Development Strategy, 1952–1970," in Podeh and Winckler, *Rethinking Nasserism,* 253–62.

28. Rostow, *Diffusion of Power,* 198; Little, "New Frontier," 509–10.

29. "Paper Presented in the Department of State," May 24, 1962, *FRUS 1961–1963,* 17: 677–82.

30. Kaufman, *Arab Middle East,* 34–35; Burns, *Economic Aid,* 134–35.

31. Burns, *Economic Aid,* 135; Little, "New Frontier," 511; Kaufman, *Arab Middle East,* 35; Jesse Ferris, "Soviet Support for Egypt's Intervention in Yemen, 1962–1963," *Journal of Cold War Studies* 10 (Fall 2008): 5–36.

32. Little, "New Frontier," 513–19.

33. Memorandum, Phillip Talbot to Dean Rusk, January 2, 1963, *FRUS 1961–1963*, 18: 292; Little, "New Frontier," 519–21.

34. Little, "New Frontier," 524; Kaufman, *Arab Middle East*, 39–40; Mufti, "United States and Nasserist Pan-Arabism," 155; Burns, *Economic Aid*, 159.

35. Douglas Little, *American Orientalism: The United States and the Middle East since 1945* (Chapel Hill: University of North Carolina Press, 2002), 185–88.

36. Rostow, *Diffusion of Power*, 199; John S. Badeau, *The American Approach to the Arab World* (New York: Harper and Row, 1968), 66.

37. Kwame Nkrumah, *Ghana: The Autobiography of Kwame Nkrumah* (New York: International Publishers, 1957), x.

38. Ibid., 290.

39. James H. Meriwether, "'A Torrent Running over Everything': Africa and the Eisenhower Administration," in Statler and Johns, *Eisenhower Administration,* 184; Ebere Nwaubani, *The United States and Decolonization in West Africa, 1950–1960* (Rochester, NY: University of Rochester Press, 2001), 119; Report from Nixon to Eisenhower, April 5, 1957, *FRUS 1955–1957*, 18: 60.

40. Ebere Nwaubani, "Eisenhower, Nkrumah, and the Congo Crisis," *Journal of Contemporary History* 36, no. 4 (2001): 600.

41. Nwaubani, *United States and Decolonization,* 130; Telegram transmitting letter from Nkrumah to Eisenhower, November 15, 1957, *FRUS 1955–1957*, 18: 384–86.

42. Nwaubani, "Eisenhower, Nkrumah, and the Congo Crisis," 602, 605; Nwaubani, *United States and Decolonization,* 130, 132–33, 136.

43. Westad, *Global Cold War,* 137–40.

44. Richard D. Mahoney, *JFK: Ordeal in Africa* (New York: Oxford University Press, 1983), 163; Nwaubani, "Eisenhower, Nkrumah, and the Congo Crisis," 611–12, 614, 616.

45. Thomas J. Noer, "The New Frontier and African Neutralism: Kennedy, Nkrumah, and the Volta River Project," *Diplomatic History* 8, no. 1 (1984): 63, 65.

46. Kennedy, Speech of October 12, 1960, in Sorensen, *"Let the World Go Forth,"* 366–68; Noer, "New Frontier," 65.

47. Noer, "New Frontier," 68, Rostow, *Diffusion of Power,* 185, 200.

48. Noer, "New Frontier," 70–76; NSC Meeting Minutes, December 5, 1961, *FRUS 1961–1963,* 21: 369–70.

49. Akwasi P. Osei, *Ghana: Recurrence and Change in a Post-Independence African State* (New York: Peter Lang, 1999), 59–60; Roger S. Gocking, *The History of Ghana* (Westport, CT: Greenwood Press, 2005), 119–20; W. Arthur Lewis, "Economic Development with Unlimited Supplies of Labor," *Manchester School* 22 (May 1954): 139–91; Michael E. Latham, "W. Arthur Lewis," in *The American National Biography,* ed. John A. Garraty and Marc C. Carnes (New York: Oxford University Press, 1999), 13: 609–11.

50. David Rooney, *Kwame Nkrumah: The Political Kingdom in the Third World* (New York: St. Martin's Press, 1988), 183–87; Tony Killick, *Development Economics in Action: A Study of Economic Policies in Ghana* (London: Heinemann, 1978), 37–38.

51. W. Scott Thompson, *Ghana's Foreign Policy, 1957–1966: Diplomacy, Ideology, and the New State* (Princeton, NJ: Princeton University Press, 1969), 300–304, 395; Gocking, *History of Ghana,* 130; Central Intelligence Agency, Memorandum of Conversation, March 11, 1965, *FRUS 1964–1968,* 24: 442–44.

TECHNOCRATIC FAITH

From Birth Control to the Green Revolution

In early 1944, in the normally placid pages of the *American Sociological Review*, the Princeton demographer Dudley Kirk identified a most alarming trend. For centuries, he noted, in backward areas "relatively untouched by Western influences," high fertility and high mortality rates had kept population levels in a merciless equilibrium. Large numbers of children were born, but amid disease and destitution few survived into adulthood, making human life cheap "both in its inception and in its destruction." The spread of modern advances in medicine, sanitation, and public health, however, had now started to produce a sharp decline in the death toll without a corresponding reduction in the birthrate. Already evident in the world's British, Dutch, and U.S. colonies, this common pattern was emerging across Asia, Africa, Latin America, and the Middle East. As a result, Kirk warned, soaring population growth might soon outstrip global food supplies and dramatically alter the world's essential geopolitical structure.

Writing as Allied armies converged on Berlin and U.S. forces fought their way across the Pacific, Kirk feared that the power of human reproduction could trigger an even more devastating struggle. As the hungry, surging masses of the colonized world learned to forge the tools of war, they would no longer tolerate their oppression. "The day is rapidly passing," he declared, "when a handful of Europeans, equipped with superior weapons and a complacent and somehow contagious faith in white supremacy, can expect indefinitely to dominate the half of the world that is occupied by the colored peoples." Unless the Western powers agreed to "meet the emerging peoples halfway, helping them willingly along the road [the West has] traveled to higher standards of living, and the more efficient creation of a better human product," they would soon face "the prospect of an inter-continental conflict that might well dwarf the present war in ferocity and in its threat to the values that are considered the foundation of [Western] society."[1]

In this fearful forecast, modernization was framed as both the cause of the problem and the essence of its solution. U.S. foundation leaders, demographers, agricultural experts, and government officials recognized that it was the diffusion of Western science in the colonized world that had triggered the sudden burst of population growth by reducing disease and improving health and longevity. And it was the promise of rapidly accelerated development, they hoped, that would produce larger harvests, promote smaller families, and alleviate the poverty that threatened to generate cataclysmic political upheaval. Like modernization theorists, the proponents of population control and agricultural development believed that the transformation of entire societies would have to be carefully guided and controlled. Having defined an overarching pattern of historical change, they also prescribed interventions that relied heavily on methods of social engineering, seeking to transform supposedly traditional peasants into modern citizens capable of producing more resources while also wishing to bear fewer children.

Most strikingly, U.S. experts tried to address the twin perils of population growth and global hunger through technological solutions. While they hoped that modernization would ultimately produce social and cultural transformations leading to smaller families, demographers and family planners also tried to accelerate that process by developing and distributing more effective, cheaper, and longer-lasting contraceptives. Worried that population growth would outrun advances in productivity, agricultural researchers turned to genetic engineering and plant breeding to increase crop yields and fend off the danger of scarcity. Reducing human fertility through birth control, and increasing food supplies through genetically modified plants, experts believed, would help ensure modernization's success.

It is important to note that philanthropic foundations and nongovernment organizations often played the most decisive roles in promoting these technological approaches. U.S. government agencies certainly became involved, especially during the late 1960s, but much of the research, planning, and funding went forward outside the boundaries of official authority. Demographers and agricultural scientists in the United States also grafted their concerns about modernization onto much older transnational movements. Neither the campaign for expanded birth control nor the drive to develop high-yielding rice, wheat, and corn were wholly concerns of the United States, suddenly appearing in the years following 1945. Attempts to expand the use of contraceptives among impoverished populations had deep roots in politically diverse eugenics, women's rights, and public health movements on both sides of the Atlantic. In the early twentieth century, the scientific pursuit of improved crop varieties had developed in East Asia as well as North America. In the postwar era, U.S. experts pursued their own particular objectives through a growing global network of philanthropic foundations, universities, nongovernment organizations, United Nations agencies, and foreign governments.

Working in the name of progress, many liberals in the United States envisioned a time in which their technological solutions would bring concrete and immediate benefits to a world afflicted by immense poverty and suffering. By developing and distributing contraceptives, they would empower women to gain control over their own fertility, improving their health and enabling them to take better care of their families. Through high-yielding staple crops they would sharply increase the caloric intake of populations that struggled at the margins of malnutrition and starvation. Their technologies, they also hoped, would promote development. They would allow decolonizing countries to curtail social welfare costs, redirect scarce foreign exchange away from food imports and into industrial growth, reduce the number of people needed for agricultural labor, and create a larger supply of workers for newly built factories.

Those ambitions, however, often produced unintended consequences. While promising to respect the voluntary choices of individuals regarding fertility and childbirth, and constantly stressing their commitment to women's rights in particular, U.S. experts also promoted a contraceptive technology that was used in starkly coercive ways. As crop yields rose across much of Asia and parts of Latin America, genetically engineered seeds and the package of technical inputs associated with them generated unexpected economic, social, and environmental effects. Postcolonial countries produced record amounts of rice and wheat, but in many regions they also harvested greater inequality, deeper poverty, and a severely damaged landscape. In aiming for what Kirk called "the more efficient creation of a better human product," modernizers promoted technological solutions with little regard for the conditions in which they would be deployed. In pursuing a very aggressive form of social engineering, they also unleashed forces that betrayed their own stated principles and goals.

Modernization and Demographic Transition

The end of World War II created an intense demand for knowledge about the past and projected future of the world's population. With much of Europe in rubble, markets and food supplies devastated, and colonized nations demanding independence, population trends became crucial variables in plans for the post-war world. In response to the problems of postwar recovery and development, population experts in the United States produced an overarching model of historical change that fit squarely within the dominant framework of modernization theory. While many scholars accepted its assumptions, work done at Princeton University's Office of Population Research by demographers Frank W. Notestein, Kingsley Davis, Irene Taeuber, and Dudley Kirk proved especially influential. In a landmark article drafted for a 1944 conference marking the creation of the United Nations Food and Agriculture Organization, Notestein described a universal process of "demographic evolution" in which all societies passed through a common series of three historical stages. In traditional societies, high death rates and high birthrates kept overall population levels in check. With the arrival of modern technology, advances in medicine, and the beginnings of industrialization, societies entered a "transitional" phase in which mortality declined but fertility remained high, leading to rapid population expansion. In the final, modern stage, fertility finally decreased to match mortality, restoring the balance and slowing overall population growth.

According to Notestein, the key factor driving the process forward was the impact of modernization on human reproductive behavior. Using the demographic history of Europe and North America as his template, Notestein argued that as industrialization started, and the role of the family in economic and social life was altered by the rise of schools, factories, and commerce, parents decided to have fewer children. Where large numbers of offspring were previously seen as essential providers for security in old age, necessary elements of a family's labor force, or important signs of social status and prestige, they were eventually regarded as expensive liabilities in a forward-thinking society "freed from older taboos and increasingly willing to solve its problems rather than to accept them." In the West, in other words, modernization had created new opportunities and aspirations for social mobility, leading parents to focus their resources on the goal of "promoting the health, education, and material welfare of the individual child." While "transitional" societies would experience a temporary surge in population, as they modernized they would eventually move toward a new point of equilibrium.[2]

Like modernization theory, demographic transition theory reassuringly suggested that the rest of the world would eventually follow the same path as the industrialized West. It cast traditional parents as passive and conservative, and framed modernization as a process of psychological as well as sociological transformation. The problem, however, was that in transitional societies modernization affected death rates far more rapidly than birthrates. In that intermediate stage, the Western imports of antibiotics, vaccines, medical procedures, and improved sanitary practices all enabled more infants to survive into adult-hood, reproduce, and have still more children. They did so, moreover, before modernization could transform social practices and lead parents to want fewer offspring. As Notestein commented, traditional societies, profoundly shaped by ancient "religious doctrines" and "community customs," were "focused toward maintaining high fertility." Their cultural practices, moreover, often proved quite durable. While imported medicine and colonial public health programs might keep more people alive, during the transitional phase birthrates would fall very slowly, and only "in response to the strongest stimulation." The result, therefore, was a crucial "cultural lag" that slowed the transition to modernity and promised sharp population increases in the more backward regions of the world.[3]

Many U.S. demographers found that prospect deeply troubling. In 1945, Notestein's colleague Davis forecast a "tremendous explosion of the Asiatic population." By spreading their "modern mode of life," he argued, Europeans had also "become its victims." As Davis put it, "the possibility that Asia's teem-ing millions will double or even triple within the next few decades, acquiring Western instrumentalities at the same time" appeared to many as an appalling "Frankenstein." Nor did Japan's aggressive imperial drive during World War II "lighten the somber picture." India, Java, and Malaya, Davis suggested, were all now in the "heavy growth phase," while Iran, China, and Borneo were just start-ing it. How would global resources be divided among these new nations, Davis and his colleagues asked? What new political threats might emerge if runaway growth resulted in greater inequalities, despair, and desperation? What could be done to reverse the trend?[4]

At first, leading demographic analysts had little to offer in the way of im-mediate answers. Interestingly enough, they also explicitly rejected proposals for increased family planning and birth control programs. As Notestein explained in 1945, although European populations had used contraceptive practices to lower their birthrates, their methods "were widely known for centuries before they were generally used." Merely improving access to contraception in the decolo-nizing world, therefore, would achieve little without "drastic changes in the social and economic setting that radically altered the motives and aims of the people with respect to family size." Because declines in fertility rates were contingent on slow-moving cultural changes, the only real way to check the forthcoming popu-lation explosion was to promote modernization itself in hopes that economic development, improved communications, urbanization, and industrialization would transform traditional values and preferences. The process of moderniza-tion would be difficult and disruptive but, as Davis observed, the "best that can be done is to use modern knowledge to make the transition as quick and smooth as possible."[5]

By the late 1940s, however, the desire for more immediate, policy-relevant solutions and a greater sense of geopolitical danger led prominent demographers to revise their earlier positions. Where they had previously defined fertility as a *dependent* variable, shaped by the wider process of modernization itself, they now gradually reframed their arguments to suggest that more aggressive, interventionist approaches could transform reproductive behavior. In 1948, following a three-month tour of six Asian countries, Notestein concluded that while modernization's effect on human motivations remained the key factor in explaining the differential fertility rates *between* separate societies, *within* a particular society there were always pioneering dissidents who would eagerly embrace new technologies ahead of the general trend. Providing contraceptives, he suggested, might actually trigger changes in behavior among those who conformed to the dominant cultural practices only because they had no other option. As Notestein argued in a most curious choice of words, cheap and effective contraceptives could help the "small family ideal" become "implanted directly in the rural population." Davis also agreed that reductions in fertility could not wait for industrialization to go forward. An "all-out governmental campaign backed by every economic inducement, educational device, and technical assistance to diffuse contraception," he mused, had never been tried. There were, of course, potential moral objections to such an intrusive approach, but the possible alternatives— "internal revolution" or a "world struggle several times more deadly than the last"—were obviously far less desirable.[6]

The quest for more rapid solutions was also driven forward by a growing fear that postcolonial population growth might ultimately derail modernization itself. In 1954, demographer Ansley J. Coale and economist Edgar M. Hoover began an influential, highly publicized project exploring the relationship between population and economic development. Their conclusions, based on a case study of India and the analysis of data from Mexico, were not optimistic. The fundamental problem, they argued, was that "a *higher rate* of population growth implies a *higher level* of needed investment to achieve a given per capita output, while there is nothing about faster growth that generates a greater *supply* of investible resources." Rapidly expanding populations, they concluded, were more often than not a serious barrier to economic advances. While a highly educated and technically trained adult population might provide essential labor for industrial and commercial progress, in most postcolonial areas high birthrates produced an impoverished, illiterate, juvenile mass that siphoned scarce savings out of investment pools and into social welfare channels. As population growth rates surged past investment rates, the immediate demands for education, housing, medical care, and food made longer-term progress extremely difficult. Falling levels of per capita consumption also destroyed living standards and eliminated incentives for more productive work. Lowering fertility, Coale and

Hoover pointed out, would produce "important economic advantages." Furthermore, "since these advantages are cumulative, the ultimate benefits of fertility reduction are greater, the sooner it occurs."[7]

By the mid-1950s, therefore, U.S. population experts had made the case for an immediate effort to transform human reproductive practices in the decolonizing world. Their warnings also tapped into growing anxieties shared by Western policymakers, foundations, nongovernment organizations, and corporate leaders. If rapid population growth halted development and increased poverty, it could trigger Communist revolutions. Fleeing from destitution and famine, desperate, hungry populations might migrate across borders, creating floods of unwanted, nonwhite arrivals and straining the resources of more affluent, fairer-skinned societies. As observers like Kirk had warned, finally, over the long run, global conflict might also erupt between the world's haves and have-nots, raising the prospect that the Cold War between East and West might in time be eclipsed by a more punishing struggle between North and South.

Those arguments shaped the agenda of a powerful network of institutions. Since the 1920s and 1930s, philanthropic foundations in the United States had promoted development programs in Asia and Latin America, but their leaders now came to believe that population growth would wipe out the tenuous progress they had made in agriculture, medical care, and education. The troubling possibility that their support for public health programs had actually helped create the very conditions for a population explosion also led them toward greater interest in contraceptive research and family planning. Demographic studies at Princeton's Office of Population Research were backed by the Milbank Memorial Fund, the Rockefeller Foundation, the Carnegie Corporation, the World Bank, and the U.S. State Department. Notestein himself became the first director of the United Nations Population Division, a body that published the first official projections of global population growth and warned that the rising human tide might soon require major increases in food production. In 1952, John D. Rockefeller III also founded the Population Council, an especially influential group that brought foundation directors, demographic experts, and UN officials together with pharmaceutical company executives and the leaders of the International Planned Parenthood Foundation. Together, these varied organizations threw their full weight behind a massive campaign to promote birth control and jump-start the process of modernization around the world.[8]

The Birth Control Campaign

The campaign for postcolonial birth control got off to an inauspicious start. In 1952, India announced the decolonizing world's first explicit policy to limit population growth. Encouraged by the government's goal to reduce the birthrate to "a level consistent with the requirements of national economy," U.S. and international organizations viewed India as a crucial testing ground. Most famously, Harvard University's School of Public Health launched one of the earliest and most widely reported population control projects, the "Khanna Study." Based on fieldwork conducted in Punjab between 1953 and 1960, and eventually backed by the Indian government, the Rockefeller Foundation, the Ford Foundation, the Population Council, and several pharmaceutical companies, the study ultimately cost roughly $1 million. Harvard epidemiologist John E. Gordon, the principal investigator, hoped to "test the power of existing contraceptive methods to change birth rates," but his results were profoundly discouraging. Dividing a set of local villages into three groups, Gordon and his colleagues defined a "test population" and two control populations. In the seven villages that made up the "test population," Punjabi workers trained by the project staff made regular visits, discussed family planning, and distributed vaginal foam contraceptive tablets. They also conducted personal and often intrusive interviews to gather information regarding births, deaths, marriages, menstruation, sexual habits, postpartum amenorrhea, abortion, stillbirths, and contraceptive practices. In the control populations, data were gathered through interviews or collected from village officials, but no discussion of family planning or contraceptive distribution took place.[9]

Gordon and his colleagues anticipated high demand for the tablets, but within a few years they discovered that "after active field work stopped, acceptance of all contraceptive methods declined rapidly." Even when villagers accepted contraceptives, they rarely used them, and in the end the birthrates in the test population actually exceeded those in the control groups. The problem, the researchers reluctantly concluded, was one of motivation. The Punjabi villagers, an Indian field director reported, "could see no compelling reasons for achieving a sharp reduction in births." As an insightful critic of the study later argued, economic factors made large families a virtual necessity. Punjabi farmers relied on their offspring to work in their fields, earn income outside the village, and help raise money to purchase additional land. Even landless citizens benefited from the wage income of sons and daughters, and they also considered children essential for security in old age. While villagers might accept contraceptive items in a polite gesture of deference to visiting strangers—an investigator found one creative soul using the tablets to build a sculpture—they wanted large families and had no desire to limit fertility.[10]

In addition to reversals in the field, American birth controllers also faced substantial political opposition at home. In 1958, Dwight David Eisenhower appointed the investment banker and retired general William H. Draper, Jr., to head the President's Committee to Study the United States Military Assistance Program. Charged with evaluating American foreign aid priorities, the group included such Washington heavyweights as John J. McCloy, the former president of the World Bank and then chairman of the boards of the Chase Manhattan Bank and the Ford Foundation; Admiral Arthur Radford, former chair of the Joint Chiefs of Staff; and James E. Webb, former director of the Bureau of the Budget. When Draper's committee dared to raise demographic questions, however, it triggered a storm of protest. Although the final version of the committee report carefully avoided language about the study of human reproduction, it did recommend that foreign aid recipients form "plans designed to deal with the problem of rapid population growth." Draper himself also acknowledged that U.S.-sponsored programs might distribute birth control information, and warned of the dangers posed by surging birthrates abroad.[11]

In the face of a furious Catholic dissent, U.S. government officials quickly disavowed those recommendations. In the fall of 1959, the U.S. Catholic bishops declared that the "promotion of artificial birth control is a morally, humanly, psychologically and politically disastrous approach to the population problem" and warned that Catholics in the United States were resolutely opposed to any government support for "artificial birth prevention, abortion or sterilization, whether through direct aid or by means of international organizations." While denying that the position of his church determined his own views, Senator John F. Kennedy also backed away from the issue while campaigning for the presidency. "I think it would be the greatest psychological mistake," he averred, "for us to appear to advocate limitation of the black or brown or yellow peoples whose population was increasing no faster than in the United States." Eisenhower was even more explicit, declaring that "this government will not, as long as I am here, have a positive political doctrine in its program that has to deal with the problem of birth control." While he privately admitted to the National Security Council that the "real menace here was the one and a half billion hungry people in the world," Eisenhower was clearly unwilling to challenge the country's Catholic leadership.[12]

The most ardent advocates of international birth control programs, however, remained undaunted by either practical or political reversals. They also pinned their hopes on the development of new contraceptive technologies that would be inexpensive, long lasting, and, above all, require minimal motivation on the part of their users. Scientific breakthroughs also appeared to be forthcoming. In 1956, physiologist Gregory Pincus announced the creation of an oral contraceptive based on synthetic steroids. Backed by the philanthropist Katharine Dexter McCormick and the Planned Parenthood Federation of America, Pincus also received support from organizations deeply engaged in the international population control movement. The Population Council and the Rockefeller Foundation, in particular, hoped he might develop a promising contraceptive for use in family planning programs abroad, and Pincus himself was eager to test the birth control pill among women in an "overpopulated area." In collaboration with the Searle pharmaceutical company, the University of Puerto Rico's Medical School, and the Puerto Rican Family Planning Association, researchers implemented two large-scale trials among housing project residents and hospital patients in the suburbs of San Juan in 1956. The initial results were decidedly mixed. Roughly half of the participants dropped out of the studies, complaining of side effects ranging from midcycle bleeding to headaches, nausea, and vomiting, and as reports of the side effects spread, it became more difficult for researchers to find additional experimental subjects. A significant number of pregnancies also plagued both trials.[13]

Confident that the pill would be steadily improved, however, Pincus pressed forward. After the Food and Drug Administration approved the pill for marketing in 1960, it quickly became a commercial success in affluent countries. Advocates declared that the pill would allow parents to space the births of their children, prevent unwanted pregnancies, reduce abortions, and enable women to pursue work and education on their own terms. Dr. John Rock, one of Pincus's colleagues, also claimed that by regulating the body's natural hormones, the pill provided Catholics with a means to promote family planning without violating the church's prohibition against "artificial" methods. Among those seeking to limit birthrates in the postcolonial world, the pill appeared to present a major opportunity. Concerns about its comparatively high cost and the fact that patients had to use it on an unfailing, daily basis limited the pill's use in overseas family planning programs in the early 1960s. By the middle of the decade, however, the U.S. government would press hard for its increased distribution and use abroad.[14]

Other technologies seemed to offer great promise as well. Intrauterine devices (IUDs) made of silk sutures and silver wire appeared in Germany and Japan prior to World War II, but in the late 1950s most physicians believed that the risks of infection or damage to the uterine wall made them too dangerous for general use. Because insertion required the dilation of the uterus under local anesthesia by a physician, IUDs seemed particularly unsuited for rapid, efficient deployment in postcolonial countries. In 1958, however, Dr. Lazar Margulies showed his colleague Alan Guttmacher, a leading obstetrician at New York's Mount Sinai Hospital and a member of the Population Council's advisory board, a new innovation. A coiled plastic spiral, he demonstrated, could be unwound and inserted through a thin rod into an undilated uterus where it would then recover its original shape. The plastic molded IUDs could also be mass-produced very cheaply and put in place without anesthetic.[15]

Although the IUDs presented numerous health risks, many population controllers believed that they had finally found the holy grail. The Population Council held an international conference on the devices in 1962 and poured more than $2.5 million into clinical trials, evaluation, and further IUD development by 1968. Physicians testing IUDs in eighteen different countries reported that the devices were more effective than condoms or diaphragms, but observed that some patients spontaneously expelled them or experienced bleeding and infections. They also advised that IUDs should be inserted only by doctors after a thorough physical exam. The Population Council, however, shrugged off the warnings, arguing that the devices were so simple that technicians, nurses, or midwives should be able to insert them as well. Though they still paid lip service to the goal of promoting voluntary family planning and respecting personal choice, they now celebrated the apparent reduction in the level of patient compliance required for success. "No contraceptive could be cheaper," Guttmacher argued, "and also, once the damn thing is in there the patient cannot change her mind. In fact, we can hope she will forget it's there and perhaps in several months wonder why she has not conceived." As former State Department intelligence officer and Population Council staff member Christopher Tietze recalled, even in the absence of clear demand for the devices, population control advocates believed that "something had to be done." As he explained further, "this was something that you could do to the people rather than something people could do for themselves. So it made it very attractive to the doers." The IUD, a World Bank paper agreed, was "superior to more conventional forms of contraception" because it did not "rely on the user for its success."[16]

The need for urgent, centrally planned action also appeared more compelling than ever. In the years following World War II, Notestein had estimated that the world's population would rise to three billion by 2000. But that mark was surpassed by 1960, and experts now feared that more than twice that number was possible by century's end. Demographers warned that spiraling growth was contributing to dangerous political volatility as well. Davis argued in *Foreign Affairs* that in the "underdeveloped majority of the world" nationalist leaders were trapped between "the squeeze of population growth and adverse economics on the one hand, and rising aspirations and popular discontent on the other." Figures like Nasser, Davis noted, pursued reckless foreign policies in response to these pressures. As Egypt's population leapt from 14.2 million in 1927 to 24 million in 1958, straining food supplies and creating vast city slums, Nasser ramped up his anti-imperialist and anti-Zionist attacks in a desperate bid to preserve his popularity. Unchecked birthrates, demographers argued, were preventing modernization and creating a far more dangerous world. To contain communism and radical nationalism, the United States would also have to contain populations.[17]

As such arguments mounted, U.S. policymakers finally began to throw their weight behind the movement. In the summer of 1963, J. William Fulbright, chair of the Senate Foreign Relations Committee, proposed an amendment to a foreign aid bill providing for "research into the problems of controlling population growth" as well as "technical assistance to cooperating countries in carrying out programs of population control." Opposition in the House led by Democrat Clement Zablocki, a Wisconsin Catholic, eliminated the provision for aid, but the Agency for International Development quietly established a Population Office in 1964. In contrast to Eisenhower and Kennedy, Lyndon Johnson also came out strongly in favor of population control. In his 1965 State of the Union address he declared a commitment to "seek new ways to help deal with the explosion in world population and the growing scarcity in world resources." Persuaded by arguments that high growth rates deepened poverty and fomented revolutions, Johnson was convinced that population control would decrease social welfare burdens, reduce the need for foreign aid, and accelerate modernization. In a 1965 speech, Johnson even went so far as to quantify the social value of each unborn child, arguing that "less than five dollars invested in population control is worth a hundred dollars invested in economic growth."[18]

With firm White House support, the cause made additional headway in Congress. Senator Ernest Gruening, an Alaska Democrat, initiated highly publicized hearings on international birth control that brought forward 120 witnesses from mid-1965 through early 1968. A physician, Gruening had tried to promote contraception while leading the Puerto Rico Reconstruction Administration during the New Deal, and his work now helped shift public discourse in favor of birth control. An agricultural crisis in the mid-1960s, complicated by the failure of the monsoon rains in South Asia in the fall of 1965 and 1966, spotlighted the issue, leading activists to warn of global famine and helping secure a congressional amendment to use funds from the sale of surplus food for family planning programs abroad. Political resistance also began to fade away, and government officials proved more willing to ignore dissenting voices. Although Pope Paul VI rejected the majority opinion of his papal study commission and forbade contraception in the 1968 encyclical *Humanae Vitae*, Gallup polls showed that the majority of American Catholics disagreed with his position and hoped it might change. In March 1967, Senator Fulbright introduced a bill to earmark federal funding for family planning overseas. Approved in November, it reserved $35 million for AID to spend on family planning before the following June. Over the next few years the agency's spending on international family planning and birth control continued to climb, rising to $45.4 million in 1969, $74.5 million in 1970, and $95.9 million in 1971.[19]

By the mid-1960s, researchers, foundations, and government agencies plunged fully into the international campaign to reduce fertility in the "developing world." Some key figures, including AID population program director Reimert Ravenholt, advocated "supply side" approaches. AID, Ravenholt declared, would back only voluntary programs in its attempt to provide all people with the "fundamental freedom of controlling their reproduction, health, and welfare as they desire." Although AID defended its work in population planning by stressing its links to development, figures like Ravenholt paid little attention to the idea of trying to transform social institutions in order to create higher demand for contraceptive use. As modernization went forward, he expected, parents would naturally want fewer children, and in the meantime a flood of cheap, effective, and easily used contraceptives would reduce fertility rates by tapping the "latent demand" for birth control that already existed. With that aim in mind, by 1968 AID funded contraceptive research at several universities in the United States and backed national family planning programs across the postcolonial world, including Pakistan, Turkey, India, Nepal, Afghanistan, Korea, Indonesia, Thailand, and the Philippines.[20]

As the distribution of IUDs and oral contraceptives went forward, however, AID began to support national programs that aggressively tried to *create* demand. Many population controllers also began to edge farther away from their public commitments to respect the wholly voluntary, uncoerced choice of individuals, insisting that the threat of escalating population rates was so severe that birth control technologies had to be coupled with legal and financial policies designed to produce a desire to use them. This tension between an emphasis on the empowerment of particular families and the objective of shaping the future of an entire society was complicated by the forms of measurement used by demographic experts and their sponsors. As they calculated the probable effects of population growth on gross national products, U.S. social scientists and foundation officials constantly focused on aggregates and pursued solutions most appealing to central planners. They also pushed aside critical questions about the fate of individual families, and the effects that specific policies might have on them.[21]

The issue, Davis argued in calling for a more aggressive approach, was one of competing objectives. "By stressing the right of parents to have the number of children they want," he lamented, family planning "evades the basic question of population policy, which is how to give societies the number of children they need. By offering only the means for *couples* to control fertility, it neglects the means for societies to do so." Technologically sophisticated contraception, Davis insisted, had to be complemented by changes in social policy to make citizens more willing to use it. Changes in tax rates to reduce family allowances, incentive payments for contraceptive use or sterilization, reduction of maternity leave, increases in the cost of marriage licenses, and policies designed to require women to work outside the home, Davis thought, could all be effective tools.[22]

Population Council president Bernard Berelson held similar views. Since high fertility prevented development, and there was a clear "time penalty" in failing to reduce it, he urged: "Everything that can be done to lower population growth rates should be done, now." Although it was most politically acceptable, voluntary fertility control was probably insufficient to the task. Besides, Berelson argued, in many impoverished countries the supposedly "free" choices of couples were already compromised by their lack of "information, services, and supplies needed to implement a free wish in this regard." Shifting away from the concept of inviolable, individual rights, Berelson declared that many of the world's poor were "restrained by ignorance, not only of contraceptive practice but of the consequences of high fertility for themselves, their children, and their country." In those conditions, he implied, there really was no meaningful concept of voluntary consent worth protecting. Though not explicitly endorsing any of them, Berelson suggested that tax policies limiting child support, restrictions on marriage, and "marketable licenses to have children" could all be valuable instruments. In a suggestion that might have come from Stanley Kubrick's Dr. Strangelove, Berelson also mused that "a fertility control agent" could be "included in the water supply in urban areas and administered by 'other methods' elsewhere."[23]

Convinced that they possessed the ideal technical methods, and increasingly unconcerned with the rights of the individuals who would be affected by them, U.S. population planners eagerly joined forces with postcolonial elites seeking to limit fertility in the name of development. As examples drawn from Kenya, the Philippines, and India suggest, the results often ranged from ineffective to disastrous. The Kenyan Ministry of Economic Planning and Development instituted sub-Saharan Africa's first official family planning program in 1966. After a three-week visit, advisers from the Population Council promoted the IUD because of its low cost and apparent advantage in requiring only a "single motivation" at the time of insertion. Defined as a public health service, family planning information and contraceptives were dispensed through government hospitals and clinics. While foreigners were delighted with the program, and Kenya's credit rating with international donors increased because of it, substantial domestic opposition quickly emerged. Kenyan religious leaders argued that contraception would increase promiscuity and erode morality, and those wary of neocolonial intervention condemned what they viewed as racist schemes to prevent the birth of black Africans. Advisers from the Population Council also noted that the Kenyan "value systems" generally favored high fertility and that collaborative child care among large extended families reduced the burdens of parenthood and the motivation for family planning. The results, unsurprisingly, were disappointing. While many women used the government clinics for pre-natal and postpartum care, few were interested in family planning. Even when Kenyan health workers avoided mentioning the potential side effects of pills and IUDs, fearing that they would lose their patients, contraceptive acceptance and use rates remained low.[24]

In the Philippines, after President Ferdinand Marcos declared martial law in 1972, the government took a more aggressive approach, promoting birth con-trol pills and IUDs in addition to sterilization. Instructed to fill assigned quotas of "acceptors," Filipino field staff often concealed evidence of side effects and disregarded questions about the informed consent of clients they considered ig-norant, uninformed, and irresponsible. One program administrator argued: "If you are really serious about the costs of population, you should not promote the less effective methods.... There are times when somebody has to decide for the people." The Philippine government and foreign donors also emphasized birth control so strongly that they often neglected other public concerns, leading rural health workers to complain that while they had more contraceptives than they could possibly dispense, they lacked the medication to treat common respiratory and gastrointestinal infections.[25]

The most troubling evidence of abuse and coercion, however, was found in India. In the late 1950s, the Indian government had integrated population con-trol into its overall development planning and started to distribute contraceptive foam tablets through a network of primary health centers. According to an In-dian health ministry report, the voluntary program's goal was to "raise the stan-dard of living of the people" and "ensure the health and happiness of the family." Although the emphasis on family welfare continued, in the early 1960s Indian officials also began to worry about creating sufficient demand for birth control in order to lower population rates and hit economic development targets. Orga-nizations like the Family Planning Association of India, the All-India Women's Conference, and the Indian Red Cross mounted educational campaigns, while the Population Council shipped the first installment of a total of more than one million IUDs. Most of them arrived unsterilized, and often only one inserter was provided for every twenty devices, requiring Indian technicians to resteril-ize them after each use. By the late 1960s, an Indian IUD factory designed by the Population Council and funded by the Ford Foundation was producing up to twenty thousand of the devices each day. As reports mounted of widespread pain, bleeding, uterus perforation, and ectopic pregnancy, the government con-tinued to promote IUD use, instructing village leaders in some Indian states to tell women that the devices were entirely safe. Patients also received little in the way of follow-up care.[26]

Determined to lower the birthrate, the U.S. government, philanthropic foundations, and international organizations helped push the Indian government toward more aggressive measures. Indian prime minister Indira Gandhi was personally committed to population control, and with funding from the World Bank, UN agencies, and the International Planned Parenthood Federation, her government began to offer patients incentive payments for sterilization or IUD insertion. The Johnson administration applauded and promoted that move. As national security staff member Robert Komer explained to Lyndon Johnson, if India and Pakistan pushed family planning, "the process of getting these countries to the stage of self-sustaining growth, *and thus reducing the longer term foreign aid burden on us*—could be greatly foreshortened." Johnson agreed wholeheartedly, declaring: "I'm not going to piss away foreign aid in nations where they refuse to deal with their population problems." By refusing to grant additional food aid and famine relief to India unless population control went forward, Johnson encouraged the process whereby voluntary family planning became steadily reformulated as a more compulsory project. In June 1966, Indira Gandhi announced that year's target of 6 million IUD insertions and 1.23 million sterilizations. After three years of drought and facing the prospect of famine, many Indians also came to believe that they had little choice but to accept the cash payments offered in exchange for surrendering their ability to bear children. Indian government doctors, working in mobile camps, were expected to meet performance standards based on the number of vasectomies and IUD insertions per month, and little provision was made for follow-up care in the event of side effects or infection. In the fall of 1967, Indira Gandhi declared that the country's failure to become more "prosperous and self-sufficient" since independence was primarily due to the fact that [India's] "population [had] gone up by 160 million." Population control, therefore, was a national imperative. By October of that year, India's Central Family Planning Council, the highest official body in the field, recommended mandatory sterilization for couples with two or more children. Although that measure was not put in place, several Indian states introduced penalties for those with large families, including increases in rents for public housing, the withdrawal of government scholarships, and the elimination of maternity leave.[27]

After Indira Gandhi declared a state of national emergency in June 1975, family planning became fully institutionalized, and, as one Indian analyst put it, "even the façade of voluntarism was ripped off." Impatient with the IUD, and even less concerned with respecting the will of individuals, the government moved strongly toward sterilization. In April 1976 the cabinet approved a national policy making the amount of central government aid available to states contingent on family planning performance, established penalties for central government employees with large families, and raised incentive payments for sterilization. In turn, Indian states pursued a range of coercive practices, including the denial of public food rations to families with more than three children, the delivery of irrigation water at subsidized rates only to villages that met sterilization quotas, and legislation requiring that teachers be sterilized or forfeit a month's pay. States warned program workers that their salaries were dependent on meeting sterilization targets, and the entire range of government employees was enlisted in the campaign. Train conductors allowed unticketed passengers to avoid fines if they submitted to sterilization, teachers warned parents that additional children would not be admitted to schools, labor contractors made employment contingent on the possession of sterilization certificates, and police pressed criminals into vasectomies. When the Muslim village of Uttawar resisted the campaign, police in the state of Haryana rounded up all men over fifteen and forcibly sent four hundred of them to be sterilized. As repression grew, Indians began to sleep overnight in fields and avoided government buses in fear of being detained and sent off to clinics. More than eight million Indians were ultimately sterilized in the campaign, and public resentment of the program contributed strongly to the Congress Party's stunning defeat in the elections of March 1977.[28]

By the 1980s, it became clear to demographers that fertility rates across much of the postcolonial world were starting to fall. There was little evidence, however, that population control campaigns had strongly influenced that development. Many critics argued that declines in fertility rates had often *preceded* the widespread use of contraception, a fact suggesting that it was the choices of individual families in particular social environments that made the greatest difference. Increased access to contraception undoubtedly benefited many women, allowing them greater control over their own bodies and lives, a point that should not be forgotten. But the belief that population growth was a fundamental obstacle to modernization and the expectation that technology would allow planners to override the frustrating "cultural lag" of supposedly traditional peoples also led to crash programs in which concerns about the rights and welfare of individuals fell by the wayside. The vision of technology as a key catalyst for modernization, and the unintended consequences it produced, were equally clear in the history of the Green Revolution.[29]

Miracle Seeds and the Green Revolution

In 1970, the American agronomist Norman Borlaug received the Nobel Peace Prize. Credited with important breakthroughs in developing new varieties of food crops and promoting their adoption across Asia, Latin America, and parts of Africa, Borlaug described the Green Revolution as a stunning accomplishment, observing in his Nobel Prize address: "Never before in the history of agriculture has a transplantation of high-yielding varieties coupled with an entirely new technology and strategy been achieved on such a massive scale, in so short a period of time, and with such great success." For the 50 percent of the world's population that lived in hunger, larger harvests of crops like wheat, rice, and maize represented new opportunities and new hopes. Famine would be averted, incomes would grow, and the technologies of genetically improved seeds, fertilizer, pesticides, and machinery would help peasants gain electricity, consumer goods, schools, transportation, and communications. If "the frightening power of human reproduction" and the consequent "population monster" were contained, the Green Revolution would transform the world.[30]

The promise of agricultural technology had great appeal for U.S. modernizers. Until populations could be brought under control, scientists and policymakers believed, it would be essential to find more effective ways to feed them. Genetically engineered, high-yielding crops, altruistic liberals expected, would reduce poverty and raise standards of living. Such crops would facilitate modernization by lightening food import burdens, increasing revenue for investment, and allowing greater numbers of people to move into urban settings and industrial work. As larger harvests raised farmers' incomes, rural areas would provide larger markets for newly produced industrial goods, allowing overall national development to go forward more rapidly. In the long run, increased prosperity would also trigger changes in local culture and individual psychology, satisfying rising expectations and ensuring that "green" revolutions would prevent red ones.

The Green Revolution's central focus on raising productivity allowed modernizers to recast complex social problems in an appealingly simple way. Setting aside questions about the structure of the global agricultural economy, the distribution of food within countries and regions, and the dilemmas caused by inequalities in wealth and consumption, U.S. experts focused instead on the discrete technical problem of increasing the yield of a given crop per unit of area planted. If that problem could be solved, advocates of the Green Revolution believed, rapid, comprehensive transformations would naturally follow. Thus plant breeding and the pursuit of "miracle seeds" were envisioned as especially potent social levers. The cultural and political environment in which the new technology was to be deployed, moreover, was deemed malleable and transitory, and was rarely considered closely.[31]

The idea of using scientific and technical advances to transform foreign agriculture and foreign societies, of course, was not new in the Cold War era. According to historian Nick Cullather, the concept of the calorie and the rise of standardized measurement conventions in the early twentieth century "allowed

Americans to see food as an instrument of power, and to envisage a 'world food problem' amenable to political and scientific intervention." As director of the American Relief Administration in the aftermath of World War I, Herbert Hoover distributed food to prevent the spread of bolshevism and warned that "famine breeds anarchy." During the interwar period, U.S. experts also hoped that improving agriculture would ensure social stability in Asia. Until its work was interrupted by the Japanese invasion, the Rockefeller Foundation tried to raise rural productivity in China, funding the use of improved seeds and mechanization in hopes of promoting a new republican government.[32]

During World War II, questions of international food production received much greater attention. Under the direction of British physiologist John Boyd Orr, the UN Food and Agriculture Organization (FAO) proposed a comprehensive effort to raise agricultural production in the decolonizing world. Although the U.S. and British governments rejected FAO proposals for a World Food Board that would prevent famine and stabilize prices by distributing reserve stocks, the idea of using technical assistance, fertilizers, and new hybrid seeds to increase crop yields gained broad approval. While defining their goals in terms of improving nutrition for the poor, experts also believed that spreading market-driven, capitalist agriculture would dramatically accelerate postwar development. As agronomist Richard Bradfield observed on returning from a survey trip to Mexico, "the leaders of some of our large philanthropic foundations have become convinced that the best way to improve the health and well-being of people is first to improve their agriculture."[33]

As the Cold War began, therefore, U.S. agricultural experts and foundation officials were quick to draw clear connections between hunger and political danger. Food scarcity, a major Rockefeller Foundation report claimed in 1951, was "the cause of much of the world's present tension and unrest." "Agitators from Communist countries," moreover, were "making the most of the situation." "The time is now ripe, in places possibly over-ripe," the report insisted, "for sharing some of our technical knowledge with these people. Appropriate action now may help them to attain by evolution the improvements, including those in agriculture, which otherwise may have to come by revolution." University of Chicago economist Theodore Shultz agreed: "Once there are investment opportunities and efficient incentives, farmers will turn sand into gold."[34]

Those convictions about agriculture, hunger, and security resulted in a massive project promoted across several continents from the 1960s through the 1980s. The modernizing assumptions and objectives of the Green Revolution are especially clear in the history of two specialized research facilities, the International Rice Research Institute (IRRI), established near Manila, and the International Center for Wheat and Maize Improvement (CIMMYT), based in the outskirts

of Mexico City. At both locations, U.S. foundations and scientists joined foreign governments and experts to produce new crop varieties that would respond
vigorously to a technological package involving chemical fertilizers, pesticides,
mechanization, and irrigation. By the early 1960s, both institutes exported their
products throughout the decolonizing world, reshaping agricultural systems in
ways that were expected to increase production, transform traditional cultures,
and ensure social stability. The work of the two institutes also produced important unintended consequences that undercut many of their original goals. While
crop yields and overall productivity rose dramatically, the Green Revolution contributed to greater socioeconomic inequalities, damaged the environment, and
generated conflict in unforeseen ways.

During the 1950s, U.S. analysts agreed that the combination of population increases and strategic dangers demanded advances in Asian agriculture. Worried
by the Chinese Revolution, a rebellion in the Philippines, and the French collapse in Indochina, officials at the Rockefeller and Ford foundations concluded
that local community development programs were helpful but insufficient. The
best solutions, they thought, would be found in new, universally applicable technologies that could raise crop yields and stimulate much broader social transformations wherever they were deployed. As one Rockefeller Foundation advisory
committee member noted in 1951, "agriculture is nothing more than the application of the principles of biology and other natural sciences to the art of growing food." If better solutions to that specific technical problem could be achieved,
then it would be possible to direct social change in liberal directions instead of
revolutionary ones.

In late 1953, the Rockefeller Foundation decided to begin a research program in the Philippines and soon allocated an expenditure of $5 million per
year for the period 1955 to 1960. A single regional research center, staffed by
a team of outstanding international experts backed by first-rate equipment,
foundation planners hoped, would also provide for greater financial savings
and efficiency. Rockefeller officials J. George Harrar and Warren Weaver argued that since the "fundamental physiological, biochemical, and genetic
problems" were "essentially independent of geography and are certainly independent of political boundaries," research done at one key site could be
applied universally. In the fall of 1958, the Ford Foundation agreed to join
the effort. Ford Foundation administrators Forrest Hill and George Gant told
their board of trustees that supporting the International Rice Research Institute was an absolute imperative. The global problems of population and
food supply, they contended, ranked second only to the "possibility of all-out
nuclear war." "At best," they lamented, "the world food outlook for the decades
ahead is grave; at worst it is frightening." Finally, with the endorsement of the

Philippine government, a facility was planned at the University of the Philippines campus near Manila.[35]

Officially dedicated in 1962, the IRRI focused heavily on one key task, the creation and promotion of high-yielding rice strains suited to tropical Asian climates. The problem, in some ways, was easy to understand. Common varieties of tropical rice responded well to fertilizer and irrigation. But as the heads of the plants grew thick and heavy with grain, their long, weak stems collapsed, and they fell or "lodged" into wet paddy fields, producing poor harvests. As early as 1910, Japanese rice breeders had started a program to develop short, stiff-stalked "dwarf" varieties that flourished in cooler climates without lodging. During the 1930s and 1940s, working in occupied Taiwan, they had also raised wartime exports to the home islands by developing plants suited to shorter day lengths and warmer temperatures. Following World War II, Taiwanese researchers had continued that work, producing an improved dwarf strain that grew well there. Building on that progress, the IRRI's plant geneticists set out to create a tropical rice seed of greater versatility, a variety that would respond to fertilizer and irrigation to produce a high yield "almost any time and anywhere in the torrid zone."[36]

Under pressure from their sponsors to deliver quick results, IRRI scientists crossed short Taiwanese plants with tall tropical varieties to produce a high-performing seed they labeled IR-8 in 1965. According to Robert Chandler, the IRRI's first director, IR-8 possessed great advantages. Under optimum conditions of irrigation and with the liberal application of nitrogen fertilizers it produced very high yields. Its short, sturdy stems prevented lodging, it possessed at least moderate disease resistance, and the fact that it was insensitive to photoperiod and matured quickly meant that it could potentially grow well at different latitudes and in different seasons, allowing farmers to grow multiple crops in a single year. When initial test results proved favorable, in 1966 the IRRI multiplied the seeds and sent them to Asian governments and Western development organizations for the widest distribution possible. As Chandler recalled, IR-8 "opened new vistas for rice yields in the tropic and subtropics and stimulated rice breeding programs in many countries where yields had stagnated at pitifully low levels."[37]

IRRI scientists, promoters, and sponsors also expected that the new seed would trigger changes in the psychology and worldviews of the farmers that adopted it. Rapidly planted throughout Asia in 1966 and 1967, IR-8 did indeed produce shocking results, sometimes yielding two to three times as much grain per hectare than common varieties. Comparing their fields to those planted with IR-8, Asian farmers were expected to recognize the obvious and immediate advantages of the new technology, and as they embraced the new "miracle seeds," proponents hoped that they would embrace new, progressive values as well. Eager to promote changes in rice paddies as well as people's minds, in 1967 AID replaced the Rockefeller and Ford foundations as the primary funding source for the IRRI. Distributing IR-8 in packages, along with farm chemicals produced by the Atlas and Esso companies, AID brought U.S. corporations into the picture, too. But AID's greatest hope was that the new rice seed would help ensure greater political security. In the Philippines, President Marcos took full credit for the advances in productivity, claiming national self-sufficiency even as his government secretly imported large amounts of rice through Hong Kong. In Vietnam, U.S. planners also hoped that the rice would provide peasants with a graphic illustration of the greater advantages to be enjoyed under the Saigon regime. IR-8, they believed, would enable South Vietnamese farmers to produce surpluses for sale on the market, allowing them to buy consumer goods, raising their living standards, and making them far less interested in a revolution that promised to redistribute wealth and power. In 1969, leaflets dropped over North Vietnam also proclaimed: "South Vietnam is Experiencing a Rice Revolution." "IR-8," they declared, was "South Vietnam's miracle rice: All Vietnamese can enjoy this rice when peace comes."[38]

The IRRI worked hard to preach the gospel of technological revolution. Trips into the IRRI's rice fields by U.S. President Johnson, Philippine President Marcos, and UN Secretary-General U Thant, along with other heads of state, leaders of international agencies, research institutions, and hundreds of tour groups bolstered the institute's prestige. As reports of its accomplishments spread, the IRRI's budget climbed from $2.46 million in 1965, largely provided by the Ford and Rockefeller foundations, to $13.8 million in 1978, covered primarily by AID. From a staff of 18 senior scientists in 1962, the IRRI grew into an international team of 58 scientists by 1980, backed by over 1,500 support staff on an 835-acre experimental site. Throughout the period, the IRRI continued to focus on a "technology first" response to the question of agricultural change, developing new plants under ideal conditions and releasing fifteen more high-yield varieties in the decade after producing IR-8. Determined to spread its knowledge, the IRRI trained hundreds of production specialists from more than forty different countries and placed its own "liaison scientists" at research sites in Pakistan, India, and Sri Lanka. By 1969, the institute also assembled thousands of "minikits," cardboard boxes containing enough seed, fertilizer, herbicide, and pesticide to plant fifty square meters with a new rice variety. Sent to foreign extension officers for immediate distribution to farmers, the kits were designed to sidestep the cumbersome approval process by foreign agencies. Conveniently sent out from the production site, the IRRI's technology promised to work its magic in any field, anywhere.[39]

Work at the International Center for Wheat and Maize Improvement (CIMMYT), near Mexico City, proceeded in a similar fashion. In 1943, following a request from Vice President and former Secretary of Agriculture Henry Wallace, the Rockefeller Foundation created the forerunner of the CIMMYT—the Mexican Agricultural Program (MAP), an effort to develop disease-resistant wheat and higher-yielding corn varieties. A more productive agricultural sector, Mexican officials and Rockefeller Foundation planners believed, would lower food prices, limit the need for food imports, and help generate funds necessary to purchase capital equipment for industrialization. As with the IRRI, broader issues regarding the socioeconomic and cultural context in which new technologies might be deployed were given minimal attention. Hired by the Rockefeller Foundation and sent to work at the MAP in 1945, Norman Borlaug proudly recalled: "Research from the start was production-oriented and restricted to that which was relevant to increasing wheat production. Researches in the pursuit of irrelevant academic butterflies were discouraged, both because of the acute shortage of manpower and because of the need to have data and materials available as soon as possible for use in the production program."[40]

The technical task for the MAP's work with wheat was similar to that faced by the IRRI's experiments in rice. Once more, Japan also proved a crucial source of genetic materials. Working there during the postwar occupation, U.S. Department of Agriculture (USDA) scientist Samuel Cecil Salmon sent hardy, high-yielding dwarf wheat samples back to the United States, where they were crossed with American varieties in a project run by the USDA and Washington State University. Borlaug then used seeds from the Washington State project to introduce dwarfing genes into indigenous Mexican varieties, hoping to create plants that would respond well to fertilizer and irrigation without lodging. The plants that Borlaug produced were spectacularly successful in the Mexican environment. By the late 1950s, their introduction sharply reduced the country's need for wheat imports by roughly 90 percent over World War II levels. By 1962, Mexico's wheat production had climbed so rapidly that it was possible to begin exporting the crop, allowing the country to start earning the foreign exchange needed to finance industrial ventures. By 1966, the project was so successful that the Rockefeller Foundation closed its original office and then, with funding from the Ford Foundation and the Mexican government, reconstituted the venture as an international research center along the same lines as the IRRI, creating the CIMMYT.[41]

The CIMMYT's wheat also produced impressive results in Asia, and particularly in India. After a visit there in the spring of 1963, Borlaug sent samples of the Mexican wheat for sowing in the fall season. When they proved up to three times as productive as local varieties, and serious droughts forced India to import large amounts of U.S. grain, Indian officials began a national campaign to distribute the new seeds. Announcements in the press, radio, and cinemas increased demand, and eighteen thousand metric tons were imported and sold at subsidized rates in the 1965–66 season. As the new varieties produced much larger yields, India's reliance on imported food also decreased sharply, falling from 4.7 percent of total imports in 1960–61 to only 0.8 percent in 1972–73 and making self-sufficiency a reasonable goal.[42]

By 1968, collaboration among institutes like the IRRI, the CIMMYT, and national research programs raised hopes for major long-term gains. Praising "harvests of unprecedented size" in India, Pakistan, Turkey, and the Philippines, AID administrator William Gaud coined the term "Green Revolution." The transformation of agriculture, he claimed, could become "as significant and as beneficial to mankind as the industrial revolution of a century and a half ago." USDA official Lester Brown was equally rhapsodic, declaring that the "exciting new cereal varieties are so superior to the traditional varieties and so dramatic in their impact that they are becoming 'engines of change' wherever used." Even "rural Asians," he observed, would "change and innovate—when it is in their advantage to do so." Linking the Green Revolution to the campaign for population control, Brown also suggested that "family planners should take heart." Once farmers learn that they "can indeed influence their destiny," he noted, "they may become much more susceptible to family planning and other 'radical' departures."[43]

Over the next three decades, the Green Revolution continued to advance. In 1971, a new Consultative Group on International Agricultural Research (CGIAR) was created to coordinate financial support for a growing network of international centers patterned on the IRRI and CIMMYT. By 1981, thirteen different international agricultural institutes were at work, with a combined budget of $145 million. The adoption of high-yielding varieties also accelerated. In 1970, roughly 10 to 15 percent of the wheat and rice crops in the postcolonial world were planted in the new varieties. By 1991, more than three-fourths were. Between 1961 and 1992, across ninety-three different countries, wheat yields rose by a factor of 2.7, while rice yields rose by a factor of 1.9. The Green Revolution certainly did enable the postcolonial world to produce much more food.[44]

The Green Revolution did not, however, produce the thoroughgoing, modernizing revolution that its proponents envisioned. Because so much agricultural research was focused on production and the problem of increasing yields per unit of area under ideal conditions, experts paid far less attention to the potential impact of the new technology on the lives of those adopting it. Dismissing the "traditional" agricultural sector as a way of life that would soon be swept away, they imagined a liberating process in which the transition to market-based agriculture would benefit all concerned, uplifting local farmers, promoting industrialization, and preventing radical upheavals. By ignoring questions regarding the likely impact of the technology on conditions of social and economic inequality, both within nations and between them, they also failed to recognize that in many cases the Green Revolution would generate increased poverty and social conflict.

These issues are the subject of a vast, complex, and contentious literature, but examples drawn from South Asia, a region in which the Green Revolution had an enormous impact, illustrate the unintended consequences produced. In Pakistan, the Green Revolution served both political and developmental ends. The country's founding party, the Muslim League, sought to preserve its power by promising land to poorer peasants and, at the same time, inviting elite landowners into the governing coalition. The need to appeal to both of those diverse constituencies and their competing interests made land reform politically unattractive if not impossible, since it would have required expropriating the property of the influential class that dominated the country's legislature. Promising rapid agricultural growth, however, was a more acceptable solution, and President Ayub Khan's decision to introduce high-yielding Mexican wheat and modified rice seeds into Pakistan took place in that context. The overall historical results, at the aggregate level, were impressive. Between the 1959–60 and 1996–97 harvests, Pakistani wheat yields climbed dramatically from 801 kilograms per hectare to 2,026 kilograms per hectare, and per hectare rice yields rose from 826 kilograms to 1,912 kilograms. Over the same period, farmers also increased the area under wheat cultivation from 4.9 million to 8 million hectares, and that under rice cultivation from 1.2 million to 2.25 million hectares. As a result of higher yields and increased farmland, Pakistan's annual rice and wheat harvests quadrupled in size. The Green Revolution also allowed that country's food production to increase faster than its population did.[45]

Those increases, however, did not alleviate poverty or promote political stability. In fact, the reverse was often the case. In Pakistan, as in other regions, the expensive technological package required to grow the high-yielding varieties, including fertilizer, pesticides, and herbicides, raised the costs of farm production, often making it difficult for smaller, less affluent landholders to compete with wealthier ones owning larger fields. The increased energy costs required for those inputs, and for irrigation and agricultural machinery, also hit poorer farmers hard, especially as oil prices jumped in the 1970s. As poorer, peasant farmers were priced out of the market, the concentration of landholding increased. Large landholders also discovered that even though high-yielding varieties required more expensive inputs, their higher profit margins enabled them to invest in labor-saving machinery and chemicals that made it less necessary to rely on tenants for the tasks of ploughing, sowing, weeding, and harvesting. As yields rose, land increased in value, and since government banks used land as collateral in advancing the credit needed to pay for the expensive capital inputs, the Green Revolution compounded the socioeconomic inequalities. As a result, large numbers of poor peasants and agricultural workers were displaced, losing their land, work, or both. Rural poverty increased, and token gestures toward land reform did little to ensure the security of the country's military regimes.[46]

In India, the results of the Green Revolution were similar, with increases in aggregate production often accompanied by rising inequality. After high-yielding varieties were introduced there in the mid-1960s, they were widely planted and achieved striking results. By the late 1970s, India became the single largest area of high-yield crop adoption in the world, with more than half of the total world area planted in improved varieties of wheat and rice. In the first five years after high-yielding crops were planted, Indian wheat harvests rose by 150 percent, and rice harvests by nearly 32 percent. Some local studies also reported widespread benefits. Anthropologist Murray Leaf, working in a Punjabi village in the mid-1960s and late 1970s, described substantial increases in the use of hybrid varieties of wheat seed received from the local university extension service. A government-supported village cooperative system, he noted, also obtained fertilizer and irrigation pumps at affordable prices and bought much of the food grains that farmers produced, making it "far more reasonable for small farmers to adopt new crops and methods at the same time larger farmers do." Other studies claimed that even among the poor and landless the increases in general rural prosperity allowed displaced peasants and tenants to find profitable nonfarm work.[47]

Such broadly favorable responses, however, were exceptional. The new varieties flourished most successfully in areas where irrigation was already established, and their introduction benefited those that had the resources to adopt them first. In those cases, farmers experienced rich returns, as they were able to raise yields before market prices fell. As adoption spread, however, and prices declined, less affluent producers entering the market later achieved thinner returns. Even in comparatively wealthy parts of the country, moreover, the Green Revolution often triggered negative results. As socioeconomic inequality grew in Punjab, for example, ethnic tensions hardened, leading not to political stability but instead increased conflict along the lines of race, religion, and culture. During the late 1970s and early 1980s, technological input costs climbed, and returns on investment in high-yielding wheat declined, causing many farmers to fall into debt and lose their land. When Sikh farmers began protests, boycotted grain markets, and tried to prevent the delivery of their harvests to the government-run food corporation, Indian prime minister Indira Gandhi sent in the army, contributing to a violent conflict in which more than 15,000 people died by 1991.[48]

The technology of the Green Revolution, finally, produced many unanticipated environmental problems. The mass distribution of high-yielding seeds and the replacement of many indigenous varieties contributed to a reduction of genetic diversity, making harvests far more vulnerable to attacks by disease and insects. Higher demands for irrigation raised water tables, increased salinization, and reduced soil fertility. High-yield varieties exhausted soil nutrients, and rising global demands for fertilizer raised energy consumption and oil prices. As farmers tried to protect their investments from insects, bacteria, fungi, and viruses, they also used increasing amounts of pesticide and herbicide, exposing themselves to dangerous toxins, inadvertently contributing to the rise of drug-resistant pests, and polluting rivers, streams, and lakes.[49]

Unintended Consequences

U.S. experts perceived the promotion of birth control and the spread of the Green Revolution as twin responses to the overriding problem of postcolonial population growth. Limiting birthrates and raising food production, they believed, would help reduce the length of the critical "transitional" phase, allowing modernization to proceed before it could be derailed by escalating social welfare costs or political upheavals. They also imagined that technological solutions, in the form of improved contraception or genetically engineered seeds, would be crucial instruments in that process, making economic development easier to accomplish and producing changes of psychology and values as well. While these technologies were presented as means to reduce poverty, improve health, and give "traditional" peoples greater control over their own lives, their actual use often produced strikingly different results. Strategies to limit fertility, focused on aggregate change and unmoored from a concern with individual families, frequently took highly coercive forms. Green Revolution technology, designed to produce more food, also contributed to growing socioeconomic inequalities.

In the end, birthrates did fall, and agricultural productivity did increase. Yet here too the picture was more complex than modernizers assumed. Demographers have argued that declines in fertility in the postcolonial world have been much more closely correlated to increases in women's education and work opportunities than the mere availability of contraception. Indeed, women's individual desires regarding the number of children they wanted proved to be the most crucial variable. U.S. agricultural experts also tended to view improved seeds, fertilizer, and related inputs as a single, exogenous package, and they impatiently described failures to accept all of its components as evidence of ignorance or traditional intransigence, setting aside the specific socioeconomic factors at work. A careful analysis reveals, however, that even at the aggregate level the Green Revolution did not close the broader, global gap. While agricultural productivity rose in many parts of Asia and Latin America, it still lagged behind the more rapid increases in Europe, North America, and Japan. Net exporters of food until 1981, postcolonial countries became net importers after that date.[50]

As they envisioned a pattern of direct technology transfer, modernizers misread or ignored the social, cultural, and economic environments in which the technology would be deployed. Assuming the existence of "latent demand," they promoted contraception in ways that failed to recognize the motivations of parents for having larger families. Sending "minikits" of seed and fertilizer off for planting in South Asia, they paid little attention to the wider questions of who would benefit from the technology at whose expense, and how it might even create the kind of political turmoil they sought to avoid. The vision of development as a process that could be catalyzed from outside, often without any real understanding of the cultural and political dynamics at work on the ground, was also clear in the U.S. attempt to direct the course of change in Guatemala, Vietnam, and Iran. In those cases, however, the results were not mixed, and the failure was both unmitigated and unmistakable.

NOTES

1. Dudley Kirk, "Population Changes and the Postwar World," *American Sociological Review* 9, no. 1 (1944): 29–30, 33, 35.

2. Susan Greenhalgh, "The Social Construction of Population Science: An Intellectual, Institutional, and Political History of Twentieth-Century Demography," *Comparative Studies in Society and History* 38, no. 1 (1996): 31, 33–34; Dennis Hodgson, "Demography as Social Science and Policy Science," *Population and Development Review* 9, no. 1 (1983): 1–2; Frank W. Notestein, "Population— The Long View," in *Food for the World,* ed. Theodore W. Schultz (Chicago: University of Chicago Press, 1945), 40–57.

3. Notestein, "Population," 39–40.

4. Kingsley Davis, "The World Demographic Transition," *Annals of the American Academy of Political Science* 237 (January 1945): 1, 7.

5. Notestein, "Population," 40; Davis, "World Demographic Transition," 11.

6. Simon Szreter, "The Idea of Demographic Transition and the Study of Fertility Change: A Critical Intellectual History," *Population and Development Review* 19, no. 4 (1993): 673–74; Frank W. Notestein, "The Reduction of Human Fertility as a Aid to Programs of Economic Development in Densely Settled Agrarian Regions," in *Modernization Programs in Relation to Human Resources and Population Problems,* ed. Milbank Memorial Fund, (New York: Milbank Memorial Fund, 1950), 96–97, 99; Kingsley Davis, "Population and the Further Spread of Industrial Society," *Proceedings of the American Philosophical Society* 95, no. 1 (1951): 17–18.

7. Ansley J. Coale and Edgar M. Hoover, *Population Growth and Economic Development in Low-Income Countries: A Case Study of India's Prospects* (Princeton, NJ: Princeton University Press, 1958), 19, 335, emphasis in original.

8. Matthew Connelly, *Fatal Misconception: The Struggle to Control World Population* (Cambridge, MA: Harvard University Press, 2008), 123–26, 154, 158–60; John Sharpless, "Population Science, Private Foundations, and Development Aid: The Transformation of Demographic Knowledge in the United States, 1945–1965," in *International Development and the Social Sciences,* ed. Frederick Cooper and Randall Packard (Berkeley: University of California Press, 1997), 182–83.

9. Connelly, *Fatal Misconception,* 168–69; John B. Wyon and John E. Gordon, *The Khanna Study: Population Problems in the Rural Punjab* (Cambridge, MA: Harvard University Press, 1971), 13–14, 18; Mamood Mamdani, *The Myth of Population Control: Family, Caste, and Class in an Indian Village* (New York: Monthly Review Press, 1972), 15–17, 24.

10. Wyon and Gordon, *Khanna Study,* 44, 47, 314; Mamdani, *Myth of Population Control,* 33, 43–44, 77–78, 94, 111.

11. Phyllis Tilson Piotrow, *World Population Crisis: The United States Response* (New York: Praeger, 1973), 37–41.

12. Ibid., 43–46; Connelly, *Fatal Misconception,* 187.

13. Connelly, *Fatal Misconception,* 61, 96; James Reed, *From Private Vice to Public Virtue: The Birth Control Movement and American Society since 1830* (New York: Basic Books, 1978), 302–3, 359–60; Laura Briggs, *Reproducing Empire: Race, Sex, Science, and U.S. Imperialism in Puerto Rico* (Berkeley: University of California Press, 2002), 124–25, 137.

14. Reed, *Private Vice to Public Virtue,* 351–52, 364–65; Connelly, *Fatal Misconception,* 201.

15. Oscar Harkavy, *Curbing Population Growth: An Insider's Perspective on the Population Movement* (New York: Plenum Press, 1995), 94; Reed, *Private Vice to Public Virtue,* 305–6; Connelly, *Fatal Misconception,* 201–3.

16. Connelly, *Fatal Misconception,* 201–5; Reed, *Private Vice to Public Virtue,* 307; World Bank, *Population Planning Sector Working Paper* (New York: World Bank, 1972), 57.

17. Paul Demeny, "Social Science and Population Policy," *Population and Development Review* 14, no. 3 (1988): 456; Kingsley Davis, "The Political Impact of New Population Trends," *Foreign Affairs* 36, no. 2 (1958): 296, 298–99.

18. Piotrow, *World Population Crisis,* 77–78, 90; Peter J. Donaldson, *Nature against Us: The United States and the World Population Crisis, 1965–1980* (Chapel Hill: University of North Carolina Press, 1990), 35–38.

19. Piotrow, *World Population Crisis,* 103–38, 148, 160.

20. R. T. Ravenholt, "The A.I.D. Population and Family Planning Program—Goals, Scope, and Progress," *Demography* 5, no. 2 (1968): 562, 564–71; Donaldson, *Nature against Us,* 110–11; Connelly, *Fatal Misconception,* 242.

21. Demeny, "Social Science and Population Policy," 456.

22. Kingsley Davis, "Population Policy: Will Current Programs Succeed?" *Science* 158, no. 802 (1967): 738, emphasis in original.

23. Bernard Berelson, "Beyond Family Planning," *Science* 163 (1969): 533–34, 537–38.

24. Donald P. Warwick, *Bitter Pills: Population Policies and Their Implementation in Eight Developing Countries* (Cambridge: Cambridge University Press, 1982), 12–15, 74–78, 168.

25. Ibid., 15–19, 85–88, 165–69.

26. K. Raghavendra Rao, *Society, Culture, and Population Policy in India* (Delhi: Ajanta, 1989), 95–100; Connelly, *Fatal Misconception,* 217–20, 228–29.

27. Rao, *Population Policy in India,* 103–14; Connelly, *Fatal Misconception,* 211–13, 221–23, 228–29, emphasis in original.

28. Rao, *Population Policy in India,* 106, 135–43; Davidson R. Gwatkin, "Political Will and Family Planning: The Implications of India's Emergency Experience," *Population and Development Review* 5, no. 1 (1979): 29–59.

29. Paul Demeny, "On the End of the Population Explosion," *Population and Development Review* 5, no. 1 (1979): 149–51; Connelly, *Fatal Misconception,* 327, 338.

30. Norman E. Borlaug, "The Green Revolution: For Bread and Peace," *Bulletin of the Atomic Scientists* 27, no. 6 (1971): 7, 42, 48.

31. Robert S. Anderson, Edwin Levy, and Barrie M. Morrison, *Rice Science and Development Politics: Research Strategies and IRRI's Technologies Confront Asian Diversity, 1950–1980* (Oxford: Oxford University Press, 1991), 39–40.

32. Nick Cullather, "The Foreign Policy of the Calorie," *American Historical Review* 112 (April 2007): 339, 349–52, 356–57.

33. Staples, *Birth of Development*, 82–104; Jack Ralph Kloppenburg, Jr., *First the Seed: The Political Economy of Plant Biotechnology, 1492–2000* (Cambridge: Cambridge University Press, 1988), 158.

34. John H. Perkins, *Geopolitics and the Green Revolution: Wheat, Genes, and the Cold War* (New York: Oxford University Press, 1997), 119, 138, 150; Theodore W. Schultz, *Transforming Traditional Agriculture* (New Haven, CT: Yale University Press, 1964), 5.

35. Anderson, Levy, and Morrison, *Rice Science and Development Politics*, 39–50; Robert F. Chandler, Jr., *An Adventure in Applied Science: A History of the International Rice Research Institute* (Manila: International Rice Research Institute, 1982), 2.

36. Chandler, *Adventure in Applied Science*, 51–52; Anderson, Levy, and Morrison, *Rice Science and Development Politics*, 65.

37. Chandler, *Adventure in Applied Science*, 107.

38. James Lang, *Feeding a Hungry Planet: Rice, Research, and Development in Asia and Latin America* (Chapel Hill: University of North Carolina Press, 1996), 11; Nick Cullather, "Miracles of Modernization: The Green Revolution and the Apotheosis of Technology," *Diplomatic History* 28, no. 2 (2004): 227–30, 241–53; Anderson, Levy, and Morrison, *Rice Science and Development Politics*, 127–28.

39. Anderson, Levy, and Morrison, *Rice Science and Development Politics*, 68, 72–75, 81–82, 118–19, 127–28, 130; Chandler, *Adventure in Applied Science*, 146.

40. Perkins, *Geopolitics and the Green Revolution*, 103–15; Borlaug, "Green Revolution," 44.

41. Perkins, *Geopolitics and the Green Revolution*, 217–23, 230–31.

42. Govindan Parayil, "The Green Revolution in India: A Case Study of Technological Change," *Technology and Culture* 33, no. 4 (1992): 744–52; Perkins, *Geopolitics and the Green Revolution*, 235–45.

43. Speech by William S. Gaud, "The Green Revolution: Accomplishments and Apprehensions," March 8, 1968, Washington, D.C., www.agbioworld.org/biotech-info/topics/borlaug/borlaug-green.html; Lester R. Brown, "The Agricultural Revolution in Asia," *Foreign Affairs* 46, no. 4 (1968): 688–98.

44. Chandler, *Adventure in Applied Science*, 157–63; J. R. McNeill, *Something New under the Sun: An Environmental History of the Twentieth-Century World* (New York: Norton, 2000), 222–23.

45. Tarique Niazi, "Rural Poverty and the Green Revolution: The Lessons from Pakistan," *Journal of Peasant Studies* 31, no. 2 (2004): 246–48, 251.

46. Ibid., 250–56; Ernest L. Schusky, *Culture and Agriculture: An Ecological Introduction to Traditional and Modern Farming Systems* (New York: Bergin and Garvey, 1989), 125–26, 132–38.

47. Dana G. Dalrymple, "The Adoption of High-Yielding Grain Varieties in Developing Nations," *Agricultural History* 53, no. 4 (1979): 708, 714; Murray J. Leaf, "The Green Revolution and Cultural Change in a Punjab Village, 1965–1978," *Economic Development and Cultural Change* 31, no. 2 (1983): 250; Peter B. R. Hazell and C. Ramasamy, *The Green Revolution Reconsidered: The Impact of High-Yielding Rice Varieties in South India* (Baltimore: Johns Hopkins University Press, 1991).

48. Dalrymple, "Adoption of High-Yielding Grain Varieties," 720; Vandana Shiva, *The Violence of the Green Revolution: Third World Agriculture, Ecology, and Politics* (London: Zed, 1991), 45, 171–92.

49. Shiva, *Violence of the Green Revolution*, chaps. 2–4; Schusky, *Culture and Agriculture*, 133; McNeill, *Something New under the Sun*, 224.

50. Connelly, *Fatal Misconception*, 373–74; B. H. Farmer, "Perspectives on the 'Green Revolution' in South Asia," *Modern Asian Studies* 20, no. 1 (1986): 184–85; McNeill, *Something New under the Sun*, 225–26.

5

COUNTERINSURGENCY AND REPRESSION
Guatemala, South Vietnam, and Iran

Modernization was a fundamentally liberal ideal. As part of the wider discourse of development so deeply embedded in U.S. political and intellectual life from the late 1950s through the early 1970s, it promised to raise economic productivity, elevate living standards, and stimulate cultural transformations to create a more humane, just, and safer world. Thus modernization's promoters in government, foundations, and academia believed that they were engaged in a profoundly altruistic enterprise. At the height of the Cold War, however, they also envisioned modernization as part of an essential and often deadly struggle, a contest that required a resolute commitment to the use of coercive, lethal force. "Like all revolutions," Walt Rostow insisted, "the revolution of modernization is disturbing. Individual men are torn between the old and familiar way of life and the attractions of a modern way of life.... Power moves towards those who can command the tools of modern technology, including modern weapons." Amid the anxieties and strains of the great transition, Communists and other radicals would prey on the new nations, offering their models of development as superior paths to modernity "even at the cost of surrendering human liberty." With the future of the postcolonial world in the balance, American modernizers were determined to direct its progress through foreign aid and development programs where possible, and through violence where necessary.[1]

The cases of Guatemala, South Vietnam, and Iran illustrate the extent to which commitments to democracy, so often repeated in the declarations of theorists and policymakers, were readily cast aside in favor of more authoritarian solutions. American modernizers imagined that they were promoting liberal, *contradicted themselves*

why?

pluralistic outcomes, but their ambivalence toward nationalism and their obsession with communism frequently led them to undermine their own stated priorities. Counterinsurgency warfare and the deployment of repressive internal police forces, U.S. policymakers came to believe, were often essential to create the conditions of social and political stability required for modernization to proceed along its natural course. The forceful expansion of state surveillance and bureaucratic control over remote, rural populations, they argued, were integral parts of the nation-building process. Distrustful of populist politics, many U.S. officials also came to see the creation of modern, professional militaries as a progressive step. Such forces, they imagined, would defend societies in transition and create new sources of rational, enlightened authority as well.

These hard-line solutions, moreover, were not simply imposed by Washington on postcolonial states. By casting themselves as progressive modernizers, postcolonial leaders found a ready vocabulary with which to legitimate their authority, identify threats, and demand increased U.S. economic and security assistance. Guatemalan military leaders, South Vietnamese dictators, and the shah of Iran quickly seized on modernization to reach domestic and foreign audiences. Economic and social development, in their hands, became a vehicle through which they could compete with alternative visions of progress and win increased support for regimes that had no interest in liberal reform.

Guatemala and the Alliance for Progress

As the Kennedy administration took office in January 1961, Latin America stood out as an arena of Cold War anxiety. Although increased U.S. demands for natural and strategic resources helped the region's economies expand during World War II, since the late 1940s the boom had subsided. As foreign exchange earnings in primary exports, like coffee, sugar, copper, and tin, continued to fall behind the costs of manufactured imports, Latin American nations accumulated little domestic savings to invest in development programs. Affluent commercial elites benefited by supplying North American markets, but little of their wealth reached destitute peasants and urban workers. During the early 1950s the region's annual per capita income remained less than $250, and Latin American life expectancies averaged only forty-three years, a full twenty-five years less than in the United States. In most countries, moreover, oligarchies perpetuated tremendous social and political inequalities, holding large majorities of the arable land and enjoying greatly disproportionate shares of the nation's income.[2]

The Eisenhower administration did little to address this situation. While progressive Latin American leaders like Chile's Eduardo Frei and Brazil's Juscelino

Kubitschek requested long-term, multibillion dollar development assistance programs, Eisenhower and his advisers stressed the need for growth through free market capitalism and private enterprise, rejecting programs that would involve significant public investment or state planning. Preferring stability to reform, they also saw little cause to advance policies that would potentially undermine the faithfully anticommunist dictators they supported. Rather than expanded economic aid or proposals for social reform, the Eisenhower administration showered its regional favorites with military assistance, awarding the Legion of Merit medal to right-wing stalwarts like Peru's Manuel Odría and Venezuela's Marcos Pérez Jiménez.[3]

By 1960, however, the costs of those policies became starkly apparent. In 1958, angry students in Lima interrupted Vice President Richard Nixon's regional "goodwill tour," and a rock-throwing crowd in Caracas nearly killed him. These events drove home the reality of deep anti-American resentment in the region, but it was the Cuban Revolution of 1959 that truly riveted Washington policymakers. If a figure like Cuba's Fulgencio Batista was vulnerable to revolutionary overthrow, they worried, what might happen to the likes of Rafael Trujillo's dictatorship in the Dominican Republic or the Nicaraguan regime of Anastasio Somoza? Faced with those questions, the Eisenhower administration began to rethink its approach, listening with new attention to the arguments of progressive Latin American leaders that popular destitution and misery were at least as dangerous as Communist conspiracy. In September 1960 the administration also agreed to contribute $500 million for the creation of a Social Progress Trust Fund to promote agricultural reforms and programs in public health, education, and housing. The wider questions, however, still remained. How could the United States define a new regional strategy to ensure that a second Cuba would not emerge, and that the prospect of revolutionary nationalism and Soviet-sponsored "wars of national liberation" would not be realized throughout the rest of the Western Hemisphere?

For Kennedy and his advisers, the answer was a comprehensive program of accelerated development. Harvard historian and White House special assistant Arthur Schlesinger, Jr., told the new president that "the problem of political ferment in Latin America" was rooted in the struggle to bring the region's invisible masses "into the 20th century." "To put it most concisely," Schlesinger emphasized, "it is the problem of modernization." Kennedy's Latin American Task Force, including the New Deal veteran Adolf Berle, economist Robert Alexander, historian Arthur Whitaker, and Puerto Rican development experts Teodoro Moscoso and Arturo Morales Carrión, concurred with that perspective. "The present ferment in Latin America, which facilitates Communist penetration," they stressed, "is the outward sign of a tide of social and political change which the United States cannot and should not check." The key to preventing revolution would be to promote an integrated, long-range hemispheric plan that would direct those forces "into channels that are or ought to be, acceptable as well as beneficial to the peoples involved."[4]

On March 13, 1961, in a White House speech to the Latin American diplomatic corps, Kennedy announced the Alliance for Progress. Drawing directly on the concepts and promise of modernization, the president boldly predicted a regional "take-off." By the end of the decade, he declared, "the living standards of every American family will be on the rise, basic education will be available to all, hunger will be a forgotten experience, the need for massive outside help will have passed, most nations will have entered a period of self-sustaining growth, and, although there will be still much to do, every American Republic will be the master of its own revolution and its own hope and progress." Radically increasing the level of economic aid, the United States pledged to provide $1 billion in public funds for the program in the first year, and to raise $20 billion from international lending and private investment over the rest of the decade. Internal investment was projected to generate an additional $80 billion by the end of the 1960s, allowing the region to achieve a much improved annual economic growth rate of 2.5 percent.[5]

The Alliance for Progress was expected to promote political transformations as well, supporting democracy over dictatorship, and ultimately alleviating the social and political conditions that fed radical nationalism and Marxist insurgency. Kennedy maintained that the Alliance would "demonstrate to the entire world that man's unsatisfied aspirations for economic progress and social justice can be achieved by free men within a framework of democratic institutions." Ratified by all the members of the Organization of American States (OAS) except Cuba, the program's official charter repeated that emphasis on the integration of political and economic change. The Alliance, OAS members declared, would seek to "accelerate the economic and social development of the participating countries of Latin America, so that they may achieve levels of well being, with equal opportunities for all, in democratic societies adapted to their own needs and desires."[6]

The Alliance's emphasis on democratic development, however, stood in direct contradiction to the immediate U.S. preoccupation with security and counterinsurgency. Kennedy's liberal advisers insisted that the Alliance for Progress should promote a "middle-class revolution," empowering doctors, lawyers, teachers, and small businessmen to mobilize broader public support for progressive, reformist movements. The president himself, speaking on the first anniversary of the program's founding, made the point most dramatically, declaring that "those who make peaceful revolution impossible will make violent revolution inevitable."

The region's elites, he warned, would have to embrace democratic reforms and liberal social policies in order to address the destitution and political repression that gave Cuban and Soviet-sponsored insurgencies a golden opportunity to derail the "natural" course of modernization. But the idea of promoting "revolution" of any kind was anathema to Latin America's conservative oligarchs. While glad to receive development funds, and eager to present themselves as benevolent, far-sighted leaders, they insisted that any progress would depend on the security they alone ensured.

In countries like Guatemala, this tension produced devastating results. As the Alliance helped fund rural cooperatives, literacy campaigns, and political training programs it also enabled Indians and poor peasants to challenge the authority of the merchants and landowners who exploited their labor. At the same time, the overriding anti-Communist policies of the Kennedy and Johnson administrations accelerated the country's descent into unrelenting conflict. Drawing on the ample supply of U.S. military and counterinsurgency aid, elites went to war against their impoverished countrymen. In the end, U.S.-sponsored repression in Guatemala prevented any real development and helped turn the "peaceful revolution" into a violent cataclysm.[7]

Guatemala emerged as a focus of Cold War concern in the early 1950s, as President Jacobo Arbenz Guzmán launched a nationalist program to create an economy that would be less beholden to U.S. capital. In addition to constructing highways and power plants that threatened the profits of U.S. transportation and utility companies, Arbenz put forward a sweeping Agrarian Reform Law in June 1952. Issued at a moment when 2 percent of the population owned a full 72 percent of farmland, and annual per capita incomes in rural areas stood at a mere $89, the decree expropriated all uncultivated land on private farms and estates over 672 acres in size. Large landholders were compensated with bonds based on their own undervalued tax returns, while new owners, many of them peasants, purchased small farms by promising to pay 5 percent of their annual harvest over the next twenty-five years. Under the law, 1.4 million acres were distributed, benefiting more than 500,000 people.[8]

Guatemala's large landowners, including the powerful U.S.-owned United Fruit Company, condemned the measure vociferously, and Washington policymakers were deeply alarmed. Beyond the complaints of United Fruit, the Eisenhower administration also worried about the enthusiastic support for Arbenz among Guatemalan Communists and feared that his land reform measures might generate revolutionary ambitions among an increasingly radicalized peasantry. While Arbenz himself was not a Communist, his collaboration with Communist Party members and attempts to create what he termed a "more collective society" aroused U.S. anxieties, as did his decision to purchase arms from Czechoslovakia after Washington cut off military aid to his country in 1949. More profoundly, the Eisenhower administration feared that his ardently nationalist economic course would embolden other Central American countries to follow similar paths, jeopardizing U.S. economic dominance and empowering an insurgent political left.[9]

Troubled by Guatemalan nationalism, and unwilling to tolerate *any* risk of growing Communist influence in Latin America, the Eisenhower administration and the Central Intelligence Agency launched a military coup against Arbenz in June 1954, putting in power Colonel Carlos Castillo Armas and starting a concerted effort to redirect the country's developmental course. Firmly backed by the United States, Castillo Armas quickly returned Guatemala to a free market economy dominated by landowning elites and open to unrestricted foreign investment. A new five-year plan in 1955 emphasized the development of infrastructure for transportation, communications, and power generation but allocated only token amounts for social programs in health and education. Unsurprisingly, the majority of the new construction contracts went to U.S. firms, many of which violated labor codes, paid less than legal minimum wages, and provided workers with inadequate housing. Determined to roll back the Arbenz reforms, the Castillo Armas regime also returned nearly 80 percent of all previously expropriated land. Through the end of the decade illiteracy remained a steady 60 to 70 percent nationwide, and three-fourths of Guatemalans experienced a decline in income.[10]

The Eisenhower administration also made little pretense of supporting democracy. Relying on the CIA for help, the Guatemalan government authorized the imprisonment of dissidents for up to six months without trial, arrested thousands of peasants and workers on charges of supporting Communists, and encouraged the formation of right-wing vigilante groups. After Castillo Armas was assassinated by a member of his own palace guard in 1957, the United States increased its military support to his successor, the conservative military officer and engineer Miguel Ydígoras Fuentes. Ydígoras promised stability and order, and though many U.S. officials doubted his competence, Washington sent him $300,000 in military aid between 1958 and 1961.[11]

Thus, as the Alliance for Progress began, Guatemala epitomized the volatile situation Kennedy and his advisers worried most about. Led by a repressive oligarchy and plagued with deep inequalities of wealth, the country seemed an ideal place for a revolutionary insurgency to take root. In November 1960, moreover, four hundred nationalist military officers, embittered by Ydígoras's decision to allow Cuban exiles to train on Guatemalan soil in preparation for the Bay of Pigs invasion, had rebelled against the government. While the CIA helped suppress the insurgents, their remnants allied with the Guatemalan Communist Party to create a new guerrilla movement, the Fuerzas Armadas Rebeldes (FAR). In early

1962, Ydígoras brutally suppressed antigovernment demonstrations, but as his term in office drew to a close in 1963, he promised to permit open elections and allowed the reformist former president Juan José Arévalo to return from exile to participate in them. In response, the Guatemalan military condemned Ydígoras as "soft on communism" and Defense Minister Enrique Peralta Azurdia mounted a successful coup. Declaring that the government was infected by Communists, Peralta then suspended the constitution, dissolved the congress, and took full control as the head of state. Guatemala became more politically polarized than ever before. As historian Rachel May observed, by 1963 the military "no longer seemed to be simply at the service of the traditional landed elites—the military itself was becoming the most influential 'elite' group in the country."[12]

The Kennedy administration's response to this turmoil reflected the fundamental contradictions at the core of the Alliance's modernizing project. While trying to promote a "controlled" revolution, U.S. policymakers were also determined to maintain internal stability. During the course of the Alliance the United States poured $27 million into Guatemala, much of which supported large infrastructure projects. A substantial portion of U.S. aid, however, was spent in attempts to intervene directly in the country's internal political and economic order. The tensions became especially clear in the Guatemalan countryside. If modernization were to go forward, many experts believed, it would have to restructure rural life, alleviating the poverty and desperation that made peasant populations susceptible to insurgent movements. The culture of Guatemala's indigenous, rural poor also seemed a fundamental barrier to development. Since the 1950s, State Department reports had bemoaned the presence of an "illiterate Indian majority [which] has continued to live separated from the main currents of modern life, entrenched in the ancient customs of the Mayan era." One report patronizingly lamented: "[The Indians] have little ambition and less opportunity to rise above a subsistence level...[they] throw away what little they can on liquor and fireworks and often prevent their children from attending school lest they forsake the ways of their forefathers."[13]

Under the Alliance for Progress, AID now sought to modernize that population, and in the process it helped mobilize some of the very groups that the oligarchy sought most to contain. Guatemalan landowners had long benefited from the oppression of the country's highland, predominantly Indian peasantry. With few opportunities to own land and little chance to grow enough food for their families, the poverty of Guatemala's highland Indians often forced them to rent from absentee landlords and make annual migrations to the Pacific coast to work on coffee, cotton, and banana plantations. Labor contractors loaded hundreds of thousands of migrants into trucks and sent them off to work fourteen-hour days on massive farms where they received minimal wages, lived in open shelters with dirt floors and no electricity, and suffered from high rates of malnutrition, malaria, dysentery, and pesticide poisoning. Tied to labor contracts by loans they struggled to repay, highland Indian peasants became a ruthlessly exploited, captive workforce.[14]

Landowning elites justified this arrangement by insisting that Indian peasants were unproductive, lacked initiative, and could never become independent farmers. The Alliance for Progress, however, began to sponsor policies that promised to alter the basic structures of rural life and labor. In 1962, U.S. funding promoted a program to organize 14,000 peasant families into producing and marketing cooperatives. AID expected to foster economic growth by integrating highland peasants into the cash economy, allowing them to produce for broader markets, and making them more active consumers of manufactured goods. By providing peasants with new means to gain credit and build savings the cooperatives helped make peasants less dependent on landlords and merchants for crop marketing, loans, and farm inputs like tools and fertilizer. U.S. Peace Corps volunteers also supported cooperatives with literacy projects, some of which fostered independent political organizing.[15]

Many of the most important impacts were brought about through collaboration with Catholic missionaries. During the 1950s the Castillo Armas regime had invited missionaries into the country to make up for a shortage of priests. Closely aligned with a conservative Catholic Church, the Guatemalan oligarchy welcomed their arrival, expecting that their pursuit of Indian converts might contribute to the creation of a more docile labor force. As a more liberal-minded "Catholic Action" movement took hold, however, priests defied the church hierarchy and combined their evangelism with community development work, establishing schools and medical clinics and organizing cooperatives and literacy campaigns. Following the Second Vatican Council's strong emphasis on the obligations of the faithful to respect human rights and create humane living standards, Maryknoll and Jesuit missionaries also organized peasant discussions of social and economic problems. During the early to mid-1960s, moreover, the U.S. Agency for International Development supported many of these efforts. Lacking experience in the country, AID officials relied on priests to establish "village improvement committees" that would propose projects and apply for U.S. development funds. Jesuits working at the Universidad Landívar in Guatemala City used AID money to train students as "social promoters," sending their comparatively affluent graduates into the countryside to organize "consciousness-raising" groups and development programs among the poor. In 1965, funds obtained through the U.S. Foreign Assistance Act also sponsored a Guatemalan leadership training program at the Inter-American Center of Loyola University in New Orleans. After being screened by the State Department, Guatemalan participants trained on U.S. farms and agricultural extension projects, met local chamber of commerce members, and returned to work in their country's villages as community organizers, union leaders, and Christian Democratic Party politicians.[16]

While some U.S. officials may have anticipated that the teaching of Catholic social doctrine would provide an attractive alternative to Marxism, Guatemala's oligarchs feared that the AID and Catholic-sponsored projects would upend the existing social order. In the department of Santa Cruz del Quiché, for example, an Indian peasant cooperative managed to purchase fertilizer at discounted prices, allowing its members to undermine the power of local merchants and labor contractors. Complaints to the governor resulted in the expulsion of the missionaries, but the cooperative was undaunted, quickly doubling its membership. In response to these sorts of challenges, elites moved quickly. Red-baiting anyone who attempted to organize upland peasants and any program that threatened to disrupt the existing patterns of class and ethnic exploitation, the elites condemned the interference of "subversives" and "Communists." When radical students arranged meetings between Maryknoll missionaries and FAR guerrillas, and the two parties found common ground in their commitment to sweeping social change on behalf of the poor, the oligarchy's worst fears were confirmed. After successfully demanding the deportation of the offending priests and nuns, the Guatemalan military searched missionary schools and targeted cooperative leaders and Mayan converts for arrest. Resenting challenges to their authority, landowners and merchants also provided the Guatemalan military with blacklists, facilitating a campaign of kidnapping and assassination that accelerated over the next two decades.[17]

The U.S. commitment to "peaceful revolution" and democracy soon evaporated. When liberal reforms created political conflict, the United States abandoned them in favor of immediate security goals. Where the Alliance had promised progressive structural change in opposition to oligarchic control, U.S. policymakers came to embrace visions of "military modernization" and threw their support behind a brutal counterinsurgency war. The idea that postcolonial militaries could play pivotal roles in accelerating modernization provided an easy way to reconcile support for development with the empowerment of security forces. A broad range of U.S. experts also provided the rationale for a more repressive turn. According to sociologist Edward Shils, as "major representatives of modernity in technology and administration," military forces could "integrate diverse ethnic groups into a national community," "teach skills useful in economic development," "widen horizons beyond village and locality," and "keep young men from being infected by nationalistic demagoguery." As one State Department intelligence report argued in early 1962, the Latin American military could play a most beneficial role if it "[became] directly involved in bringing the benefits of the Alliance to the people, especially in rural areas."[18]

Expanding military control over the countryside, of course, was precisely what Guatemala's government intended. While its policies had nothing to do with social reform or democratic development, they enjoyed strong U.S. support. Between 1961 and 1963 the United States delivered $4.3 million in military aid to Guatemala, more than four times the amount supplied by the Eisenhower administration in the previous four years. After seizing power in 1963, Colonel Peralta Azudia also defined his own vision of modernization. "Security and order," he declared in his first major speech, "are the indispensable prerequisites for the realization of the values of economic and social evolution. Whoever disturbs the public order will be rigorously repressed." Although that formulation fully inverted the Kennedy administration's argument that immediate progressive change was essential for the long-term achievement of security, U.S. government support for the Guatemalan regime increased. After briefly suspending relations to express its official disapproval of Peralta's coup, the Kennedy administration quickly restored relations even as Peralta refused U.S. requests to schedule presidential elections and end an extralegal system of military tribunals. AID support for the Guatemalan "civic action" and police training programs also funded the delivery of pistols, machine guns, mortars, and helicopters, while U.S. Special Forces troops traveled to Guatemala to train army officers in counterinsurgency techniques.[19]

That U.S. assistance helped the Guatemalan military unleash a relentless campaign against all forms of opposition. Making full use of the tools the United States supplied, military forces arbitrarily exiled, imprisoned, and tortured union organizers, cooperative leaders, and opposition party members. A new Mobile Military Police and a network of military commissioners expanded state control in rural areas, providing surveillance, conducting interrogations, and collaborating with large plantation owners to discipline the indigenous workforce. Just prior to the 1966 elections, military intelligence and judicial police also captured and secretly executed more than thirty political activists and Communist Party members in Guatemala City—the start of a wider pattern of mass "disappearances." In October 1966 the army went on to deploy U.S.-supplied arms and aircraft in a "scorched earth" campaign, killing up to 8,000 in peasant communities thought to be aligned with guerrilla forces. In the same year right-wing death squads such as the infamous Mano Blanca began to operate, murdering political opponents with military collaboration.[20]

These developments, of course, were patently clear to U.S. officials. Yet between 1964 and 1966 the United States provided an additional $34 million in development aid to Guatemala, even as U.S. ambassador John Bell warned that all proposals for social reform had stalled in the face of determined opposition by the military and conservative oligarchs. In October 1967, Thomas Hughes of the State Department's intelligence branch warned Secretary of State Dean Rusk that the counterinsurgency program was "running wild" as Guatemalan security forces employed methods that "resembled those of the guerrillas themselves: kidnappings, torture, and summary executions." Rural and urban counterinsurgency units, Hughes reported, not only attacked "known" Communists and sympathizers, but "threatened and acted against an alarmingly broad range of Guatemalans of all social sectors and political persuasions." According to Hughes, "labor leaders, businessmen, students and intellectuals, government officials, and politicians have all been included at various times on the 'target lists' of clandestine anti-communist organizations."[21]

As frustrations mounted, U.S. policymakers blamed the Alliance's failures on the oligarchy's intransigence. "What is wrong," one official lamented, "is that you are dealing with a society here that has a concept of mankind opposed to that of Western civilization. In Guatemala, the educated, the people of means, and their children, are interested only in amassing as much as they can for themselves and their families. They have no sense of obligation for the rest of society." The cycles of violence and oppression that devastated Guatemala, leading to civil war, three decades of military dictatorship, and the deaths of approximately 200,000 citizens between 1966 and 1996, certainly had deep domestic roots. The failure of the United States to resolve the fundamental contradictions at the core of its vision of modernization, however, helped accelerate the tragedy. When programs intended to promote progressive economic and political change generated conflict in Guatemala's deeply stratified society, U.S. policymakers quietly abandoned them in favor of shoring up the forces they identified with the preservation of security and order. Unwilling to go where destabilizing interventions might lead, the Kennedy and Johnson administrations dispensed with their reformist ambitions and fueled the forces of reaction, ultimately achieving neither democracy nor stability, and contributing to precisely the kind of revolutionary violence they wished to prevent.[22]

Nation Building in South Vietnam

The presidential palace in Saigon was a long way from his office in East Lansing, but Wesley Fishel had little doubt about the path to progress in South Vietnam. A political scientist at Michigan State University (MSU), Fishel became one of South Vietnamese prime minister Ngo Dinh Diem's closest U.S. advisers and confidants during the late 1950s and early 1960s. Between 1954 and 1955, Fishel served as a liaison between Diem and General Lawton Collins, President Eisenhower's personal envoy to South Vietnam. From 1955 through 1962, he helped lead an MSU team that assisted Diem's government with training and advice on matters of refugee resettlement, civil service education, and police administration. But, above all, in a flood of government memoranda, public speeches, scholarly articles, and popular essays, Fishel conveyed to U.S. audiences an optimistic vision of Vietnamese modernization that elided the increasing repression by Diem's corrupt, dictatorial regime. ↳ left out

As Fishel conceded in 1961, Diem's government was not yet a model of liberal democracy. The press remained subject to government intervention, the executive branch held far greater power than either the judiciary or the legislature, and the country's constitution included a clause permitting the abrogation of the bill *abolish by authoritarian action* of rights in conditions of emergency. It was important to understand, however, that South Vietnam was in the midst of a great nation-building struggle. French colonialism had devastated Vietnam, and "the resultant society was a product *mixture of races* of political miscegenation: one with a traditional base, influenced by Confucian, Taoist, and Buddhist ideas and values, topped by a weighty superstructure of Western organizations, principles, laws and techniques." The stunning defeat and departure of the French in 1954 had also "left a sudden, and nearly disastrous political vacuum" as the new government sought to defeat a dangerous revolutionary insurgency. Yet Diem remained committed to programs that would "stimulate a rapid development of national consciousness and engender strong support," and he knew that the keys to victory were to be found in the countryside, among a peasantry caught up in a sweeping transition away from the traditional loyalties of family and village toward a modern desire for higher living standards, economic growth, and active, political participation. By "journeying about their zones of responsibility, learning the problems of the people," Fishel claimed, Diem's province and district chiefs would bridge the gap between the central government and the rural masses, build an educated electorate, and "bring every district in the country into contact with its neighbors and with the capital." The new South Vietnamese state, Fishel concluded, would overcome both the colonial legacy and the Communist threat. With the guidance and support of the United States, it would seize the moment to build a nation where none had existed before.[23]

Fishel's interpretation reflects the extent to which U.S. social scientists and policymakers envisioned nation building in South Vietnam as part of a universal process of modernization that, once it gained sufficient momentum, would become an inexorable force. In this vision of nation building, the South Vietnamese were framed as essentially malleable, and their history and culture were relegated to a seemingly irrelevant past. As "traditional" peasants became "modern" citizens, U.S. policymakers expected, a new, distinctly South Vietnamese nationalism could be created to undercut Ho Chi Minh's revolutionary appeal. The condition of war, moreover, was hardly an obstacle to the process. The National Liberation Front (NLF) could certainly challenge Diem's regime, but the sheer violence and disruption of war also appeared to provide a setting in which state-driven development might prevail.[24]

The challenge for the United States in Vietnam, modernizers believed, was to create a nation-state capable of driving that society through the essential transition before Communists might direct it down a dangerous false path. That problem remained central for much of the United States' war in Vietnam, but it can be illustrated most clearly by focusing on the early 1960s, when U.S. policymakers envisioned nation building as a way to redirect the revolution and avoid a wider war. In the immediate aftermath of World War II, U.S. policymakers knew little about Vietnam. While claiming to reject imperialism, they relied heavily on French colonial descriptions of the country's inhabitants. Viewed through a framework stressing the gap between the backward nature of nonwhite, traditional societies and Western progress, the Vietnamese appeared to be motivated more by immediate self-interest than adherence to principle, driven more by emotion than logic. Such a people, most U.S. analysts concluded, were incapable of self-government and vulnerable to foreign subversion. The need for French cooperation in the reconstruction of Europe and the formation of an anti-Soviet, Cold War alliance, moreover, led U.S. policymakers to ignore Ho Chi Minh's 1945 declaration of independence in favor of the preservation of French sovereignty over Indochina. The Chinese Revolution and war in Korea only amplified U.S. anxiety about the dangers of Communist gains, and by 1950 the United States began to provide millions of dollars in military aid to support French counterinsurgency efforts. When the revolutionaries decisively defeated France at Dienbienphu, the subsequent Geneva Accords of 1954 partitioned Vietnam into northern and southern halves, pending national elections to reunify the country in 1956. Worried that Ho Chi Minh's stature as an anticolonial hero would almost certainly enable him to prevail at the ballot box, the United States rejected reunification and began its long drive to create a viable, distinctly South Vietnamese state with a growing economy and enough political legitimacy to redirect the revolution into liberal, capitalist channels. Determined to back South Vietnamese prime minister Ngo Dinh Diem, an anti-French Catholic with an influential lobby in the United States, U.S. policymakers came to view nation building as an urgent imperative. If it failed, they feared, the United States would have to go to war in Southeast Asia.[25]

Between 1955 and 1961, the United States poured $1.65 billion into South Vietnam, making that country the fifth largest recipient of U.S. aid at the time.

The U.S. mission in Saigon was also the largest in the world. Yet rather than engineering a new sense of national solidarity, Diem and his U.S. backers were most successful in alienating the South Vietnamese public. At the time of the Geneva settlement, one-quarter of 1 percent of the rural population owned a full 40 percent of rice land in the South. Saigon's conservative land reform program, however, affected less than 10 percent of the country's tenant farmers and utterly failed to compete with the revolutionary practice of directly redistributing landlord holdings. A U.S.-sponsored Commercial Import Program proved equally unproductive as American dollars and import credits funded consumer purchases by wealthy urbanites and did nothing to promote local industrial growth. Armed with military aid from the United States, Diem created a powerful secret police, killed, imprisoned, and tortured Viet Minh sympathizers, and mounted a drive to suppress any and all dissent against his regime. In December 1960, an alliance of Diem's southern opponents, led by Communist Party members but also including anti-French Viet Minh veterans, professionals, intellectuals, students, and peasants created the NLF to lead an armed revolt.[26]

By 1961, it was increasingly clear to U.S. policymakers that their attempt to create a sense of popular loyalty to a separate, southern Vietnamese nation-state was failing miserably. American CIA operative Edward Lansdale hoped that Diem might become a compelling leader, but it soon became obvious to him and many other U.S. advisers that the United States and the South Vietnamese were losing the crucial war in the countryside. "It was a shock to me," Lansdale wrote to Secretary of Defense Robert McNamara, "to look over maps of the estimated situation with U.S. and Vietnamese intelligence personnel" and find that the NLF "had been able to infiltrate the most productive area of South Vietnam and gain control of nearly all of it except for narrow corridors protected by military actions." Other assessments that year were similarly bleak. The prominent journalist Theodore White offered this report from Saigon in a letter to his friend John F. Kennedy: "The situation gets steadily worse almost week by week....Guerrillas now control almost all the Southern delta—so much that I could find no American who would drive me outside Saigon in his car even by day without military convoy....What perplexes the hell out of me is that the Commies, on their side, seem able to find people willing to die for their cause."[27]

By this point, moreover, Vietnam had emerged as a crucial "test case" of America's ability to combat "wars of national liberation." A loss there, Kennedy and his advisers feared, would do immense damage to U.S. credibility around the world. Yet U.S. officials remained reluctant to commit American combat troops in the field. Diem's hold on his own government remained tenuous at best, and he had narrowly survived a coup attempt against him in 1960. To deploy U.S. soldiers, Kennedy worried, might create an irreversible public commitment to a figure whose leadership ability now appeared questionable at best. It might be necessary to send American troops at some point in the future, Kennedy believed, but the fact that neither France nor Britain was likely to assist in a direct military campaign and the danger that the Soviets or Chinese might respond to U.S. combat forces by sending in their own troops led the president toward another approach. While amplifying U.S. support for Diem's army and radically increasing the number of U.S. military advisers, the Kennedy administration would ultimately try to defeat the revolutionaries through a dramatically expanded nation-building program. Modernization, policymakers concluded, could prevail as a means of counterinsurgency and a weapon of war.

In thinking about the challenge they faced in Vietnam, the British struggle against the Malayan Communists seemed especially important to U.S. planners. From late 1952 through early 1953 political scientist Lucian Pye conducted fieldwork in Malaya, seeking to learn the reasons why Malayan Chinese joined the Communist Party. His conclusions, based on interviews with "surrendered enemy personnel," focused less on matters of the distribution of resources, economic conditions, and political repression and more on the universal dynamics of modernization itself. Revolutionary insurgencies, Pye argued, "[are] intimately related to a general process now going on in most underdeveloped areas of the world. Large numbers of people are losing their sense of identity with their traditional ways of life and are seeking restlessly to realize a modern way." In this setting, communism appealed to those caught up in the transition, those who, according to Pye, felt "isolated from, and even hostile to the ways of their forefathers," but were not yet "personally a part of the new." These people, he observed, "are anxious to belong to the future, but they are concerned lest it pass them by." For those whose worlds were destabilized by increasing violence and rapid economic change, the party offered a vital element of stability and a vehicle for their recently awakened ambitions. In Pye's terms, the key to competing with a revolutionary insurgency lay in an expanded state structure reaching from the capital into distant provinces and villages, one that could meet the needs of an alienated, anxious peasantry more effectively than the revolution could.[28]

Walt Rostow arrived at a similar conclusion on a visit to South Vietnam in the fall of 1961. After interviewing captured NLF soldiers, he determined that the revolution appealed most to "young men in a developing region who had been caught up for the first time—and found various degrees of satisfaction and disappointment—in a modern organizational structure reaching beyond family, hamlet and village." NLF recruits, he determined, did not join the revolution because they were inspired by Marx, Lenin, or even Ho Chi Minh. They did not fight because they espoused a historical vision of a united Vietnam or because they were alienated by Diem's regime. Instead, they were dislocated, rootless young men who wanted above all to become part of a larger, modern institution and pinned their hopes on the Vietcong. The solution, therefore, was to promote a pattern of nation building that would replace the institutions of the insurgency with those of the state and give the peasant caught in the "transition" toward modernity a renewed sense of the potential for personal advance. As the State Department's Vietnam Task Force concluded in mid-1961, the problem was to "bring the rural people of Vietnam into the body politic."[29]

Inspired by those arguments, and convinced that the war would be won or lost in the countryside, where the vast majority of Vietnam's population lived, in early 1962 the U.S. government made the strategic hamlet program the centerpiece of its nation-building efforts. Based roughly on population resettlement plans used in Malaya and promoted by Robert G. K. Thompson, head of the British Advisory Mission in Saigon, the program aimed to condense South Vietnam's roughly 16,000 hamlets (each estimated to have a population of slightly less than 1,000) into about 12,000 "strategic hamlets" more easily defended against incursion, subjected to military control, and made the target of a battery of government programs intended to create a new and vital nationalism. Designed to resettle approximately 15 million people, the strategic hamlet program was, in Vietnam expert Bernard Fall's estimation, the "most mammoth example of 'social engineering' in the non-Communist world."[30]

At Kennedy's direction, State Department intelligence chief Roger Hilsman, himself a Yale-trained political scientist and veteran of the Office of Strategic Services, outlined a design for the program in the February 1962 plan "Strategic Concept for Vietnam." On one hand, the plan heavily emphasized security measures. "Each strategic village," Hilsman proposed, "will be protected by a ditch and a fence of barbed wire. It will include one or more observation towers, guard posts, and a defense post for central storage of arms.... The area immediately around the village will be cleared for fields of fire and the area approaching the clearing, including the ditch, will be strewn with booby-traps (spikes, pits, explosives, etc.) and other personal obstacles." Hilsman recommended that each hamlet be protected by a "self-defense corps" of 75 to 100 men armed with carbines and shotguns, but he also made it clear that hamlet watchtowers faced inward as well as out. Security forces were charged with "enforcing curfews, checking identity cards, and ferreting out hard core Communists" to achieve what Thompson referred to as "the physical and political separation of the guerrillas from the population." As he vividly described it, "one must get all the 'little fishes' out of the 'water' and keep them out; then they will die."[31]

While conditions varied from case to case, in practice hamlet construction generally involved a series of steps. South Vietnamese government "Rural Reconstruction" teams of ten to twenty men would take a census of an existing village and make a map identifying families and their apparent loyalties. Villagers would then be broken into work groups, given labor schedules, and required to build fortifications for the new settlement. Houses outside the perimeter of the new hamlet would be brought in or destroyed, and a hamlet militia would be selected and trained. Finally, peasants would be issued identification cards, photos of families would be posted on the walls of homes, and a hamlet administrative center would track all population movements and enforce curfews. The space inside the hamlet would become a realm of heightened surveillance, while the territory outside it became a free-fire zone.[32]

— concentration camps

U.S. planners believed that, beyond such security benefits, the strategic hamlets would be most crucial in promoting the essential task of nation building. "The problem presented by the Viet Cong," Hilsman emphasized, "is a political and not a military problem—or, more accurately, it is a problem in civic action." "Civic Action teams" of Vietnamese backed by U.S. supplies and advice were the "most important element in eliminating the Viet Cong" because they were to build an "essential socio-political base" by forming a new set of ties between the rural peasantry and Diem's regime. Hilsman's goal was to "set up village government and tie it into the district and national levels assuring the flow of information on village needs and problems upward and the flow of government services downward." The government provision of livestock, rice seed, cooking oil, and schools, in this vision, was expected to do more than raise peasant morale. It would also transform rural consciousness and become part of a process in which "traditional" loyalties to family and formerly isolated, largely autonomous villages would be replaced by "modern" identification with a specifically South Vietnamese nation-state. While a few figures within the U.S. government remained skeptical of such an effort, and some military officers strongly dissented in favor of a more orthodox "search and destroy" approach, the plan met with widespread approval. Nation building, in this vision, would steadily proceed one hamlet at a time.[33]

The strategic hamlet program was not imposed on Ngo Dinh Diem's government. Diem's regime arrived at the concept through its own planning and experience. In 1959 and 1960 Diem and his brother Ngo Dinh Nhu had already started to relocate peasants to "prosperity and density centers" or "agrovilles" in which they could be more closely indoctrinated and controlled. In Diem's view, "communism, underdevelopment, and disunity" were all essentially related, and his government's plans for population resettlement reflected an attempt to frame an integrated response to the crisis. Alongside his British and American supporters, Diem articulated his own vision of modernization, speaking repeatedly of the need to transform peasant attitudes and worldviews. More importantly, he also believed that the strategic hamlet program would help expand the reach of his national government into remote rural areas, allowing his province chiefs to gain greater control over peasant life and replacing local leaders with cadres directly responsible to Saigon. While Diem resented what he viewed as aggressive U.S. meddling in South Vietnamese planning, he shared the broader ambition of his superpower sponsor to integrate security and development in the countryside.[34]

In contrast to such lofty expectations, in practice the program was a disaster from the start. Serious efforts to implement it began in March 1962, with Operation Sunrise—a plan to create new hamlets in part of Binh Duong, a province to the north of Saigon that was heavily infiltrated by the NLF. South Vietnamese troops swept through the area to drive the guerrillas out, and the U.S. Agency for International Development provided $300,000, about $21 per family, to compensate resettled peasants for their property losses and to equip civic action teams with medicine, fertilizer, farming implements, and ID cards. According to one report, 70 families agreed to move, and 140 others were resettled at gunpoint. All were forced to build new homes and dig trenches in the new hamlets while South Vietnamese soldiers burned their former dwellings. By May, even the government newspaper admitted that after six weeks only about 7 percent of the district's 38,000 peasants had permanently relocated either voluntarily or by force. The fact that the NLF enjoyed substantial local support also became clear as guerillas ambushed a government convoy with help from villagers, who sabotaged roads and prevented reinforcements from arriving.[35]

Throughout 1962 and 1963 further evidence accumulated demonstrating that the program was failing dramatically. CIA field reports, AID officers, and RAND Corporation studies all documented the degree to which peasants resented being forced off ancestral lands, put on corvée teams, and denied access to their crops and fields. As Bernard Fall reported, not much nation building took place in such a repressive environment: "Egress and ingress controls upon which the system hinges necessarily give the strategic village the aspect of a detention area rather than that of a harmonious socio-economic unit. *The Wall Street Journal*'s local observer, a former OSS operative who was wholly sympathetic to the cause of South Vietnam, nevertheless felt that a visit to such a hamlet left one with the impression of having 'blundered into some sort of prison camp.'" Surveys also revealed that the NLF had successfully strengthened its hold on areas in which the hamlet program was promoted. One report on Long An province noted: "Both the hamlet gate and barbed wires are 100 percent destroyed by enemies....The hamlet hall was burnt down by the VC....All the members of the service administration, the hamlet council and all the hamlet armed forces cannot carry on any more work because there is no security and their morale is rather confused, being afraid of enemies." In case after case, and in province after province, revolutionaries infiltrated or overwhelmed hamlets, frequently with the cooperation of their inhabitants.[36]

Such apparently clear evidence of failure, however, provoked little serious analysis of the possibility that the fundamental assumptions of the program might be flawed. Instead, the powerful appeal of modernization as a vehicle for nation building prevented its advocates from recognizing the significance of disconfirming evidence. U.S. intelligence reports frequently cast blame on their Vietnamese allies. Province chiefs, they lamented, embezzled funds. South Vietnamese army officers refused to respond to night attacks. Civic action cadres rigged hamlet elections to get the results they wanted. U.S. policymakers also criticized Diem's desire to implement the program as rapidly as possible as a means of appointing his political favorites to positions of provincial leadership. These abuses were indeed widespread, yet by constantly citing administrative matters such criticism effectively prevented a more thoroughgoing challenge to the possibility that modernization through a bureaucratic regime, replete with constant surveillance and rigid controls on social and economic life, was not something that Vietnamese desired. The romance of nation building and the belief that the United States could engineer a transformative revolution to create a viable new state obscured the fact that, in the end, Vietnamese society, culture, and nationalism were not so malleable. As a former U.S. adviser to the Saigon government reflected, "ways I had been taught to think about the problem subsequently proved to be the greatest obstacle to understanding." In the early 1960s, the possibility that much of Vietnam's population was attracted to the revolution because it *redistributed* political and economic power, and that Diem's repressive regime was not one that rural Vietnamese were interested in identifying with or participating in at all was rarely considered seriously.[37]

By late 1963, the U.S. government would ultimately conclude that Diem was indeed a liability, and U.S. officials would support a coup to overthrow him. Yet plans for village-level "pacification" programs blending security, violence, and nation building were soon repeated in the form of "New Life" hamlets starting in 1964 and the program for Civilian Operations and Revolutionary Development Support (CORDS) in 1966 and 1967. Building on an idea put forward by South Vietnamese prime minister Nguyen Cao Ky, U.S. policymakers endorsed a plan to send "revolutionary development" cadres into remote villages to build schools, construct dams, and transform peasant attitudes. Yet if CORDS was "revolutionary," it promoted a revolution from above. Rather than empowering peasants or promoting local autonomy, it sought to tie remote villages into a firm hierarchical structure enforced by the military and anchored in Saigon. The results, moreover, were consistently poor. Although the program deployed more than five thousand military and civilian personnel into 44 provinces and 234 districts, the CIA reported steady losses in the countryside as revolutionaries took control of one village after another.[38]

Through the mid-1960s, U.S. officials had clung to the hope that they could create a South Vietnamese government with sufficient political legitimacy to win the war. As nation building failed and the revolutionaries continued to gain the upper hand, however, U.S. policymakers ultimately abandoned their ambitions for structural change in favor of an ever-expanding war of attrition. In April 1965 Lyndon Johnson dramatically offered to construct a Tennessee Valley Authority on the Mekong Delta, promising to bring the blessings of the New Deal to Southeast Asia. But in that same year the president also began to discount plans for social engineering in favor of the deployment of overwhelming force. Even in the absence of a legitimate South Vietnamese government worth defending, Johnson believed that America's Cold War credibility demanded a sharp military escalation. In the early 1960s, modernization was framed as an alternative to direct U.S. military commitment, but as hopes for it dimmed the United States launched a massive bombing campaign and began a troop deployment that would ultimately station a half-million soldiers in South Vietnam. Recognizing the long odds for success, Lyndon Johnson and his advisers also supported a military strategy that did far more to displace rural populations than it did to resettle them. By January 1968 the intensified war in the countryside created approximately four million refugees. U.S. officials downplayed that fact, blaming it on insurgent terrorism or casting it as a political decision made by Vietnamese to "vote with their feet" and relocate to government-controlled areas. "The refugee camps," one U.S. pacification officer maintained, "bring the people in closer to the urban centers, where they can have modern experiences and learn modern practices. It's a modernization experience." In truth, however, the escalating violence did far more to obliterate South Vietnamese rural life than to modernize it.[39]

By the time Lyndon Johnson left office in 1968, U.S. policymakers had largely abandoned the attempt to create a new, viable, and independent state in South Vietnam. The construction of a massive military infrastructure and the pursuit of an expanded "search and destroy" strategy replaced visions of Vietnamese social and political transformation. Richard Nixon continued to define the defense of South Vietnam as essential for the preservation of the credibility of the United States, but the language of reform, democracy, and modernization steadily faded away. As counterinsurgency planners struggled to eliminate the NLF's leadership on the ground, the Nixon administration promoted a rapid military buildup of South Vietnamese defensive forces and a phased withdrawal of U.S. troops. The final collapse of the Saigon government in 1975, and the total failure of a war whose fundamental purposes were initially framed in terms of democratic development and nation building, would also do great damage to the ideology of modernization itself.

Iran and the White Revolution

The pattern of U.S. engagement in Iran shares striking similarities with that in Guatemala and Vietnam. As in those two countries, the United States intervened directly in Iran to fend off nationalist and revolutionary challenges in the early 1950s. It then backed a repressive, dictatorial regime, providing military and economic aid through the rest of the decade. By the early 1960s, as political instability grew, U.S. policymakers turned to policies of modernization, hoping that moderate reforms and economic growth would alleviate insurgent pressures and that accelerated development would achieve long-term security. As in Guatemala and Vietnam, U.S. enthusiasm for accelerated development in Iran also lacked any real commitment to democracy. U.S. policymakers embraced the shah of Iran's authoritarian vision of modernization, throwing their resources behind a regime that remained most interested in preserving a system of political oppression and social control. As in the other cases, moreover, the results were disastrous. While U.S. policies helped push Guatemala into a prolonged civil war and failed to slow the revolutionary Communist advance in Vietnam, in Iran they contributed to the social forces that enabled the Islamic Revolution to triumph in 1979.

In Iran the nationalist challenge emerged in the form of Mohammad Mosaddeq, a venerable statesman and powerful member of the Iranian parliament, the Majlis. Though he came from an elite, privileged family, Mosaddeq's sincere commitment to constitutional government made him an enemy of the ruling Pahlavi autocracy. His ardent conviction that Iran should free itself from the shackles of foreign control also aroused the ire of Great Britain, which controlled Iran's vast oil wealth through the massive Anglo-Iranian Oil Company (AIOC). In the wake of World War II, the terms of Britain's exclusive oil concession in Iran, the product of a deal first struck in 1901, became an increasing source of populist anger. By 1947, the AIOC enjoyed after-tax profits equivalent to $112 million annually, while Iran received only about one-sixth that amount in royalties. The AIOC's refusal to modify the terms of its contract, and its brutal treatment of Iranian workers, triggered growing protests on the streets and in the Majlis. As the leader of the National Front, a coalition of secular and religious parties opposed to British influence and determined to curb the power of Shah Mohammad Reza Pahlavi, Mossadeq demanded that the AIOC split its profits with Iran on a fifty-fifty basis, as Western oil companies did with Saudi Arabia. When the AIOC refused to even consider such proposals, the Majlis responded by nationalizing Iran's oil reserves and electing Mossadeq prime minister in the spring of 1951. Over the shah's objections, Mossadeq then stunned the British by expropriating the AIOC without compensation and demanding that all British businessmen and military personnel leave the country. As long as a foreign power controlled Iran's most valuable

resource and repeatedly intervened in its internal affairs, he argued, Iran's sovereignty would be in jeopardy.[40]

U.S. officials watched the situation unfold with growing dismay. Frustrated by
the AIOC's intransigence, they tried to encourage the British to accept a greater
degree of profit sharing. But they worried that Mossadeq's actions would inspire
further nationalist challenges and threaten lucrative oil concessions held by the
United States and its allies across the Middle East. Roughly 70 percent of the oil
used for the post–World War II reconstruction of Western Europe and Japan
came from the region. U.S. officials also feared the possibility of subversion
from within. Although banned by the shah in 1949, the leftist, Soviet-supported
Tudeh Party led popular demonstrations against the monarchy and the AIOC,
proposing that Iran end its trade with the West and rely on Soviet markets and
economic aid instead. The shah soon proved unable to retain control of his own
government. After he dismissed Mossadeq in mid-1952, mass protests and rioting forced him to return the prime minister to office.[41]

Distrustful of Mossadeq's intentions and unwilling to accept any risk of expanded Soviet influence, the United States ultimately joined forces with Britain
to launch a coup in August 1953. After supporting a global boycott of Iranian oil
and severely damaging Iran's economy, the Eisenhower administration worked
with conservative landowners and alienated military officers to force Mossadeq from office. With the shah's power safely restored, the United States then
brokered a new oil deal. The AIOC, now renamed British Petroleum, retained
40 percent of its original concession. Another 40 percent went to several U.S.-
owned firms, and the remaining 20 percent was divided between French and
Dutch companies. The agreement also provided for the fifty-fifty profit sharing that Mossadeq had originally sought, but because the consortium of foreign
firms retained full authority over matters of pricing and production, it denied
Iran the power that would have come with real nationalization. The shah, for
his part, moved quickly to consolidate his authority. His government declared
martial law, arrested National Front leaders, purged the army of Tudeh members,
and forcefully put down demonstrations among students at Tehran University.
Pro-government mobs and organized gangs intimidated voters, loyal provincial
governors deployed police to supervise elections, and a carefully rigged process
ensured that pro-shah politicians would dominate the Majlis.[42]

Determined to keep the oil flowing, keep the Soviets out, and preserve stability in Iran, Washington bolstered the shah's royal dictatorship. Between 1954 and
1961, the United States provided an average of $64.5 million in economic aid to
Iran per year. In the first decade following the coup, U.S. financial support con-
stituted about 80 percent of the total spending by Iran's Plan Organization, the
country's main development body. An ambitious seven-year development plan

focused on major "showcase" projects, including highways, dams, and power plants, but little was done to increase the productivity of the country's large peasant population and working class. The shah refused calls for land reform, and government repression prevented the formation of effective labor unions, keeping wages low. With foreign investment in the oil industry and access to Western markets restored following the boycott, Iran's petroleum revenues climbed steeply from $34 million in 1954–55 to $181 million by 1956–57 and $358 million in 1960–61. Encouraged by gains in the country's gross national product and by the steady flow of U.S. aid, the shah concluded that no major structural changes in the country's political economy were necessary.[43]

U.S. support also helped the shah build a formidable defense and internal security apparatus. After Iran joined Iraq, Turkey, Pakistan, and Britain in the anti-Soviet Baghdad Pact in 1955, U.S. policymakers began to think of the country as a valuable regional barrier to Communist expansion and Nasserist radicalism. Between 1954 and 1961 annual U.S. military aid averaged $60 million, the beginning of a program that would steadily grow and involve Iranian purchases of increasingly sophisticated U.S. weaponry. In 1957, U.S. aid and technical training by the CIA helped the shah create a "National Security and Information Organization," better known by its Persian acronym, SAVAK. Given sweeping powers of arrest and prolonged detention, SAVAK routinely employed torture as a method of interrogation. It also helped the shah's regime penetrate trade unions, investigate university and civil service applicants, and control political activity among the intelligentsia and the middle and working classes.[44]

By the end of the decade, however, the combination of an economic crisis and rising political turmoil led U.S. policymakers to reassess their relationship with Iran. In 1958, just over the border in Iraq, the ardent nationalist Colonel Abdel Karim Qassim overthrew that country's pro-Western monarchy, raising questions about the stability of the Tehran government as well. Iran's heavy foreign borrowing, deficit financing, importation of luxury goods, and a poor harvest also led to high inflation and a growing gap in living standards. New entrepreneurial classes joined old-line landowners in elite circles, but rising prices for consumer staples damaged popular living standards while a fiscal austerity program, imposed as a condition for loans from the International Monetary Fund, froze government wages. Blatant corruption fed rising discontent, and a revived National Front condemned the clearly fraudulent 1960 Majlis elections. In May 1961 schoolteachers went on strike, and massive protests erupted in front of the Majlis buildings. Police opened fire on the crowd, killing a demonstrator, and deepening the shah's political crisis.[45]

In Washington these developments aroused concern. While the shah constantly demanded increased military aid, he seemed oblivious to the sources fueling internal dissent. In late 1958, Eisenhower's National Security Council noted the shah's support base in "large landowners and their conservative business associates, the top ranks of the government bureaucracy, and senior military officers" but worried about the "awakening popular expectations for reform of Iran's archaic social, economic, and political structure." Yet the Eisenhower administration did little to press for changes, fearing that there was no reliable, firmly anti-Communist alternative to the shah's regime. In cases like Iran, Eisenhower reflected, the United States was trapped. U.S. aid policies often supported ruling classes unwilling to consider progressive reforms and deepened inequalities of income, leading to further unrest. But to turn away from dictatorships like the shah's, he feared, would open the floodgates for Soviet-sponsored subversion, leaving the United States to "stand by and watch a wave of revolution sweeping around the world." Unable to solve the problem, Eisenhower left it for the Kennedy administration to consider.[46]

The shah hoped that unqualified U.S. support would continue, sending John F. Kennedy a letter describing Iran as "the one country that enjoys a democratic regime with all the freedoms except freedom to commit treason and to betray the interests of the Fatherland." But the new president delayed further aid and began a review of U.S. policy. He found his advisers divided on the matter. Conservative voices within the State Department worried about the possibility that reform might unleash radical forces capable of driving the shah from power. Pushing the shah too far, too fast, figures like Secretary of State Dean Rusk and Ambassador-Designate Julius Holmes suggested, might lead the shah to embrace a neutralist policy, turning away from the West and playing the United States and the USSR against each other in pursuit of trade deals and increased aid. While noting that National Front members and former associates of Mossadeq still commanded the support of Iran's educated classes, several prominent analysts feared that Communists could gain greater influence. The State Department's Iran desk officer at the time, John Bowling, gave Kennedy a pessimistic assessment. The status quo in Iran wasn't optimal, he admitted, but it was about the best that could be achieved there.[47]

Other influential advisers disagreed and insisted that Iran's problems demanded a more comprehensive policy of modernization. Kenneth Hansen, an assistant director of the Bureau of the Budget who had spent several years in Iran with a U.S. economic advisory group, insisted that any new aid program had to address "the vital areas of productivity and social and institutional change." U.S. experts on Iran, including political scientists Richard Cottam and Manfred Halpern, also argued that liberal reforms were essential and that the United States should try to reduce the shah's power, possibly relegating him to the role of a constitutional monarch. Robert Komer, working at that point on Middle

East affairs for the National Security Council, warned that without accelerated development "the continued slide towards chaos in Iran could result in as great a setback as in South Vietnam." Critical of what he called State Department "Do-Nothingism," Komer soon insisted that the overriding objective of U.S. policy should be to achieve a "'controlled revolution' in Iran."[48]

Worried by the delay in U.S. aid, and hoping to appeal to the new U.S. administration, the shah decided to make a reformist gesture. In May 1961 he appointed Ali Amini, a former ambassador to the United States, as prime minister. A "maverick aristocrat" and proponent of land reform, Amini was respected in Washington and enjoyed credibility among National Front members as well. Within the Kennedy administration, the advocates of modernization were encouraged. Kennedy's Iran Task Force argued that "profound political and social change in one form or another is virtually inevitable" and recommended support for Amini. Convinced by those arguments, Kennedy's National Security Council decided that the administration should back the Amini government as "the best instrument in sight for promoting orderly political, economic, and social evolution in Iran." In November 1961, U.S. aid to Iran resumed.[49]

Amini soon ran into difficulty. The new prime minister moved quickly to exile the head of SAVAK, opened discussions with the National Front, and put middle-class figures into the Ministries of Justice and Education. Most dramatically, he appointed the radical journalist Hassan Arsanjani as minister of agriculture and supported a sweeping land reform program designed to create a new class of independent small farmers among the country's rural peasants and sharecrop-pers. But Amini never secured a substantial base of political support. While conservative landowners protested against the agrarian reforms, the National Front resented his failure to call new, free elections for the Majlis. The shah, for his part, remained unwilling to allow a potential rival too much power. When Amini tried to control inflation and limit government spending, the shah refused to cut the expanding military budget. Attacked from both the right and the left and lacking the shah's support, Amini's position became increasingly untenable. In July 1962, after only fourteen months in office, he resigned.[50]

—Throughout this period the modernizers within the Kennedy administration continued to press their case. As Washington prepared to welcome the shah for a visit in April 1962, Hansen recommended that the United States fully endorse Amini's program, emphasizing the need to "provide the impetus toward faster economic progress, reform, and the beginnings of a political synthesis which will speed the process of modernization." Komer concurred, asking the president to tell the shah that U.S. aid would focus on "development and reform, together with improved counter-insurgency capabilities." In his meetings with the Iranian monarch, Kennedy himself also emphasized the need for the shah to meet the needs of the country's impoverished masses. Franklin Delano Roosevelt, he explained, was "still regarded almost as a god in places like West Virginia," and the shah could learn from his example. Iran, U.S. policymakers suggested, might launch a New Deal of its own.[51]

Responding to the Kennedy administration's focus on modernization, the shah moved decisively to adapt the concept to his own purposes. In January 1963 he dramatically unveiled the "White Revolution," a six-point plan to place Iran on a transformative course. Land reform, the nationalization of forests, the sale of state-owned factories to entrepreneurs, profit sharing for industrial workers, the advancement of women's suffrage, and the creation of a new literacy corps, he argued, would all restructure Iranian society and politics. Peasants and workers, he claimed, would gain a stake in society, becoming more productive, independent citizens. New women's voting rights and greater popular education would also deepen democracy, while forward-looking middle classes gained new authority. The White Revolution, the shah declared, would create "a social transformation unprecedented in Iran's three-thousand-year history." "We mean," he proclaimed, "for Iran to march in step, shoulder to shoulder, with the most progressive countries of the world."[52]

Although they knew that Mohammad Reza Pahlavi was no FDR, U.S. policymakers embraced his new approach. The shah, one State Department analyst argued, had "launched and pushed with boldness and determination a reform program which is drastically and irrevocably altering the political situation and prospects of Iran." The previously "ineffectual" monarch had long presided over "an apathetic, poverty-ridden peasant and proletarian mass [that] presented a rich target for would-be revolutionary agitators." Now, however, his daring move had made him "a savior and hero" in peasant eyes. While landowning elites and conservative Islamic leaders would certainly fight him, and the ultimate results remained unclear, U.S. economic, technical, and food aid could help Iran through a "dramatic but dangerous transition." Komer also believed that the shah had finally accepted U.S. advice. While the future was uncertain, after "encouraging the shah to take [the] reform track," he remarked, "we're going to have to ride this tiger." The shah's program, Komer concluded, was pushing Iran out of the traditional past and into a modern era. Despite the "dislocations" created, "tribal dissidence and [the] opposition of mullahs seem [to be] vestigial remnants of yesterday's business, not today's." Rusk now agreed as well, holding that "support and encouragement of the shah and his reform program is correct."[53]

While a few U.S. officials lamented the absence of any real democratic advances, noting that the shah's program was proceeding hand in hand with dictatorial repression, the Kennedy administration cast aside such concerns. When the shah claimed victory in a national referendum on the White Revolution, claiming 99.9 percent approval, U.S. policymakers chose to ignore the obviously fraudulent results. In a congratulatory telegram Kennedy instead praised the dictator, emphasizing his pleasure at learning that "a vast majority has supported your leadership in a clear and open expression of their will." As the shah's security forces rounded up and incarcerated National Front leaders, the United States remained silent, quietly dropping its previously stated goal of moving Iran toward a constitutional monarchy.[54]

U.S. policymakers also downplayed the significance of growing opposition to the shah's program. Islamic clerics resented provisions in the land reform legislation that affected the property of religious foundations, and objected to proposals that women be allowed to vote or enter political campaigns. When the influential Ayatollah Ruhollah Khomeini spoke out against the shah's dictatorship and condemned U.S. influence in Iran from the main madrasa in the city of Qom, Iranian paratroopers and SAVAK operatives attacked the school, killing students, arresting the cleric, and triggering widespread protests. As massive antigovernment demonstrations and riots spread to Tehran and other cities in the early summer of 1963, the shah ordered his troops to shoot to kill, taking the lives of hundreds, perhaps thousands of demonstrators. U.S. convictions that the shah had finally embraced a modernizing agenda, however, led the United States to disregard this growing wave of dissent. Reading his U.S. audience well, the shah described his opponents as "black reactionaries," intransigent obstacles in the path toward Iranian modernity. Many U.S. officials accepted that perspective. In an accommodating, supportive letter, Kennedy told the shah that he shared "the regret you must feel over the loss of life connected with the recent unfortunate attempts to block your reform programs." The president expressed his confidence, however, "that such manifestations will gradually disappear as your people realize the importance of the measures you are taking to establish social justice and equal opportunity for all Iranians."[55]

Although some U.S. experts still dissented, modernization under the shah's authority was increasingly perceived as an ideal means to ensure the goal of Iranian security. As the historian James Goode put it, by 1963 "the White Revolution had coopted the New Frontier." With the United States now fully behind him and calls for political liberalization long discarded, the shah put forward his own authoritarian vision of development. In addition to securing uncritical U.S. support, the shah expected that land reform, the central element of his program, would accomplish several domestic objectives. It would weaken the power of the landholding and clerical classes that dominated the Majlis, securing the shah greater personal control. It would undercut the appeal of the Left and the National Front, appropriating their calls for socioeconomic change. By distributing land to peasants, it would also solidify a new alliance between the monarchy and the Iranian masses, creating a populist base of support. Where liberals and radicals like Amini and Arsanjani imagined a process that would curtail or even eliminate the sphere of royal authority in favor of a genuinely democratic transition, the shah cast himself as a "modernizing monarch" and defined a process that could unfold only through his own benevolent authority and control. The White Revolution, in his terms, was framed as the "Shah-People Revolution," a platform that stressed the maintenance of social order and rejected all political opposition as illegitimate. "We have been able to achieve all these outstanding successes," the shah insisted, "because traitors, subversives and demagogues have been kept out of affairs." Standing between the traditionalist forces of "black reaction" and the Communist proponents of "red subversion," the shah declared that only he could lead Iran into modernity, accelerating a universal transformation that took other nations hundreds of years.[56]

The shah's authoritarian development program unfolded in ways that expanded state control far more than it empowered Iran's peasant and working classes. Through the White Revolution, the shah intended to replace the power of landlords with the power of the state, consolidating his royal dictatorship and preventing the emergence of affluent rivals. Absentee landlords dominated the countryside, often owning entire villages through which they provided the government with military recruits, taxes, and food supplies, all drawn from the peasantry. With 55 percent of farmland owned by 1 percent of the population, landlords also controlled rural politics, wielding vast influence in voting for the Majlis. Radicals like Arsanjani hoped that breaking up large estates and turning sharecroppers into landowners would create a new, independent class that would play a leading role in shaping village life. Drawn together through membership in local cooperatives, small farmers would gain independent access to credit, and as their productivity rose they would form new political associations that would allow them to run their own schools, improve health care, and elect their own representatives. The shah, however, wanted nothing less than total, undivided authority. After forcing Arsanjani to resign in March 1963, he redirected the function of the cooperatives, requiring their members to join the shah's ruling Iran Novin or "New Iran" political party. Government officials claimed the power to appoint the committee members of local cooperatives, and the shah's literacy corps, health corps, and extension services sent thousands of military-trained high school graduates into villages to complete eighteen-month terms of service. These urban arrivals knew little about farming or agrarian society, but their presence was intended to secure state power in rural areas. Alongside them, SAVAK also deployed agents in remote towns, all contributing to a sharp increase in the state's capabilities for surveillance and social control.[57]

While the power of large landowners was replaced by greater central authority, the shah's reform program did little to improve rural life. Through the 1960s, the Iranian government steadily throttled back the speed and scale of land redistribution. By the early 1970s, convinced of the need to raise agricultural productivity through mechanization and hoping to further state control, the shah also began to promote corporate farms, forcing peasants to surrender their newly received land in exchange for shares of collective profit. In other cases, the government pressured peasants to sell their plots, evicted those that refused, and bulldozed entire villages before leasing large landholdings to Iranian and multinational agribusinesses.[58]

By the mid-1970s, the White Revolution contributed to growing social and political instability. While landlord control was indeed weakened, most peasants who received land were left with allotments far too small to support their families, and rural wage laborers often received no land at all. Chronically underfunded, government-managed cooperatives provided little credit, and hundreds of thousands of villagers found that the shah's agrarian reforms had deepened their poverty. Moving into overcrowded, polluted slums in Tehran and other major cities, they sought low-paying, unskilled work in construction and manufacturing, or survived as servants, porters, and street vendors. By the eve of the Islamic Revolution, millions of alienated migrant workers also began to play significant roles in the growing political opposition to the shah, organizing the poor for demonstrations in slum areas and spreading revolutionary ideology back to their former villages in the countryside. In trying to break the authority of powerful landlords and simultaneously prevent the rise of a politically independent peasant class, the shah helped create the conditions for his eventual overthrow.[59]

Following the Kennedy period, the Johnson, Nixon, Ford, and Carter administrations all lined up in support of Iran's authoritarian regime. Preoccupied with Vietnam and glad to have Iran's endorsement there, Johnson praised the shah for "the heartening economic and social progress Iran has made under your leadership." U.S. ambassador Armin Meyer described Iran as a "show-case of modernization in this part of the world," and Walt Rostow, now Johnson's national security adviser, suggested the country was "at that point on the development ladder where the 'take off' is just about finished."[60]

A longtime admirer of the shah, Nixon defined Iranian power in the Persian Gulf as "the key pillar of support for American interests in an increasingly important part of the world." He also offered Iran a virtually unlimited opportunity to purchase conventional arms and aircraft from the United States and stood by as the shah built an increasingly repressive security apparatus. By 1977 SAVAK employed more than five thousand full-time agents and a much larger number of part-time informers. Speaking in 1975, the secretary-general of Amnesty International concluded that "no country in the world has a worse record of human rights than Iran."[61]

By the time Jimmy Carter took office in 1977, the failures of the White Revolution were hard to miss. Although the shah had built the fifth largest military in the world, Iran's health care system was among the worst in the Middle East. Nearly 70 percent of the population remained illiterate, 96 percent of those living in rural areas lacked electricity, and agricultural productivity had fallen behind population growth. Swelling with rural migrants, 42 percent of Tehran's population lacked adequate housing, and many lived without a functioning sewage system or public transportation. The shah's continued denunciation of Islamic leaders as "reactionary," his extension of the power of secular courts over religious ones, and his deployment of a government "religious corps" into the countryside stimulated strong clerical opposition. Alarmed by the rapid influx into the cities and the resulting social problems, including alcoholism, drug use, crime, and prostitution, Islamic clerics condemned the state for policies that, in their view, led to moral failings. The most radical among them demanded not a constitutional monarchy, as the National Front had once hoped to achieve, but instead a political revolution and the creation of a clergy-led government under Islamic law.[62]

Although Jimmy Carter urged the shah to embrace political reforms in November of 1977, he did little to alter the long-standing pattern of firm U.S. support and watched in frustration as the Iranian regime collapsed in late 1978. By that point the shah's repression had thrown a diverse range of groups together, bringing large landowners, the Left, the remnants of the National Front, students, workers, and Islamist activists into combined opposition. Although State Department reports noted unmet "rising expectations," and White House officials warned of growing clerical opposition, most U.S. advisers still worried more about the possibility of Soviet-sponsored subversion than Islamist radicalism. The ideology of political Islam, of course, predated the Cold War and was not merely a reaction to the shah's repression. Attempts to overhaul the economic and social life of the region also drew inspiration from the periods of British and even Ottoman domination. But the shah's policies provided fertile ground for his radical opponents. Still working within a Cold War framework, his U.S. supporters ignored the possibility that modernization could trigger revolutions in which supposedly irrational and traditional forces, thought to have been swept aside by the acceleration of history, might return to seize power.[63]

Toward a Crossroads

In Guatemala, Vietnam, and Iran, U.S. policymakers pursued remarkably similar approaches. After intervening in the 1950s to prevent nationalist and revolutionary forces from taking power, the United States backed repressive dictatorships. When political and economic crises emerged in the early 1960s, U.S. policymakers turned to strategies of modernization, expecting to alleviate the underlying structural conditions that gave rise to insurgencies and radical opposition. Police training programs and deliveries of military equipment were presented as tools for the defense of democracy, but in each country U.S. policymakers abandoned any commitment to political liberalization, choosing instead to back governments that devastated their own populations in the name of development.[64]

U.S. officials anticipated that these approaches would satisfy immediate economic and security goals. As in Indonesia, another important case in which the United States backed a brutally repressive form of modernization, policymakers aimed to ensure containment, keep markets open, and promote the flow of strategic resources into U.S. and allied hands. The concept of modernization provided dictatorial regimes with a powerful narrative, useful for defending their legitimacy, seeking external support, and crushing opposition. Yet the lasting results were uniformly tragic as authoritarian policies of modernization empowered governments that destroyed democratic institutions and contributed to cultures of corruption and rampant violence, deepening problems that endured in many societies long after the Cold War ended.[65]

The stunning failures in Vietnam and Iran, moreover, also helped stimulate a broader intellectual and political debate over modernization through the 1970s. As both a social scientific theory and an option for government policy, modernization became the focus of searing criticism. Where its liberal defenders had described modernization as a way to comprehend the course of universal social change, promote development, and ensure security, critics on both the left and the right would attack its intellectual fallacies as well as its longer-run effects. The result would be a dramatic reorientation in thinking and policy.

NOTES

1. Walt W. Rostow, "Countering Guerrilla Attack," in *Modern Guerrilla Warfare: Fighting Communist Guerrilla Movements, 1941–1961*, ed. Franklin Mark Osanka (New York: Free Press, 1962), 465–66.

2. Stephen G. Rabe, *Eisenhower and Latin America: The Foreign Policy of Anticommunism* (Chapel Hill: University of North Carolina Press, 1988), 74–75.

3. Ibid., 75, 86–87.

4. Memorandum, Schlesinger to Kennedy, March 10, 1961, *FRUS 1961–1963*, 12: 11; Task Force Report, January 4, 1961, Teodoro Moscoso Papers, box 9, "Report of the Task Force on Immediate Latin American Problems, Winter, 1960," John F. Kennedy Library [hereafter JFKL]. For a broader treatment of the Alliance for Progress, see Latham, *Modernization as Ideology,* 69–108.

5. John F. Kennedy, *Public Papers of the President* (Washington, DC: U.S. Government Printing Office, 1962), 1: 172; Stephen G. Rabe, *The Most Dangerous Area in the World: John F. Kennedy Confronts Communist Revolution in Latin America* (Chapel Hill: University of North Carolina Press, 1999), 2.

6. Rabe, *Most Dangerous Area,* 10; U.S. Congress, House, Committee on Foreign Affairs, *Regional and Other Documents concerning United States Relations with Latin America* (Washington, DC: U.S. Government Printing Office, 1962), 101–3.

7. Stephen M. Streeter, "Nation-Building in the Land of Eternal Counterinsurgency: Guatemala and the Contradictions of the Alliance for Progress," *Third World Quarterly* 27, no. 1 (2006): 57–68.

8. James F. Siekmeier, "'The Most Generous Assistance': U.S. Economic Aid to Guatemala and Bolivia, 1944–1959," *Journal of American and Canadian Studies* 11 (1993): 7; Stephen M. Streeter, *Managing the Counterrevolution: The United States and Guatemala, 1954–1961* (Athens, OH: Ohio University Center for International Studies, 2000), 17–19; Walter LaFeber, *Inevitable Revolutions: The United States in Central America* (New York: Norton, 1984), 115–16.

9. Streeter, *Managing the Counterrevolution,* 19–23.

10. Stephen M. Streeter, "The Failure of 'Liberal Developmentalism': The United States's Anti-Communist Showcase in Guatemala, 1954–1960," *International History Review* 21, no. 2 (1999): 386–413.

11. Streeter, *Managing the Counterrevolution,* 38–41, 91–93, 103–7.

12. Rachel A. May, *Terror in the Countryside: Campesino Responses to Political Violence in Guatemala, 1954–1985* (Athens, OH: Ohio University Center for International Studies, 2001), 52–56.

13. Rabe, *Most Dangerous Area,* 72–3; Streeter, *Managing the Counterrevolution,* 406.

14. Jim Handy, *Gift of the Devil: A History of Guatemala* (Boston: South End Press, 1984), 205–11.

15. Handy, *Gift of the Devil,* 213; Streeter, "Nation-Building," 61.

16. Streeter, "Nation-Building," 61–62; Susan Fitzpatrick Behrens, "From Symbols of the Sacred to Symbols of Subversion to Simply Obscure: Maryknoll Women Religious in Guatemala, 1953–1967," *The Americas* 61, no. 2 (2004): 207–10.

17. Behrens, "Symbols of the Sacred," 210–16; Arturo Arias, "Changing Indian Identity: Guatemala's Violent Transition to Modernity," in *Guatemalan Indians and the State, 1540–1988,* ed. Carol A. Smith (Austin: University of Texas Press), 233–34, 247–48.

18. Edward Shils, "The Military in the Political Development of the New States," in *The Role of the Military in Underdeveloped Countries,* ed. John J. Johnson (Princeton, NJ: Princeton University Press, 1962), 17, 23, 33; Memorandum, State Department Bureau of Intelligence and Research, January 19, 1962, *FRUS 1961–1963,* 12: 90.

19. Rabe, *Most Dangerous Area,* 76–77; Michael McClintock, *The American Connection,* vol. 2, *State Terror and Popular Resistance in Guatemala* (London: Zed, 1985), 53–57.

20. McClintock, *American Connection,* 67–68, 78–91.

21. Memorandum, Thomas L. Hughes to Dean Rusk, October 23, 1967, National Security Archive, George Washington University, http://www.gwu.edu/~nsarchiv/NSAEBB/NSAEBB11/docs/.

22. "Where Reds May Take Over Next in Latin America," *U.S. News and World Report,* March 18, 1963, 50; Charles D. Brockett, *Political Movements and Violence in Central America* (Cambridge: Cambridge University Press, 2005), 3–4.

23. Wesley R. Fishel, "Problems of Democratic Growth in Free Vietnam," in *Problems of Freedom: South Vietnam since Independence,* ed. Wesley R. Fishel (New York: Free Press, 1961), 9–28.

24. For a broader treatment of this argument, see Latham, *Modernization as Ideology,* 151–207.

25. Mark Philip Bradley, *Imagining Vietnam and America: The Making of Postcolonial Vietnam, 1919–1950* (Chapel Hill: University of North Carolina Press, 2000), 47; Robert D. Schulzinger, *A Time for War: The United States and Vietnam, 1941–1975* (New York: Oxford University Press, 1997), 87.

26. James S. Olson and Randy Roberts, *Where the Domino Fell: America and Vietnam, 1945–1990* (New York: St. Martin's Press, 1991), 87; George C. Herring, *America's Longest War: The United States and Vietnam, 1950–1975,* 3rd ed. (New York: McGraw-Hill, 1996), 62; James P. Harrison, *The Endless War: Vietnam's Struggle for Independence* (New York: Columbia University Press, 1989), 183–84; Nancy Wiegersma, *Vietnam: Peasant Land, Peasant Revolution* (New York: St. Martin's Press, 1988), 116, 180–83, 202–3.

27. Memorandum, Lansdale to McNamara, January 17, 1961, Lansdale Papers, box 42, "Memoranda, 1950–1961," Hoover Institution Archives [hereafter HIA]; Olson and Roberts, *Where the Domino Fell,* 87.

28. Pye, *Guerrilla Communism,* 7, 201–2.

29. Rostow, *Diffusion of Power,* 273–74; Memorandum, Sterling Cottrell to National Security Council, May 9, 1961, National Security Files, box 330, "NSAM 52, Vietnam," JFKL.

30. Bernard Fall, *The Two Viet-Nams: A Political and Military Analysis* (New York: Praeger, 1963), 373.

31. Roger Hilsman, "A Strategic Concept for South Vietnam," February 2, 1962, Hilsman Papers, box 3, Vietnam, "Strategic Concept," JFKL; Robert Thompson, *Defeating Communist Insurgency: Experiences from Malaya and Vietnam* (London: Chatto and Windus, 1966), 123–24.

32. William A. Nighswonger, *Rural Pacification in Vietnam* (New York: Praeger, 1966), 99–100; John C. Donnell and Gerald C. Hickey, *The Vietnamese "Strategic Hamlets": A Preliminary Report, Memorandum RM-3208-ARPA* (Santa Monica: Rand Corporation, 1962).

33. Hilsman, "Strategic Concept."

34. Philip E. Catton, "Parallel Agendas: The Ngo Dinh Diem Regime, the United States, and the Strategic Hamlet Program, 1961–1963" (PhD diss., Ohio University, 1998), 78, 153.

35. Fall, *Two Viet-Nams,* 376–79; Memorandum, Sterling Cottrell to Special Group for Counterinsurgency, March 22, 1962, National Security Files, box 319, "Special Group (Ci), 1/61–6/62," JFKL.

36. Fall, *Two Viet-Nams,* 378; U.S. Information Service, Long An Province Survey, January 1964, Lansdale Papers, box 23, "Pacification and Land Reform/General, 1964–1969," HIA.

37. Jeffrey Race, *War Comes to Long An: Revolutionary Conflict in a Vietnamese Province* (Berkeley: University of California Press, 1972), ix-x.

38. Harrison, *Endless War,* 236–39; Christopher T. Fisher, "The Illusion of Progress: CORDS and the Crisis of Modernization in South Vietnam, 1965–1968," *Pacific Historical Review* 75, no. 1 (2006): 39–43.

39. James M. Carter, *Inventing Vietnam: The United States and State Building, 1954–1968* (Cambridge: Cambridge University Press, 2008), 210–11.

40. Stephen Kinzer, *All the Shah's Men: An American Coup and the Roots of Middle East Terror* (Hoboken, NJ: Wiley, 2003), 67.

41. Malcolm Byrne, "The Road to Intervention: Factors Influencing U.S. Policy toward Iran, 1945–1953," in *Mohammad Mossadeq and the 1953 Coup in Iran,* ed. Mark J. Gasiorowski and Malcolm Byrne, (Syracuse, NY: Syracuse University Press, 2004), 214.

42. Nikki R. Keddie, *Roots of Revolution: An Interpretive History of Modern Iran* (New Haven, CT: Yale University Press, 1981), 147; Ervand Abrahamian, *Iran: Between Two Revolutions* (Princeton, NJ: Princeton University Press, 1982), 419–21; Mark J. Gasiorowski, *U.S. Foreign Policy and the Shah: Building a Client State in Iran* (Ithaca, NY: Cornell University Press, 1991), 86–89.

43. Keddie, *Roots of Revolution,* 148–49; Abrahamian, *Iran,* 419–20; Gasiorowski, *U.S. Foreign Policy and the Shah,* 104–5.

44. Abrahamian, *Iran,* 419–20; Gasiorowski, *U.S. Foreign Policy and the Shah,* 104–5.

45. Keddie, *Roots of Revolution,* 150–53; Gholam Reza Afkhami, *The Life and Times of the Shah* (Berkeley: University of California Press, 2009), 211–12.

46. Gasiorowski, *U.S. Foreign Policy and the Shah*, 96–97; Little, *American Orientalism*, 218–19.

47. James F. Goode, *The United States and Iran: In the Shadow of Musaddiq* (New York: St. Martin's Press, 1997), 169–71.

48. Ibid., 171–75; Roland Popp, "Benign Intervention? The Kennedy Administration's Push for Reform in Iran," in *John F. Kennedy and the "Thousand Days*," ed. Manfred Berg and Andreas Etges (Heidelberg: Universitätsverlag Winter, 2007), 204–8.

49. Abrahamian, *Iran*, 422–23; Goode, *United States and Iran*, 172–73; Popp, "Benign Intervention?" 206–7.

50. Abrahamian, *Iran*, 423–24; Keddie, *Roots of Revolution*, 153–54.

51. Popp, "Benign Intervention?" 211–12; Memorandum of Conversation, Kennedy and Shah of Iran, *FRUS 1961–1963*, 17: 607–8.

52. James A. Bill, *The Eagle and the Lion: The Tragedy of American-Iranian Relations* (New Haven, CT: Yale University Press, 1988), 148; Afkhami, *Life and Times of the Shah*, 228–29.

53. Memorandum, William Brubeck to McGeorge Bundy, January 21, 1963, *FRUS 1961–1963*, 18: 311–14; Popp, "Benign Intervention?" 214–15; Goode, *United States and Iran*, 178–79.

54. Popp, "Benign Intervention?" 215.

55. Goode, *United States and Iran*, 179–80.

56. Ibid., 179; Ali M. Ansari, "The Myth of the White Revolution: Mohammad Reza Shah, 'Modernization' and the Consolidation of Power," *Middle Eastern Studies* 37, no. 3 (2001): 14. For an alternative view, see Roland Popp, "An Application of Modernization Theory during the Cold War? The Case of Pahlavi Iran," *International History Review* 30, no. 1 (2008): 76–98.

57. Ali Farazmand, *The State, Bureaucracy, and Revolution in Modern Iran: Agrarian Reforms and Regime Politics* (New York: Praeger, 1989), 67–69, 103, 111–25.

58. Ibid., 128–34; Eric J. Hooglund, *Land and Revolution in Iran, 1960–1980* (Austin: University of Texas Press, 1982), 60–87.

59. Hooglund, *Land and Revolution in Iran*, 93–97, 111–20, 148; Farazmand, *State, Bureaucracy, and Revolution*, 154–55.

60. Little, *American Orientalism*, 221; Memorandum of Conversation, W. W. Rostow and Mehdi Samii, June 13, 1968, *FRUS 1964–1968*, 22: 530; Bill, *Eagle and the Lion*, 178; Goode, *United States and Iran*, 183.

61. Abrahamian, *Iran*, 435–39; Fred Halliday, *Iran: Dictatorship and Development*, 2nd ed. (New York: Penguin, 1979), 85; Goode, *United States and Iran*, 184–85; Little, *American Orientalism*, 221–22.

62. Abrahamian, *Iran*, 444–48, 473–76.

63. Barry Rubin, *Paved with Good Intentions: The American Experience in Iran* (New York: Oxford University Press, 1980), 148–49; Westad, *Global Cold War*, 293–94; Nathan J. Citino, "The Ottoman Legacy in Cold War Modernization," *International Journal of Middle East Studies* 40 (November 2008): 579–97.

64. Jeremy Kuzmarov, "Modernizing Repression: Police Training, Political Violence, and Nation-Building in the 'American Century,'" *Diplomatic History* 33 (April 2009): 191–221.

65. Bradley R. Simpson, *Economists with Guns: Authoritarian Development and U.S.-Indonesian Relations, 1960–1968* (Stanford, CA: Stanford University Press, 2008), 4.

MODERNIZATION UNDER FIRE

Alternative Paradigms, Sustainable Development, and the Neoliberal Turn

Modernization, as a social theory and a political ideology, was at the peak of its power in the early and mid-1960s. It integrated research across social scientific disciplines, shaped the direction of U.S. efforts to promote the development of the postcolonial world, and fired the imagination of liberals. Yet over the next fifteen years the concept was largely discredited in academic and public life, challenged on the left by arguments about the devastating effects of international capitalism, and on the right by a rising neoliberal chorus condemning attempts at social engineering and proclaiming the virtue of free markets. The editors of one prominent journal reflected that in its heyday modernization embodied a spirit of tremendous optimism and enthusiasm. It was a grand project to create a "truly interdisciplinary and universal social science" that could help promote "economic growth and political development around the world." But by the mid-1970s its weaknesses were "blindingly apparent," and its aspirations seemed "tinged, or maybe poisoned, with American imperialism [and] Western ethnocentrism."[1]

How was it that a concept with such great intellectual and political appeal was so quickly disavowed and repudiated? What led many social scientists, government policymakers, and influential opinion leaders in the United States to reject modernization in favor of competing paradigms of social change, development, and foreign policy? First, modernization was seriously damaged by the broader crisis of liberalism in the late 1960s and early 1970s. A liberal ideal, modernization was grounded in the faith that government elites and experts, armed with the proper knowledge and rational techniques, could catalyze progressive change at home and abroad. By placing the United States at the apex of a single, universal scale of achievement, it also described a society that had discovered the optimum path toward affluence, liberty, and social justice and was now qualified to chart the way for an "emerging" world. Those assumptions, however, were severely challenged during the late 1960s and early 1970s as the United States' own domestic failings—persistent poverty, continued racial injustice, urban violence, and gender-based discrimination—became glaringly evident. The war in Vietnam, finally, shattered liberal claims about the promotion of democracy, development, and freedom. In that context, criticisms of modernization from within and outside of the paradigm gained new weight. As liberalism came under fire, the political and cultural foundations on which modernization stood were also seriously damaged.[2]

Second, conservative, or "neoliberal," arguments about the virtues of market capitalism ultimately triumphed in the late 1970s and early 1980s. This, ironically, was largely due to the fact that they provided an optimistic, confident vision much like that of modernization itself. Modernization, above all, had framed a compelling *narrative*, an integrated plotline of rapid, universal, linear advance promising nothing less than an *acceleration* of history. International development programs of the 1960s, however, failed to meet expectations, and by the mid-1970s the field was profoundly divided by several competing models. Postcolonial nations lamented declining terms of trade, World Bank experts called for a focus on basic needs, and other critics advocated policies of "sustainable development." Given the intractable problems of inequality, poverty, and environmental degradation, liberal experts now described development as a potentially *infinite* struggle, and one that had achieved far less than it had originally promised. When global economic crises emerged in the 1970s, the more diffuse, fragmented vision of development also proved vulnerable to a powerful challenge from the right. With modernization discredited and no single, overriding narrative of progress to replace it, neoliberals took the field with their own promises of accelerated, benevolent change. They also insisted that their methods would be more essentially natural, rejecting "social engineering" and replacing the liberal, visible hand of the modernizer with the classical, invisible hand of the market. Above all, neoliberals provided the kind of appealing, reassuring answers that modernizers once did. Like modernizers, they defined development as something that could be achieved quickly and comparatively cheaply, driving the world down a common, historical path toward a single, utopian end point. Neoliberalism, in other words, prevailed precisely because it revived a vision of the global mission of the United States and made the same kind of transformative claims that modernization had.

Modernization and the Crisis of Liberalism

Between the mid-1960s and the mid-1970s, political and cultural life in the United States underwent a dramatic sea change. Liberalism, as Allen Matusow aptly put it, came "unraveled." There are many ways in which that phenomenon can be illustrated, but perhaps one of the most dramatic moments took place on April 4, 1967. On that evening, Martin Luther King, Jr., delivered a searing attack on the Vietnam War from the pulpit of New York City's massive Riverside Church. While his advisers had warned him that speaking out against the war would alienate Lyndon Johnson and might jeopardize liberal support for further advances in civil rights, King argued that the war was irreconcilable with the black freedom struggle and, more deeply, with the nation's fundamental principles. The president's Great Society programs, he declared, had once offered "a real promise of hope for the poor," but Vietnam drew vital resources away from the cause of social justice at home and sent young black men "8,000 miles away to guarantee liberties in Southeast Asia which they had not found in Southwest Georgia or East Harlem." The war also created a hell for the peasants of Vietnam, King reflected: "[They watch] as we poison their water, as we kill a million acres of their crops.... They wander into the hospitals, with at least 20 casualties from American firepower for one Vietcong-inflicted injury. They wander into the towns and see thousands of children, homeless, without clothes, running in packs on the streets like animals." It would be impossible, King concluded, to "raise my voice against the violence of the oppressed in the ghettos without having first spoken clearly to the greatest purveyor of violence in the world today—my own government."[3]

In King's powerful dissent, the failures of domestic and foreign policy were clearly linked. Together, they were evidence of the crisis of liberalism and a symptom of a deep, pervasive sickness afflicting a society that had lost its way. As Cold War liberals, the proponents of modernization held fast to two essential beliefs. First, they were confident that an activist state, using the best tools of social scientific management, could generate sustained economic growth and solve the few remaining problems facing American society. Second, they envisioned the United States as standing at the leading edge of history's evolutionary course and identified it as a uniquely benevolent global force. Although not yet perfect, they believed that the nation's democratic institutions, its thriving capitalist economy, and its moderate provisions for social welfare represented the best of all possible worlds and a model for all societies. Between the late 1960s and the early 1970s, many concluded that both of those basic assumptions were clearly false. The United States' liberal establishment, it appeared, had neither the capacity nor the will to solve problems that were, in fact, severe and structural, not minor or

cosmetic. Beset with increasing evidence of domestic crises, its claims to enlightened world leadership were also betrayed by a long, brutal, and devastating war
in Southeast Asia.

Since the 1950s, policymakers had recognized that the persistence of racial
discrimination in the United States was a severe liability in the Cold War struggle, particularly among the postcolonial world's people of color. They also tried
to put the most positive spin possible on growing evidence of popular anger
and continued injustice. As the title of a U.S. exhibit at the 1958 World's Fair defined it, segregation was an example of the "Unfinished Business" of the United
States, one of the remaining flaws that would soon be addressed and eliminated.
In a similar sense, the U.S. Information Agency described the 1963 March on
Washington as an example of the vitality of American democracy, and Lyndon
Johnson heralded the Voting Rights Act of 1965 as a "triumph for freedom as
huge as any victory that has ever been won on any battlefield."[4]

Over the next several years, however, such claims were decidedly undercut by
the fact that liberal measures designed to ensure advances in formal, legal equality did little to address the realities of continued black poverty and unemployment. Liberal solutions successfully confronted the obvious and internationally
embarrassing problems of racial segregation, but they failed to grapple with the
deeper structural forces that connected race and class. Between 1965 and 1968, as
Watts, Detroit, Newark, Washington, and Cincinnati exploded in violence fueled
by persistent racial injustice, those problems became harder to rationalize away.
They also cast serious doubt on assertions that the United States was a global
model. As the mayor of Detroit commented after rioting over fourteen square
miles resulted in forty-three deaths, seven thousand arrests, and the destruction of 1,300 buildings, his city looked more like "Berlin in 1945" than a center
of urban modernity. The rise of radical nationalist movements among African
Americans, Latinos, and Native Americans rejecting the promise of assimilation
and integration also exposed the limits of liberal politics.[5]

Liberal attempts to win what Lyndon Johnson called an "unconditional war on
poverty" also produced mixed, often disappointing results. Buoyed by twenty years
of strong economic growth, declining unemployment, and low inflation, Johnson
and his planners expected that the tools of Keynesian fiscal policy would enable
them to spread U.S. affluence more widely. The key, they believed, would be to
improve the productivity of the poor to enable them to partake more fully in the
ever-increasing size of the U.S. economy. Investments in job training, education,
community action programs, and better access to health care were all expected to
produce rapid improvements. As Johnson told an aide in 1964, "I'm sick of all the
people who talk about the things we can't do. Hell, we're the richest country in the
world, the most powerful. We can do it all.... We can do it if we believe it."[6]

Yet the liberal definition of poverty in absolute terms of annual income, instead of relative terms of socioeconomic inequality, resulted in a program that failed to meet such high expectations. As federal spending on poverty rose to more than $27 billion over six years, the percentage of people in the United States living below the official "poverty line" declined from twenty to twelve. But many programs proved inefficient and incapable of assisting those they were intended to benefit. Funds targeted for the education of poor children were spent by local school boards on general overhead, medical price inflation wiped out resources expected to improve health care for the impoverished, training programs prepared candidates for entry-level positions for which there was already a surplus of job seekers, and community action programs were gutted by municipal officials determined to ensure their own control of federal funding. By design, there was also little real redistribution of wealth in a society of starkly evident and steadily increasing inequality.[7]

Even among many of the comparatively affluent, the nation's culture and society also came to appear less enlightened, progressive, and exemplary than stifling, confining, and oppressive. In her landmark book of 1963, *The Feminine Mystique*, Betty Friedan described the "problem that has no name," the gnawing frustration and depression faced by educated, skilled women who, after marriage, were expected to find personal satisfaction in a narrow sphere of suburban consumption, homemaking, and child rearing. The denial of their creative and intellectual potential, Friedan argued, left them trapped in "comfortable concentration camps," a jarring phrase that, as historian Howard Brick observed, cast U.S. modernity in the language of the Holocaust. On university campuses in the United States, affluent students also condemned a bureaucratic, alienating educational system that produced technocratic "organization men" instead of offering a vibrant setting for free, critical inquiry. Like Mario Savio, the hero of the University of California's Free Speech Movement, they concluded that the "operations of the machine" had become so oppressive that they had no choice but to put their "bodies upon the gears and upon the wheels, upon the levers, upon all the apparatus...to make it stop." For many of them, moreover, that meant rejecting liberal leadership and turning toward a radical politics of direct confrontation.[8]

Above all, however, it was the war in Vietnam that galvanized a broad rejection of the liberal and modernizing claims of the superiority and global benevolence of the United States. Through 1968, growing evidence of Saigon's dictatorial repression, the escalating U.S. and Vietnamese death tolls, and the increasing burdens of the military draft all enervated the Johnson administration's defense of a war to secure South Vietnamese freedom from totalitarianism. Radicals in the United States, of course, were quick to link the war to a broader indictment of U.S.

society. Paul Potter, president of Students for a Democratic Society, famously asked in 1965: "What kind of system is it that justifies the United States or any country seizing the destinies of the Vietnamese people and using them callously for its own purpose?" It was the same "system," he argued, that "disenfranchises people in the South," "leaves millions upon millions of people throughout the country impoverished," "creates faceless and terrible bureaucracies," "puts material values before human values—and still persists in calling itself free." Within two years, Martin Luther King's sermon at the Riverside Church made a similar, sweeping indictment, demonstrating the extent to which the failures of liberalism were increasingly part of a broader, widely shared critical discourse.[9]

The war's costs also helped dash expectations that the powerful engines of U.S. economic growth would continue to expand the horizons of liberal and modernizing capabilities at home and abroad. By early 1968, federal spending drove inflation up, worsened a serious balance of payments deficit, and led to a run on the nation's gold supplies. In 1971, as the United States ran a trade deficit for the first time since the 1890s, the Nixon administration abolished the convertibility of the dollar into gold, ending the Bretton Woods system that had made U.S. currency the benchmark for the rest of the world in the postwar period. The Arab oil embargo of 1973 also undermined the U.S. economy, compounding double-digit inflation and pushing the country into a painful recession.[10]

The optimistic assessments of a forthcoming American Century, so boldly recapitulated in the assumptions of modernization theorists, depended on the ability of the liberal state to continue to deliver the kind of prosperity that had characterized the first two decades of the postwar period. When those expectations for a constantly growing economy and an increasingly affluent society collapsed, many of those international ambitions did as well. The United States, Richard Nixon declared in 1969, would assist in the "defense and development of allies and friends," but it "cannot—and will not—conceive of all the plans, design all the programs, execute all the decisions and undertake all the defense of the free nations of the world."[11]

Challenging the Paradigm

As modernization's liberal foundations were challenged, social scientists also began a critical reassessment of the theory's core assumptions and arguments. At first, this process moved forward among scholars working within the modernization paradigm, carefully testing and assessing its specific principles across different regions and cases. Over time, however, internal criticisms gave way to more radical, alternative formulations. Many critics, examining the relationship between the production of knowledge and the imperatives of the national security state, attacked modernization's claims to scientific objectivity and rigor. Rather than an empirical theory of universal social change, they found modernization to be a Cold War product legitimating a resurgent U.S. imperialism. Others, stressing the historical impact of international capitalism, finally went on to build rival social theories based on concepts of dependency and world systems.

One of the most striking lines of criticism to emerge in the 1960s dealt with modernization's most basic assumption, the idea of discrete traditional and modern conditions, and their position as opposite poles on a single historical scale. The sociologist Joseph Gusfield pointed out that theorists assumed that "existing institutions and values, the content of tradition, are impediments to changes and are obstacles to modernization." Such perceptions, however, rested on a vision of traditional worlds as necessarily static when, in fact, they were long open to change even before the arrival of Western institutions. Older traditions, moreover, were not necessarily replaced by new ones. In fact, traditional structures often provided "sources of legitimation which are capable of being utilized in the pursuit of new goals and with new processes." Drawing on the pathbreaking work of Indian scholars M. N. Srinivas and Rajni Kothari, Gusfield and his colleagues in the United States came to understand tradition and modernity as mutually reinforcing instead of diametrically opposed. After all, Western technologies of printing, radio, and film promoted not only modern knowledge and business practices but also Hindu epics, mythology, and religious literature. Structures of caste, kinship, and village provided the social cohesion, legitimacy, and authority necessary for new, modern political parties to be organized and built. Westernization, moreover, gave birth not only to nationalism, but also to diverse forms of religious revivals, linguistic consciousness, and communal politics. Similar conclusions, drawn from research in countries like Nigeria, Ghana, and Indonesia, steadily led U.S. scholars to conclude that it was time to "reject dichotomous conceptualizations of the nature and process of change in the so-called developing areas."[12]

Other scholars, often from diverse ideological positions, came to criticize modernization's assumptions of linear, directional change. Historical and empirical research, they argued, simply did not support the claim that all societies marched along the same universal path. Even among European nations, economic historian Alexander Gerschenkron contended, countries beginning the process of industrialization at different historical periods and in different conditions of "backwardness" followed different patterns with respect to the scale of enterprises, banking structures, agricultural production, and labor systems.

Theories of uniform stages like Walt Rostow's, Gerschenkron warned, masked "conceptual and empirical deficiencies."[13]

From opposite ends of the political spectrum, radical sociologist C. Wright Mills and conservative political scientist Samuel Huntington also attacked modernization theory's assumption of universal convergence on a common point of consensual equilibrium. In one of the earliest and most devastating critiques, Mills argued that Talcott Parsons's focus on common "value orientations" and moral norms as the forces integrating modern societies eliminated the realities of class conflict and coercion. "To accept his scheme," Mills lamented, "we are required to read out of the picture the facts of power and indeed of all institutional structures, in particular the economic, the political, the military. In this curious 'general theory,' such structures of domination have no place." The social structure that Parsons and other theorists defined as modern, natural, and liberal, Mills argued, was instead based on coercion. Serious expressions of dissent, moreover, were simply cast aside as "pathological" or "maladjusted."[14]

For his part, Huntington doubted that the process of modernization produced any kind of stability at all, liberal or otherwise. Where Mills lamented a dearth of democracy, Huntington condemned it as leading to dangerous instability. "Rapid increases in mobilization and participation, the principal political aspects of modernization," he argued, "undermine political institutions. Rapid modernization, in brief, produces not political development but political decay." Where modernization theorists were ambivalent about democracy, often preferring antipopulist forms of elite politics and issuing apologies for authoritarian regimes, Huntington eagerly defended military dictatorship. The naïve, utopian ambitions of liberal progressives to promote economic growth and political participation, he warned, were equally likely to end in civil wars, ethnic conflict, and revolution. The real test of modernity was the preservation of social order.[15]

Other scholars dismantled the theory of modernization by critically examining the intellectual history of its assumptions and creation. According to historian Robert Nisbet, modernization theory recapitulated much older, nineteenth-century ideas about social evolution. While claiming to be empirical and scientific, it followed in the well-trod footsteps of Comte, Marx, Tocqueville, and Hegel by defining change as directional, continuous, and flowing from uniform causes. Freighted with such a high degree of abstraction, theorists produced a profoundly ahistorical history. Rather than carrying out a rigorous analysis of cause and effect in specific contexts, they simply classified foreign societies in relation to the modern template, plotting evidence of social difference as discrete points along a universal trajectory. The result, Nisbet maintained, was nothing more than "a finely graded, logically continuous series of 'stills' as in a movie film." He explained: "It is the eye—or in this instance, the disposition to believe—that creates the illusion of actual development, growth or change."[16]

Kenyan political scientist Ali Mazrui also identified modernization with a long-standing intellectual tradition. The idea of evolution toward a modernity defined in explicitly Western terms, he argued, revealed an ethnocentrism "which has strong links with older theories of Anglo-Saxon leadership as a central force of a new wave of civilization." Assumptions that the "demonstration effect" of Western contact was necessary to drive supposedly benighted, fatalistic societies out of stasis and into motion simply recapitulated imperial understandings that "human progress was possible because the more backward of the races at least had the ability to imitate."[17]

Most dramatically, modernization was also attacked as part of the broader radical campaign against war-related scholarly research. Social scientists who had enlisted in the service of the Cold War national security state, critics maintained, had abandoned their responsibility for scholarly independence. MIT linguistics professor Noam Chomsky contended that by legitimating the brutal destruction of the Vietnamese peasantry as a benevolent project, and seeking to furnish techniques for the effective manipulation and direction of Vietnamese society, scholars had forfeited the moral responsibility of intellectuals to "seek the truth lying hidden behind the veil of distortion and misrepresentation, ideology, and class interest." By the early 1970s, the accelerated bombing of Vietnam, the invasions of Cambodia and Laos, news of the massacre at My Lai, and the deaths of student protesters at Kent State and Jackson State generated massive resistance to war-related social research, and protests erupted at some of the most prestigious universities in the United States, including Columbia, MIT, Stanford, and Berkeley. Even scholars of modernization who had restricted themselves to largely abstract questions and had no contact with federal support or government policymaking found themselves criticized as having helped produce an ideology that effectively legitimized an immoral war.[18]

The criticism of modernization theory, both in terms of its empirical validity and its ideological effects, ultimately helped pave the way for the rise of alternative, left-leaning frameworks for understanding global change. Among the most influential of these was dependency theory, an argument that inverted most of modernization's central claims. Driven forward by the research of figures like Argentine economist Raúl Prebisch and the North American Marxists Paul Sweezy and Paul Baran, dependency theorists described a historical pattern of unequal capitalist exchanges between the advanced metropolitan "centers" and the exploited "peripheries" of the world. Prebisch's work at the United Nations Economic Commission for Latin America demonstrated that the "terms of trade" between the producers of primary commodities and the producers of manufactured goods had steadily shifted over time. Technological innovations and industrialization allowed Western exporters to make large profits, while "developing" countries trying to maximize their "comparative advantage" in agricultural products and natural resources steadily lost ground. Drawing on Lenin's theories of imperialism, Sweezy and Baran launched a broader, more politically charged attack, rejecting the idea that poorer nations could replicate the experience of advanced ones. Baran claimed that the raw materials and outlets for investment found in the "backward world" had always "represented the indispensable hinterland of the highly developed West." As they extracted material and natural wealth, Europeans and North Americans seized land, crushed local industry, and destroyed any real possibility of self-sufficiency.[19]

Andre Gunder Frank, a German-American living in Chile, popularized those arguments and struck directly at the concept of modernization. Rejecting the idea of sequential stages of development, Frank pointed out that while the world's advanced industrial economies were once "*un*developed," they were never "*under*developed." "Underdevelopment," he explained, was not an original or "traditional" condition deriving from internal economic, political, or cultural factors. Nor was it the bottom rung of a universal ladder toward progress. It was instead a historical product, the result of centuries of capitalist exploitation by European and North American "metropoles" and their allies among local elites. "No country, once underdeveloped," he declared, "ever managed to develop by [Walt] Rostow's stages."[20]

By the early 1970s, sociologist Immanuel Wallerstein built on the dependency critique to formulate a theory based on the idea of a single capitalist "world system." Rather than focusing on economic interactions between particular countries or the classes within them, Wallerstein emphasized the historical evolution of a global division of labor among "core," "peripheral," and "semi-peripheral" regions of the "capitalist world-economy." While core areas were marked by the rise of strong states and the accumulation of capital, skilled labor, and urbanization, peripheral areas provided primary goods at low prices and possessed little technology or capital. The "semiperiphery," finally, was made up of countries that could function as "both exploiter and exploited," seeking investments in the periphery, providing luxury goods for the core's elites, and preventing a unified, anticapitalist revolt. Like dependency theory, world systems approaches rejected assumptions of linear progress through common stages toward a utopian convergence. "Modernization," Wallerstein sarcastically declared in 1979, was a "worthy parable for the times." In the midst of global decolonization, it allowed liberal scholars and policymakers to promise rapid social and economic advance. If "the underdeveloped were clever enough to invent an indigenous version of Calvinism" or "if transistors were placed in remote villages" or "if farsighted elites mobilized benighted masses with the aid of altruistic outsiders," then the postcolonial world would "cross the river Jordan and come into a land flowing with milk and honey." It was now time, Wallerstein proclaimed, "to put away childish things, and look reality in its face."[21]

Poverty, Inequality, and Sustainable Development

While intellectuals attacked the validity of modernization as a social theory, by the early 1970s international development experts pondered its continued relevance as a guide for policy. Since the end of World War II, modernization had provided development professionals with an integrating framework. It had inspired confidence that the industrialized societies of the West possessed both the resources and the technical knowledge to transform the decolonizing world along multiple axes of progress. As national planning, new technologies, and targeted investment increased economic growth, the people of the Third World would develop new attitudes and social practices, stimulating greater productivity and contributing to the rise of democratic institutions. By the early 1970s, however, such expectations appeared wholly unrealistic.

As experts assessed the results of the 1960s, the "Decade of Development" came to look more like the "Decade of Disappointment." Attempts to increase economic growth rates, it turned out, did not make much of a dent in the persistent poverty and growing unemployment of many Latin American, Asian, African, and Middle Eastern nations. Problems surrounding the lack of technical skill, difficulties of systematic planning, cost of debt service, inequalities of international trade, and the determined resistance of oligarchies to reform all diminished expectations. The Alliance for Progress, so boldly launched as a Latin American showcase program in 1961, proved a most illustrative case. Despite the increase in public lending and campaigns for greater private investment, the regional per capita growth rate target of 2.5 percent per year was not met, and sharp inequalities of income remained largely unchanged. Modest gains in trade diversification, increased industrialization, and agricultural productivity were undercut by rising unemployment and marginal progress in agrarian reform. Social indicators in adult literacy, life expectancy, and housing construction also remained well below stated goals. The disillusionment was exacerbated by political reversals. In the first eight years of the Alliance, the region experienced sixteen military coups, destroying hopes for a progressive "middle-class revolution."[22]

A similar pattern unfolded across the global South. At the outset of the 1960s, UN Secretary-General U Thant called for a campaign to help poor nations "compress the stages of growth through which developed countries have passed." Integrated national planning and expanded funding were expected to catalyze a comprehensive advance. Approximately ninety low-income countries managed aggregate economic growth rates close to official targets, but per capita gains were disappointing, and these accomplishments brought little measurable improvement to popular living standards. Advances in health care helped reduce infant mortality and raise life expectancies, but malnutrition, hunger, and unemployment continued to grow. One expert grimly predicted that by the year 2000 much of the world's poor would be "left behind in the drive for modernization and subsist in conditions which will make present urban ghettoes and rural slums look like model settlements."[23]

With modernization's fundamental assumptions cast into question, experts in postcolonial countries, U.S. agencies, multilateral bodies, and nongovernment organizations began to pursue a range of competing approaches. One of the most striking challenges to the dominant model appeared in the call for a New International Economic Order (NIEO). Working through the new United Nations Conference on Trade and Development (UNCTAD), a large group of low-income countries, labeled the G-77, argued that the terms of international trade made development impossible. Forced to sell their primary goods on world markets with unstable prices, they were hurt by the restrictive tariffs and domestic subsidies imposed by affluent nations. Their low export earnings, in turn, limited their access to the capital goods needed to industrialize, locking them into a position of long-term inequality. In response to their protests, in 1974 the UN General Assembly adopted the "Declaration on the Establishment of a New International Economic Order," a manifesto demanding greater aid for developing states, preferential trade concessions, the right to nationalize natural resources, and the regulation of multinational corporations. At subsequent international conferences the G-77 nations sought to establish commodity cartels and gain increased decision-making power in UN and Bretton Woods institutions.[24]

With the United States, West Germany, Britain, Japan, and other leading industrialized nations strongly opposed, the NIEO's proposal for a redistribution of global economic power ultimately produced few results. But prominent development experts in the United States and Britain did begin a fundamental reevaluation of their field's practices. "Why," British economist Dudley Seers asked, "do we confuse development with economic growth?" It was certainly true that the GNP was a "convenient indicator," a quantifiable variable that could be easily plugged into models. But the modernizing assumption that "increases in national income, if they are sufficiently fast, sooner or later lead to the solution of all social and political problems" was simply wrong. Political upheavals and social crises occurred even where per capita incomes were rising, and attempts

to promote economic "take-offs" did not necessarily reduce the poverty and injustice at the root of popular anger. Stressing the value judgments inherent in
the concept of "development," Seers then went on to redefine the term. Instead
of representing a mere synonym for *growth,* he argued that *development* involved
"creating the conditions for the realization of the human personality." Instead of
systematic modernization, genuine development demanded meeting the absolute, basic needs of human beings for food, clothing, and shelter. It required direct, focused, and planned efforts to promote full employment and reduce social
and economic inequality.[25]

During the 1970s, UN agencies also called for a new, "human-centered pattern
of development." The United Nations Economic and Social Council's campaign
for literacy and universal primary education, the World Health Organization's
efforts to promote broader access to medical care, and the Food and Agriculture
Organization's "Campaign Against Hunger" all reflected a new ethos focusing on
equity and the need to reach across socioeconomic barriers. Between 1970 and
1976, the International Labor Organization also sent employment missions to
Colombia, Sri Lanka, Sudan, the Dominican Republic, Iran, and the Philippines,
contending that the best way to alleviate poverty was by diverting an increasing
share of a country's growing income toward programs specifically designed to
improve the skills, credit, and resources of the working poor.[26]

Those arguments and policy changes ultimately made a dramatic impact in
an unlikely place—the World Bank, under the direction of former U.S. Secretary
of Defense Robert McNamara. One of the principal architects of the Vietnam
War, McNamara had long subscribed to the liberal, modernizing vision of the
massive, structural transformation of "traditional" societies. Like modernization
theorists, he had also considered the reduction of poverty less a goal in its own
right than a by-product of aggregate economic growth and industrialization.
After he became the bank president, however, McNamara found himself increasingly persuaded by the new emphasis on inequality and destitution. McNamara's
long-standing concern with international security and stability also led him to
see poor, frustrated populations as a dangerous source of political instability.
On April 4, 1968, as his first official meeting with the bank's senior bureaucrats
ended, Washington erupted into rioting following the murder of Martin Luther
King, Jr. With the United States' own failure to confront poverty and injustice
on full display outside his office windows, the global problem took on added
significance.[27]

Frustrated with the relatively small scale of its programs, McNamara was determined to transform the World Bank into a leading development agency. He
moved aggressively to raise more money from foreign donors around the world,
and by the time he left office in 1981, the bank's lending had increased in real

terms by a factor of five. Persuaded that the bank's traditional projects of power plants, dams, and transportation networks did little to meet the needs of the poor, he also searched for a philosophy on which to base a new series of programs. British expatriate writer Barbara Ward, Harvard economist Hollis Chenery, and Pakistani economist and national planner Mahbub ul Haq helped provide him with one. The population making up the bottom 40 percent of a poor country's income distribution, they argued, was the essential target, and the key was to incorporate programs specifically intended to raise their productivity into overall development planning. As Chenery later explained in the landmark book of 1974 *Redistribution with Growth*, "in the early stages of development income tends to be more concentrated." As new, technologically advanced, higher-productivity sectors took hold in industry and agriculture, they absorbed a large proportion of the total pool of public and private investment. The poor, however, lacked access to land, education, and credit—factors that limited their ability to enter the "organized market economy." As aggregate economic growth continued, their opportunity was also constrained by rapid population increases, which created a surplus of unskilled labor among small farmers, rural artisans, and urban workers. The essential task, therefore, was to redirect public investment to create jobs for the poor, improve their access to education and land, and give them the skills, tools, and resources necessary to participate in the new economy.[28]

In 1972, McNamara made those arguments the basis of the World Bank's new development policy. He declared in his annual address to the bank's international board of governors that "development's most fundamental goal" was not modernization, but instead "ending the inhuman deprivation in hundreds of millions of individual lives throughout the developing world." While he still emphasized security and warned that "a decisive choice [had to] be made between the political costs of reform and the political risks of rebellion," McNamara also framed the problem of social equity as an inescapable moral challenge. Left "beyond the reach of traditional market forces and public services," the poorest 40 percent of the developing world's population were plagued by hunger, malnutrition, illiteracy, and disease. Promoting income growth and job creation for them, he concluded, was the bank's most urgent imperative.[29]

Over the next several years the World Bank became the leader of an international antipoverty campaign. Working in destitute regions of Brazil, Nigeria, Tanzania, and many other countries, the bank targeted populations with per capita incomes that were often well under $100 per year. Planners delivered integrated "packages of inputs," including credit, agricultural extension services, roads, education, and health services. They also set ambitious goals, typically aiming to double small farm incomes within five or six years. In urban areas across Africa, Asia, and Latin America, job creation programs based on small-scale industry and improved access to education, health care, and housing became priorities. "Slum upgrading" projects also went forward as bank planners tried to provide sanitation, drainage, and footpaths in the massive settlements inhabited by destitute workers on city outskirts.[30]

In many cases, planners found their projects circumscribed by a range of practical and political limitations. In rural areas, for example, most of the beneficiaries of World Bank programs were small farmers who owned their own land. Because the bank considered landless tenants, sharecroppers, and squatters too difficult to reach, the "poorest of the poor" were often ignored. Bank staff also found it difficult to determine who benefited from particular projects. In urban housing work, for example, did the greatest gains go to the poor families or to the contractors and investors who built the houses and later moved in to purchase the improved land? The bank's antipoverty objectives also ran into resistance from national elites. Although concerned with poverty, governments in countries like Nigeria, Indonesia, Mexico, and India were not enthusiastic about promoting labor-intensive approaches to small-scale industrialization and agriculture, fearing that the new emphasis on poverty reduction and job creation would leave them with inferior prospects for long-term, technologically driven growth. Recommended changes in trade policy, taxation, public spending, and agrarian reform, which went against the interests of the politically powerful classes, also limited the potential of antipoverty programs.[31]

Like the new emphasis on basic human needs, debates over the impact of development on the environment challenged the assumptions underlying modernization. The proponents of modernization, focused on the potential for "big pushes" and "take-offs," had never given much thought to questions of scarcity or environmental damage. During the mid-1960s, however, a growing environmental movement within the United States transformed the political climate. Following the publication in 1962 of Rachel Carson's classic study of chemical pesticides, *Silent Spring*, activists gained federal passage of several key measures, including the Clean Air Act, the Water Quality Act, the Noise Control Act, and the Beautification Act. By the time student radicals organized the first Earth Day in April 1970, environmentalism and its varied critique of consumption, pollution, and damaging technologies began to affect discussions of international development policy as well.[32]

Standing prominently among the environmental critics of modernization was none other than George F. Kennan, author of the Cold War concept of containment. In 1970 Kennan warned that the pollution of the oceans and atmosphere with industrial waste, car and jet exhaust, chemicals, and radioactive materials threatened to produce a "world wasteland." Development policy, accordingly, needed to take environmental questions into account. "The principle," Kennan argued, "should be that one exploits what a careful regard for the needs of conservation leaves to be exploited, not that one conserves what a liberal indulgence of the impulse of development leaves to be conserved." Recommending the creation of a supranational "International Environmental Authority" with the power to enforce common standards, Kennan urged "the great communist and Western powers" to "replace the waning fixations of the cold war" with a venture to "restore the hope, the beauty, and the salubriousness of the natural environment in which man has his being."[33]

Stark warnings were also issued in *The Limits to Growth*, a highly publicized 1972 study sponsored by the Club of Rome, a prominent international association of economists, educators, businesspeople, and government officials. Their "Project on the Predicament of Mankind," based on the computerized analysis of a global "system dynamics" model, predicted a bleak future. Given the interconnected forces of "accelerating industrialization, rapid population growth, widespread malnutrition, depletion of nonrenewable resources, and a deteriorating environment," they concluded that unless present trends of development were sharply altered, "the limits to growth on this planet will be reached sometime within the next one hundred years." If radical changes in production, consumption, and birthrates were not imposed soon, when it might still be possible to reverse the damage, a cataclysmic "resource crisis" would trigger a global "collapse into a dismal, depleted existence." Where modernization theorists had envisioned a world moving from "tradition" to "modernity," the Club of Rome now advocated a "great transition" of a very different kind—"the transition from growth to global equilibrium."[34]

Such environmental forecasts produced a wide range of political responses. Although *The Limits to Growth* received broad public attention, and more than four million copies of the book were printed in thirty languages, many critics discounted the dire predictions. Warnings about the fixed limits of arable land and exhaustible minerals, they argued, ignored the reality that while consumption grew exponentially, so too did the effects of technologies that could push limits back. Economist Carl Kaysen contended that rising market prices for resources and commodities would function as natural adjustment mechanisms. Instead of a dire, sudden collapse, human production and consumption would smoothly and gradually adjust to the limits of an eventual growth ceiling. The solution to rapid population increases in the postcolonial world, critics also insisted, was *greater* economic growth and the redistribution of it to meet human needs, not the imposition of limits, which would only exacerbate human suffering.[35]

From the early 1970s through the 1980s, debates over development and the environment were also shaped by two additional concepts, those of "appropriate technology" and "sustainability." Published in 1973, E. F. Schumacher's *Small*

Is Beautiful provided an especially popular critique. A German-born economist who spent much of his life working in Britain, Schumacher tapped into the countercultural temper of 1970s environmentalism with a sharp critique of modernization and a poetic embrace of what he called "Buddhist economics." The "modern industrial system, with all its intellectual sophistication," he declared, "consumes the very basis on which it has been erected." Depleting resources and spoiling the world's natural beauty, this system also failed to bring about its much heralded psychological transformations. Instead of converting passive, fatalistic, traditional peoples into activist citizens, modern factories and urban centers replaced personally and spiritually fulfilling labor with slavery to machines. By elevating the maximization of production over human liberation, modern social orders forced individuals off the land and into the marginal, destitute life of urban migrants. Like those focused on "basic human needs," Schumacher stressed problems of inequality and poverty. Unlike them, however, he insisted that introducing advanced, Western technologies into postcolonial countries was a disastrous mistake. Less costly, labor-intensive "intermediate technologies" geared to simple, local strategies of production could be installed, repaired, and maintained far more cheaply. Dispersed through the countryside of low-income nations, such technologies would also encourage small-scale businesses and entrepreneurship, enabling people to produce the clothing, farm tools, household goods, and building materials most needed by the poor.[36]

Among development professionals and scholars, the idea of "sustainability" proved equally influential. The distinguished political scientist Karl Deutsch observed in 1977 that long-term development could go forward only if it were environmentally sustainable. Decisions about consumption and investment, therefore, could not be left to the functioning of markets that routinely ignored environmental concerns. Prominent research and advocacy groups gave this idea broad circulation. Worldwatch Institute director Lester Brown argued that any concept of development had to accept the need for a global "transition to sustainability." Where Talcott Parsons and other theorists had once focused on the passage from tradition to modernity, Brown called for a shift from "planned obsolescence" to "durability," from "material possessions" to "personal development," and from "the domination of nature" to a harmonious existence within it.[37]

Like the basic needs approach, environmental criticism met determined resistance. The rise of laissez-faire conservatism in the United States, Great Britain, and much of Western Europe in the 1980s brought governments to power that had little to no interest in environmental concerns. This became patently clear in 1987, when the World Commission on Environment and Development presented its report to the UN General Assembly. Under the leadership of Norwegian prime minister Gro Harlem Brundtland, the commission recounted several years of crisis marked by drought and famine in Africa, the Bhopal gas disaster in India, and the death of tens of millions of children due to unsafe drinking water and malnutrition. Environmental degradation, the commission warned, was now "a survival issue for developing nations." But despite pious promises on all sides, no policies or programs offered any real hope of arresting the "downward spiral of linked ecological and economic decline in which many of the poorest nations are trapped." As the industrialized countries continued to consume a vastly disproportionate share of the world's "ecological capital," developing countries were forced to overexploit their limited natural resources.[38]

In addition to arguments about inequality, poverty, and the environment, dissenters regarding modernization also raised questions about the impact of development projects on the status of women. The concept of modernization, scholars like Ester Boserup argued, reproduced classic, liberal assumptions about gender and labor. By defining progress in terms of the division of home and workplace as well as the rise of "rational" and "achievement-oriented" men, modernization theorists defined women as repositories of backwardness. The purportedly objective, social scientific categories of tradition and modernity, feminist critics maintained, were in fact heavily gendered, contributing to the creation of policies that focused on the promotion of male opportunity and undervalued women's vital economic roles. Since the colonial period, as development schemes drew men out of villages for work on plantations, mines, and road-building projects, women's work in food production had substantially increased. Since men carried harvests to market, however, women's labor was typically unrecognized and unpaid. Development programs of the 1960s put technologically improved seeds, fertilizer, and mechanized equipment in male hands, and men held the cash proceeds deriving from the sale of larger harvests. Even as rural incomes grew, newfound wealth did not trickle down to other family members. While male heads of households bought watches, bicycles, and radios—all signs of greater prosperity—family nutritional levels actually fell. Conditions in urban areas were equally bleak. Job training programs focused on men, and sex stereotyping in employment often pushed women into the "informal sector" of the economy, where many were forced to survive through petty trading or prostitution.[39]

According to feminist critics, therefore, development policies based on theories of modernization deepened women's inequality. Even basic needs approaches—stressing health, nutrition, and improved child-care—did not go far enough. In response to those arguments, through the 1970s "Women in Development" programs appeared in UN agencies as well as AID. Rather than focusing on overall family welfare, they began to stress the need to create greater income-earning opportunities for women, including training programs, access to credit, and assistance with marketing. Major UN conferences on the status of women in

Mexico City (1975), Copenhagen (1980), and Nairobi (1985) went beyond questions of living standards to stress equality, autonomy, and the defense of women's political, economic, and civil rights.[40]

The Neoliberal Turn

The critical reassessment of development during the 1970s marked a pivotal change in the field. It exposed modernization's failures, set out new agendas, and forced professionals to reconsider their fundamental objectives, values, and goals. The intellectual challenge to modernization and the decentering of development had other implications as well. As the premium placed on unlimited growth, aggregate productivity, and high technology was replaced by an emphasis on problems of poverty and inequality within the boundaries of a fragile ecosystem, the task of accelerating progress came to appear far more complex. Modernization had embodied the tremendous optimism of liberals in the United States at the apex of their nation's power. Its narrative gave the postwar development project a clear sense of direction, speed, and feasibility, defining the economic and social levers that could be managed to produce a "take-off," after which countries would be able to move into "self-sustaining growth." It promised, in other words, that development had a clear end, that its goals could be realized within a finite period, and that the "developing" world could foresee a readily attainable future in the image of the industrialized nations. But by the 1970s all those integrating assumptions were replaced by a much greater sense of fragmentation, ambiguity, and uncertainty.

Therefore, although it addressed serious problems and deficiencies, the new, diverse, and far more complex agenda lacked the crucial attribute that modernization had once possessed—the confidence that development could be achieved rapidly and that the world would soon converge on the kind of political and economic order found most clearly in the West, and especially in the United States. Conservative, "neoliberal" arguments, however, recapitulated precisely those claims. By rejecting integrated planning and Keynesian fiscal policy as coercive interventions, neoliberals also stressed methods seemingly in harmony with the essentials of human nature. Economist Milton Friedman argued that unrestricted markets allowed citizens to pursue freely their own interests through a system of wholly voluntary exchange. That economic freedom, moreover, was "an indispensable means toward the achievement of political freedom." Development, in this light, was actually a simple matter, best accomplished by getting the state out of the way and letting the engines of capitalism run their inevitable course.[41]

Among development experts, these ideas emerged in the form of a conservative "counterrevolution." Development problems, these dissenters argued, centered fundamentally on the need to direct resources and investment to the most productive sectors of society. That task, moreover, was one that markets could always handle more effectively than governments. Like modernization theorists, the neoliberals defined aggregate economic growth as an essential goal. Unlike them, they rejected the idea of government intervention and planning intended to create a "big push" toward take-off. Optimum results, they maintained, would instead be achieved through the rational choices of individuals in the capitalist marketplace. Plans to address questions of poverty and inequality, they also believed, were ultimately misguided and wasteful. The most rapid progress, in fact, often came through natural inequality, as expanding progress eventually lifted all boats.[42]

These views gained increasing circulation among conservative scholars in the 1970s. Experts like University of Chicago economist Harry G. Johnson contended that development planning had resulted in unproductive investments in state-owned industries and allowed corrupt officials to enrich themselves by manipulating price and wage controls. British economist Ian Little took a similar tack, arguing that planners always relied on insufficient data to direct the complex workings of the economy. The situation, he explained, was "rather like an architect designing a building with no knowledge of the strength of the materials—the building blocks—that might be used." "It could thus be a redeeming feature," Little concluded, "that so many plans went unimplemented." Deepak Lal, an economist and consultant to the Indian Planning Commission and the World Bank, also rejected the idea that the particular needs of developing countries demanded a greater degree of state intervention. The economics of classical liberalism, built around free trade, price mechanisms, and the self-interested pursuit of profit, he argued, produced universally optimum solutions. Because official interventions to promote some sectors of the economy often did far greater harm to others, it was better for governments not to act. Reformist interventions in the name of social equity, he claimed, also wound up violating principles of individual liberty.[43]

British economist P. T. Bauer, perhaps the most famous of the conservative "counterrevolutionaries," pushed such arguments further. In addition to attacking the failures of planning, he assaulted the entire field of development economics itself. Its promises of rapid material progress, he claimed, were "oversold to a credulous public" plagued by "widespread feelings of guilt." In his fieldwork in British colonial Malaya and West Africa, he argued that non-Europeans created thriving local economies without the need for an expensive infrastructure or the injection of foreign aid. Relying on a remarkably sunny view of British imperialism, Bauer maintained that progress in those regions was not the result of the "forcible modernization of attitudes or behavior, nor of large-scale state-sponsored industrialization, nor of any other form of big push." Instead of "conscious efforts at nation building (as if people were lifeless bricks, to be moved about by some master builder)," rising prosperity was "the result of individual voluntary responses of millions of people to emerging or expanding opportunities created largely by external contacts and brought to their notice in a variety of ways, primarily through the market." If government would only get out of the way, unfettered capitalism could unleash long-suppressed human potential.[44]

In the United States, such antistatist ideas clearly resonated with a broader rejection of Keynesian economic policies. From the New Deal of the mid-1930s through the Great Society of the late 1960s, the idea of federal intervention in public life for the promotion of high employment levels, economic growth, and technological progress had been well established. Keynesian fiscal policy, in particular, was accepted as a successful means for the state to create the conditions in which capitalism would serve larger social objectives. By the mid-1970s, however, as inflation and unemployment rose together to new heights, conservative critics argued that liberal economic policies had produced a structural crisis. Excessive government regulation, they claimed, had shackled the economy and limited job creation, while misguided and irresponsible social welfare spending and entitlement programs had triggered runaway inflation. The tax policies needed to pay for government programs were also condemned as obstacles to productive investment. Capturing the erosion of the previous consensus, the economist and blunt-speaking Federal Reserve chairman Paul Volcker told a journalist: "We're all Keynesians now—in terms of the way we look at things. National income statistics are a Keynesian view of the world, and the language of economists tends to be Keynesian. But if you mean by Keynesian that we've got to pump up the economy, that all these relationships are pretty clear and simple, that this gives us a tool for eternal prosperity if we do it right, that's all bullshit."[45]

By the early 1980s, the ascendancy of Ronald Reagan to the White House created the conditions in which the antistatist, pro-market doctrine of the neoliberals would transform U.S. foreign development policy. With the Reagan administration turning toward supply-side economics and the massive tax cuts that would supposedly empower private entrepreneurship, the idea of spending substantial amounts of public money to promote modernization abroad came under withering fire. As conservative intellectuals and think tanks condemned the Great Society's social welfare programs for eroding market incentives, encouraging a culture of entitlement, and destroying the potential for individual initiative, critics also attacked attempts at "social engineering" abroad. Massive Western aid projects and national planning, analysts like Grace Goodell argued, were largely responsible "for the syndrome of overbearing government and popular (even middle-class) apathy that marks Third World poverty." By promoting irresponsible governments instead of free markets, modernization created paternalistic bureaucracies that contributed to "local ennui, the solidification of centralized power, [and] society's acceptance of corruption as a way of life." Since social scientists and development administrators really had "little idea about how to solve a wide range of social problems either in their own country or in less developed countries," they often did more harm than good.[46]

The international economic crises of the 1970s and early 1980s contributed to the neoliberal ascendancy and the broader turn against development. In particular, the "oil shocks" of the period produced important and unanticipated effects. The Arab oil embargo following the 1973 Arab-Israeli war quadrupled oil prices, and the cutoff of Iranian oil exports following the 1979 revolution tripled them yet again. These events plunged the United States into recession, decreasing the willingness of U.S. politicians to provide further funding for development abroad in times of economic turmoil at home. The oil shocks also rattled the global monetary system. Much of the wealth or "petrodollars" that nations belonging to the Organization of the Petroleum Exporting Countries (OPEC) gained from the industrialized countries in higher oil revenues was ultimately invested in Western commercial banks. Those banks, in turn, found ready customers among the non–oil exporting, low-income countries that were hit hard by the rising costs of oil, fertilizer, food, and manufactured imports. As industrialized economies fell into recession and cut their aid levels, the poorest nations faced economic ruin. Borrowing from commercial sources now appeared as a vital means to avoid a crisis, pursue economic recovery, and obtain development funds.[47]

The result helped pave the way for the debt crisis of the 1980s. As borrowing by lower-income countries continued, rising to a level of $165 billion in 1978, poor nations resorted to paying off their current loans with new ones, deriving less and less benefit from the capital they received. In 1981, the Latin American countries borrowed $34.6 billion, but they also paid back $28.2 billion in interest, leaving only $6.4 billion for the purposes of investment. Finally, in 1982, the bubble burst. After Argentina went to war with Britain over the Falkland Islands in May, bankers became more cautious about the political risks of lending. The Mexican government's announcement in August that it was officially broke also triggered a widespread realization that the lower-income countries, especially in Latin American and Africa, were in no position to continue carrying such heavy debt burdens.[48]

The proposed solution to this problem was a decidedly neoliberal one. Although commercial creditors agreed to reschedule debts, and bilateral agencies reduced some obligations, the industrialized countries made further assistance contingent on policies of "structural adjustment." According to the new "Washington Consensus," the countries of the developing world had lived beyond their means. Their failures, insisted Reagan administration, World Bank, and International Monetary Fund officials, were due to the unbridled government intervention and irresponsible spending that had produced unbalanced budgets and overvalued currencies. To correct this problem, they would have to turn to the right by promoting free trade, opening their doors to foreign investment, privatizing state enterprises, and deregulating domestic markets. In place of earlier calls to fight poverty and social inequality, the governments of developing countries were now ordered to embrace the market.[49]

Neoliberals also looked to the "East Asian miracle" to bolster their claims about the failures of state-led modernization. During the 1970s, the "four tigers" of Hong Kong, Singapore, South Korea, and Taiwan enjoyed tremendous economic growth rates averaging 8 to 10 percent per year. After the U.S. economy recovered from recession in the early 1980s, those high annual rates returned as the four tigers complemented their existing manufacturing base in textiles and simple consumer goods with more capital-intensive electronics products. Over the longer haul, figures for increases in real income per capita were even more impressive, quadrupling between 1960 and 1985. Comparing the thriving economies of these four East Asian countries with those of most Latin American, African, and other Asian nations, neoliberals thought that they could discern the secret of success. The "great leap from poverty to wealth," the *Economist* magazine maintained in 1987, was largely due to "the use of free markets instead of bureaucrats' orders to tell people what they ought to produce and how much of it." In a major 1993 study, the World Bank arrived at similar conclusions. The astounding success in East Asia was caused primarily by "the application of a set of common, market-friendly economic policies, leading to both higher accumulation and better allocation of resources."[50]

Such interpretations, however, radically simplified a much more complex picture. In South Korea and Taiwan, the two "tigers" in which United States intervention played a significant role, the foundations for success were set by government policies that involved a very high degree of state control over economic life. In Taiwan, the U.S. aid mission supported systematic economic intervention under the authority of the Kuomintang's one-party state from the late 1940s through the end of U.S. economic aid in 1965. U.S. advisers strongly endorsed the government's "planned free economy" over a policy of immediate economic liberalization, reasoning that since there were few prospects for private capital investment, such a strategy was necessary to promote industrialization. With U.S. support, Taiwan's Economic Stabilization Board coordinated the functioning of government-controlled or state-owned banks, sugar plantations, railroads, public utilities, and major industries. During the 1950s, the government also used a strategy of import substitution, subsidies, tariff barriers, and price controls to promote domestic textile and light manufacturing industries. Taiwan's shift toward the market, in other words, was a very gradual one, unfolding from the late 1940s through the 1970s. Only after establishing the basis for an industrial economy and guiding it toward exports, did the government pare back its role. The country's chief economic official, K. T. Li, recalled: "What we as policy makers did in Taiwan was to help various parts of the economy first to stand and then to walk. And then we let go."[51]

The pattern in South Korea was similar, with the United States strongly supporting a "developmental autocracy" heavily engaged in economic planning. Massive U.S. military and economic aid allowed Syngman Rhee to build an anti-Communist state capable of weathering the storms of the Korean War, but little economic growth took place in the country until the early 1960s. After a military junta under General Park Chung Hee took power in 1961, however, a Government Economic Planning Board worked with U.S. officials to raise domestic tax revenues and interest rates to create a pool for investment. The government also promoted exports by helping a select group of firms evolve into massive conglomerates, or *chaebols*, through low-interest loans, tax incentives, and cheap transportation rates. These large, diversified industrial groups, including giants like Hyundai, Samsung, and Daewoo, ultimately dominated the economy and helped secure their relationship with the government by providing kickbacks and contributions to Park's political machine. Only after Park's assassination in 1979 and the brutal suppression of pro-democracy demonstrations in 1980, did the South Korean government, under U.S. pressure, revise its trade and financial policies and open the economy to international markets. During the 1980s, however, neoliberals ignored that historical evidence, insisting that high rates of economic growth were solely the result of more contemporary liberalizing trends.[52]

The neoliberal attack on modernization and state-led development also dovetailed with a broader conservative rejection of the concept of postcolonial "nation building." Liberal modernizers argued that the United States could channel the ambitions of nationalists, linking the objectives of development with the attainment of security. By the 1980s, however, U.S. conservatives rejected that formulation and the political strategies that went with it. Where modernizers called for the United States to defuse revolutionary threats by accelerating a broader process of social transformation, Ronald Reagan framed the problem in far more reductive terms. As he declared in the 1980 election campaign, "let us not delude ourselves. The Soviet Union underlies all the unrest that is going on. If they weren't engaged in this game of dominoes, there wouldn't be any hot spots in the world."[53]

Through much of the 1980s, Reagan administration officials and their supporters moved toward a hard-line, militarized approach to Cold War containment. Self-abasing, apologetic, liberal attempts to conciliate postcolonial
nationalists, they argued, had produced only ungrateful, irrational calls for an
international redistribution of wealth. The poverty of postcolonial states, conservatives insisted, was primarily their own fault, and the liberal failure to stand
up to the impudent demands and radical movements of these states, conservatives believed, had led to disaster in Vietnam, resulted in the loss of the Panama Canal, and encouraged Communist aggression in Angola and Afghanistan.
Jimmy Carter's emphasis on human rights and expanded foreign aid, Reagan
insisted, was nothing more than a "foreign policy bordering on appeasement," a
strategy of standing by while friendly governments were overthrown and Iranian
radicals invaded the U.S. embassy to take American hostages. Conservatives also
had very little patience for nonalignment. Third World countries, they declared,
would have to "stand up and be counted." Rather than trying to steer the course
of their development, the United States also relied more heavily on ostentatious
displays of force, as in the invasion of Grenada, the bombing of Libya, and the
interventions in Afghanistan, Angola, Cambodia, Guatemala, Honduras, El Sal-
vador, and Nicaragua.[54]

Of course, conservatives continued to describe a world that could be driven in
the direction of the United States. The key to this, however, would certainly not be
found in the export of New Deal institutions, comprehensive development planning, or publicly funded attempts to push the trajectory of postcolonial states
in liberal directions. As U.S. ambassador to the UN Jeanne Kirkpatrick argued,
modernization theory's "shortcomings as an analytical tool" were eclipsed only
by its serious "inadequacies as a framework for thinking about foreign policy."
U.S. attempts to direct the course of development in countries like Vietnam and
Iran, she lamented, had only weakened the ability of steadfast, anti-Communist
allies to fight off dangerous revolutions. Dictatorships could gradually move in
democratic directions, but it was counterproductive to interfere in their internal
affairs and insist on sudden, overnight steps toward political reform, especially if
they were under siege by hostile revolutionaries.[55]

The correct way to produce global transformations, many Reagan-era conservatives argued, would instead be found in the blending of military force and
neoliberal ideology. During the 1960s, U.S. policymakers had sought to forge ties
to nationalists in places like India, Egypt, and Ghana, hoping to prevent them
from turning to the left, and aiming to alleviate the social and economic destitution that fed revolutionary ambitions. The Reagan administration, however,
sought to isolate such figures, directing U.S. economic and military aid only to
those with clear, unequivocal anti-Communist track records. An ever-vigilant,

forceful assault on communism, conservatives believed, would deter the Soviets and keep Third World elites in line. By eliminating radical threats, such an attack would also allow free markets and private investment to work their magic, creating businesses, stimulating entrepreneurial incentives, giving rise to middle classes, securing social justice, and eventually paving the way for the inevitable rise of democratic values and institutions. In his 1985 State of the Union address, Reagan declared: "America's economic success is freedom's success; it can be repeated a hundred times in a hundred different nations."[56]

By the 1980s, then, the ideology of modernization was in a state of near collapse. From the late 1960s through the 1970s, the crisis of U.S. liberalism, the rise of competing social scientific models, the controversial redefinition of development, and finally the neoliberal shift in political life in the United States all destroyed the essential foundations on which modernization was based. Yet even in the midst of that escalating wave of criticism and rejection, the essential conviction that the United States had a unique, global mission to transform the world in its own image survived. Ronald Reagan proclaimed in his 1989 "farewell address" that America remained a "shining city upon a hill," "still a beacon, still a magnet for all who must have freedom, for all the pilgrims from all the lost places who are hurtling through the darkness, toward home." With the triumphant end of the Cold War, the belief that the United States could lead a world converging on "market democracy" would continue to grow and deepen. Shortly after the turn of the new century, as the United States faced what its leaders described as yet another struggle of potentially infinite duration for absolute ends, a revised, reformulated vision of modernization would also stage a remarkable comeback.[57]

NOTES

1. "Editorial Foreword," *Comparative Studies in Society and History* 20, no. 2 (1978): 175–76.

2. Gilman, *Mandarins of the Future*, 205; Ekbladh, *Great American Mission*.

3. Allen J. Matusow, *The Unraveling of America: A History of Liberalism in the 1960s* (New York: Harper and Row, 1984); Martin Luther King, Jr., "Beyond Vietnam," Speech at Riverside Church Meeting, April 4, 1967, in *Lyndon B. Johnson and American Liberalism: A Brief Biography with Documents*, ed. Bruce J. Schulman (Boston: Bedford, 1995), 208–12.

4. Mary L. Dudziak, *Cold War Civil Rights: Race and the Image of American Democracy* (Princeton, NJ: Princeton University Press, 2000), 215–16, 232, 237; Borstelmann, *Cold War and the Color Line*, 180.

5. Dudziak, *Cold War Civil Rights*, 252; Matusow, *Unraveling of America*, 363.

6. Robert M. Collins, *More: The Politics of Economic Growth in Postwar America* (New York: Oxford University Press, 2000), 54, 59–60; Alice O'Connor, *Poverty Knowledge: Social Science, Social Policy, and the Poor in Twentieth-Century U.S. History* (Princeton, NJ: Princeton University Press, 2001), 152–53.

7. Matusow, *Unraveling of America*, 218–41, 270.

8. Brick, *Age of Contradiction*, 50–51; David Farber, *The Age of Great Dreams: America in the 1960s* (New York: Hill and Wang, 1994), 196.

10131517192123252729

9. Farber, *Age of Great Dreams*, 139.

10. Collins, *More*, 69–85; Kunz, *Butter and Guns*, 188–205.

11. Collins, *More*, 97; Kunz, *Butter and Guns*, 188, 216–17.

12. Joseph R. Gusfield, "Tradition and Modernity: Misplaced Polarities in the Study of Social Change," *American Journal of Sociology* 72 (January 1967): 351, 352–53, 355; M. N. Srinivas, *Social Change in Modern India* (Berkeley: University of California Press, 1966); Rajni Kothari, *Politics in India* (Boston: Little, Brown, 1970); C. S. Whitaker, Jr., "A Dysrhythmic Process of Political Change," *World Politics* 19, no. 2 (1967): 190–217.

13. Alexander Gerschenkron, *Economic Backwardness in Historical Perspective* (Cambridge, MA: Harvard University Press, 1966), 353–57.

14. C. Wright Mills, *The Sociological Imagination* (New York: Oxford University Press, 1959), 42, 86.

15. Samuel P. Huntington, "Political Development and Political Decay," *World Politics* 17, no. 2 (1965): 386, 392; Huntington, *Political Order in Changing Societies* (New Haven, CT: Yale University Press, 1968).

16. Nisbet, *Social Change and History*, 168–82, 197.

17. Ali A. Mazrui, "From Social Darwinism to Current Theories of Modernization: A Tradition of Analysis," *World Politics* 21 (October 1968), 73, 75.

18. Noam Chomsky, *American Power and the New Mandarins* (New York: Pantheon, 1969), 5, 324; Robert R. Tomes, *Apocalypse Then: American Intellectuals and the Vietnam War, 1954–1975* (New York: New York University Press, 1998), 160.

19. Raúl Prebisch, "Five Stages in My Thinking on Development," in Meier and Seers, *Pioneers in Development*, 175–78; Paul A. Baran, *The Political Economy of Growth* (New York: Monthly Review, 1957), 12, 16, 143, 249–51; Gilman, *Mandarins of the Future*, 235–36.

20. Andre Gunder Frank, *Latin America: Underdevelopment or Revolution: Essays on the Development of Underdevelopment and the Immediate Enemy* (New York: Monthly Review Press, 1969), 4, 40–42, 47.

21. Immanuel Wallerstein, "The Rise and Demise of the World Capitalist System: Concepts for Comparative Analysis," in *The Essential Wallerstein* (New York: New Press, 2000), 71–105; Wallerstein, "Modernization: Requiescat in Pace," in *The Capitalist World Economy*, ed. Wallerstein (Cambridge: Cambridge University Press, 1979), 132–33.

22. Jerome Levinson and Juan de Onís, *The Alliance That Lost Its Way* (Chicago: Quadrangle Books, 1970), 8–10, 77.

23. Richard Jolly, Louis Emmerji, Dharam Ghai, and Frédéric Lapeyre, *UN Contributions to Development Thinking and Practice* (Bloomington: Indiana University Press, 2004), 86–91, 106–7; Barbara Ward, J. D. Runnalls, and Leonore D'Anjou, eds., *The Widening Gap: Development in the 1970s* (New York: Columbia University Press, 1971), 280.

24. Jolly et al., *UN Contributions*, 105–6, 120–22; Prebisch, "Five Stages," 179; H. W. Arndt, *Economic Development: The History of an Idea* (Chicago: University of Chicago Press, 1987), 140–42.

25. Engerman, "American Knowledge and Global Power," 617–20; Dudley Seers, "What Are We Trying to Measure?" *Journal of Development Studies* 8, no. 3 (1972): 21–36.

26. Jolly et al., *UN Contributions*, 111–13.

27. Deborah Shapley, *Promise and Power: The Life and Times of Robert McNamara* (Boston: Little, Brown, 1993), 470; Martha Finnemore, "Redefining Development at the World Bank," in *International Development and the Social Sciences*, ed. Frederick Cooper and Randall Packard (Berkeley: University of California Press, 1997), 205.

28. Robert L. Ayres, *Banking on the Poor: The World Bank and World Poverty* (Cambridge, MA: MIT Press, 1983), 4; Shapley, *Promise and Power*, 499, 502, 506–9; Hollis Chenery et al., *Redistribution with Growth* (New York: Oxford University Press, 1974), xiv–xix.

29. Robert S. McNamara, *The McNamara Years at the World Bank: Major Policy Addresses of Robert S. McNamara, 1968–1981* (Baltimore: Johns Hopkins University Press, 1981), 217, 223–26.

30. Ayres, *Banking on the Poor,* 92–100, 148–61.

31. Arndt, *Economic Development,* 109–11; Ayres, *Banking on the Poor,* 101–8, 216.

32. Hettne, *Development Theory,* 180–84.

33. George F. Kennan, "To Prevent a World Wasteland," *Foreign Affairs* 48, no. 3 (1970): 408–9, 412–13.

34. Donella H. Meadows, Dennis L. Meadows, Jorgen Randers, and William W. Behrens III, *The Limits to Growth: A Report for the Club of Rome's Project on the Predicament of Mankind* (New York: Universe Books, 1972), 21–30, 66–68, 126–28.

35. Collins, *More,* 141–45; Carl Kaysen, "The Computer That Printed Out W*O*L*F*," *Foreign Affairs* 50 (July 1972): 660–68; Mahbub ul Haq, *The Poverty Curtain: Choices for the Third World* (New York: Columbia University Press, 1976), 77–105.

36. E. F. Schumacher, *Small Is Beautiful: Economics as If People Mattered* (New York: Harper and Row, 1973), 19, 50–54, 164–79.

37. Karl W. Deutsch, ed., *Ecosocial Systems and Ecopolitics: A Reader on Human and Social Implications of Environmental Management in Developing Countries* (Paris: UNESCO, 1977), 12–14; 37–40; Lester R. Brown, *Building a Sustainable Society* (New York: Norton, 1981), 280–81, 351.

38. World Commission on Environment and Development, *Our Common Future* (Oxford: Oxford University Press, 1987), xi, 3, 5–6.

39. Ester Boserup, *Woman's Role in Economic Development* (London: Allen and Unwin, 1970); Catherine V. Scott, *Gender and Development: Rethinking Modernization and Dependency Theory* (Boulder, CO: Lynne Rienner, 1995); Ingrid Palmer, "Rural Women and the Basic Needs Approach to Development," *International Labour Review* 115, no. 1 (1977): 97–107; Jane S. Jaquette, "Women and Modernization Theory: A Decade of Feminist Criticism," *World Politics* 34, no. 2 (1982): 267–84.

40. Jolly et al., *UN Contributions,* 131–35; Ilsa Schuster, "Recent Research on Women in Development: Review Article," *Journal of Development Studies* 18, no. 4 (1982): 511–35.

41. Milton Friedman, *Capitalism and Freedom* (Chicago: University of Chicago Press, 1962), 8–9.

42. John Toye, *Dilemmas of Development: Reflections on the Counter-Revolution in Development Theory and Policy* (Oxford: Blackwell, 1987).

43. Toye, *Dilemmas of Development,* 23–25, 72–81; Little, *Economic Development,* 127.

44. P. T. Bauer, *Dissent on Development: Studies and Debates in Development Economics* (Cambridge, MA: Harvard University Press, 1972), 20–21; Bauer, "Remembrance of Studies Past: Retracing First Steps," in Meier and Seers, *Pioneers in Development,* 30–31.

45. William C. Berman, *America's Right Turn: From Nixon to Bush* (Baltimore: Johns Hopkins University Press, 1994), 44–50; Collins, *More,* 167–82.

46. Grace Goodell, "Conservatism and Foreign Aid," *Policy Review* 19 (Winter 1982): 111–12, 118; Charles R. Frank and Mary Baird, "Foreign Aid: Its Speckled Past and Future Prospects," *International Organization* 29, no. 1 (1975): 145–46, 154.

47. Kunz, *Butter and Guns,* 235–46.

48. Ibid., 265, 272–76.

49. Jolly et al., *UN Contributions,* 142–43, 148–51.

50. Robert Solomon, *The Transformation of the World Economy,* 2nd ed. (New York: St. Martin's, 1999), 139; "The U.S. Recovery Has Four Asian Nations Roaring Back," *Business Week,* June 25, 1984, 42; "A Special Place," *The Economist,* July 18, 1987, 12; World Bank, *The East Asian Miracle: Economic Growth and Public Policy* (New York: Oxford University Press, 1993), v–vi, 1–4, 10, 24.

51. Westad, *Global Cold War,* 404; Nick Cullather, "'Fuel for the Good Dragon': The United States and Industrial Policy in Taiwan, 1950–1965," in *Empire and Revolution: The United States and the Third World since 1945,* ed. Peter L. Hahn and Mary Ann Heiss (Columbus: Ohio State University Press, 2001), 242–68; Daniel Yergin and Joseph Stanislaw, *The Commanding Heights: The Battle between Government and the Marketplace That Is Remaking the Modern World* (New York: Simon and Schuster, 1998), 175–79.

52. Gregg Brazinsky, *Nation Building in South Korea: Koreans, Americans, and the Making of a Democracy* (Chapel Hill: University of North Carolina Press, 2007), 4–5, 130–60, 245–46; Yergin and Stanislaw, *Commanding Heights*, 168–73; Ekbladh, *Great American Mission*.

53. David F. Schmitz, *The United States and Right-Wing Dictatorships* (Cambridge: Cambridge University Press, 2006), 200.

54. Schmitz, *United States and Right-Wing Dictatorships*, 200; John Ehrman, *The Rise of Neoconservatism: Intellectuals and Foreign Affairs, 1945–1994* (New Haven, CT: Yale University Press, 1995), 114.

55. Jeanne Kirkpatrick, "Dictatorships and Double Standards," *Commentary* 68 (November 1979): 37–39.

56. Ronald Reagan, Address before a Joint Session of the Congress on the State of the Union, February 6, 1985, Ronald Reagan Presidential Library, www.reagan.utexas.edu/archives/speeches/1985/20685e.htm; Seyom Brown, *The Faces of Power: Constancy and Change in United States Foreign Policy from Truman to Clinton* (New York: Columbia University Press, 1994), 407.

57. Ronald Reagan, Farewell Address to the Nation, January 11, 1989, Ronald Reagan Presidential Library, www.reagan.utexas.edu/archives/speeches/1989/010089i.htm.

THE GHOSTS OF MODERNIZATION
From Cold War Victory to Afghanistan and Iraq

The end of the Cold War radically altered the world's geopolitical structure. For more than four decades, U.S. foreign policymakers had waged an intense, relentless, worldwide struggle against Soviet communism. Then, between 1989 and 1991, Eastern Europe's Communist states suddenly collapsed, jubilant crowds tore down the Berlin Wall, and the Soviet Union itself dissolved. U.S. officials had long anticipated that a global strategy of military containment and economic liberalization would exacerbate internal strains within the Soviet system. In the late 1980s, however, very few U.S. analysts anticipated such a rapid turn of events. As the Soviet Union fractured into constituent republics, and the long anti-Communist crusade raced to a surprising finish, U.S. officials faced the future with an uneasy blend of triumphal celebration and nagging uncertainty. With its greatest ideological competitor gone, what principles and strategies would guide the exercise of U.S. power in a new era?

In thinking about the postcolonial world, U.S. policymakers found few easy answers to that question. Where some experts insisted that the Cold War's end marked a moment of unprecedented opportunity, the start of an era in which the United States' liberal, capitalist, and democratic institutions could be spread to every corner of the globe, others spoke in much darker tones. Although the Cold War had partially suppressed and distracted attention from them, long-festering forces of ethnic conflict, religious violence, and militant nationalism were on the rise. How would the sole remaining superpower try to shape this far less predictable environment? What could it do to confront the threats generated by deepening poverty, global migration, the instability of "failed states," and the rise of Islamic radicalism? "Until the Cold War was over," historian Ronald Steel reflected, "we did not appreciate that the conflict, for all its inequities and dangers, imposed a kind of order on the world. Now even that is gone."[1]

Amid those uncertainties Americans returned to an older set of beliefs tightly connected to deeply rooted understandings of national identity and mission. From the "nation-building" efforts of the 1990s through the invasions of Afghanistan and Iraq after September 11, 2001, U.S. policymakers, intellectuals, and opinion leaders approached the postcolonial world through a very familiar framework. Modernization, as a theory and a policy, was discredited in the wake of the U.S. failures in Vietnam and Iran, and the hope for a global New Deal was discarded in favor of a market-driven, neoliberal vision in the 1980s. Many of modernization's fundamental assumptions, however, made a startling comeback in the years following the Cold War's end. In confronting crises in Latin America, Africa, Asia, and the Middle East, U.S. policymakers once again linked the promotion of development with the enhancement of security. Just as they had during the Cold War, U.S. officials assumed that the forces of liberal, capitalist modernity would sweep all before them, transforming the political life, economies, and cultures of malleable foreign societies in predictable and ultimately benevolent ways. History, they insisted, had a clear direction, and its acceleration would create a better, freer, and ultimately more secure global order. Finally, as they had during the Cold War, U.S. policymakers blended the language of idealistic, democratizing reform with the deployment of lethal force. Where possible, the United States would encourage the spread of "market democracy" using development aid, trade policy, and the transfer of technology. Where necessary, it would impose modernity through far more direct, far more coercive means. In a period of neoliberal consensus, the original preference for state-led, government-planned development policies remained dead and buried. But in the post–Cold War era, and especially after September 11, 2001, many of modernization's essential elements rose dramatically from the grave.

"The End of History"

The Cold War's sudden end provoked a variety of competing arguments about the causes of the Soviet collapse and the meaning of the U.S. victory. For some conservative commentators, the matter was clear. The U.S. defense buildup of the 1980s had essentially driven the Soviet Union into bankruptcy. Unable to compete with the United States in a costly arms race that stretched from conventional weaponry through nuclear technology and into Ronald Reagan's Strategic

Defense Initiative, Mikhail Gorbachev had little choice but to reverse decades of Soviet policy and abandon his country's global ambitions. "When communism came down," Senator Jack Kemp declared in a tribute to Reagan, "it wasn't because it fell. It was because he pushed it." Others, however, emphasized a longer, more complex causal chain. The Soviet demise, they argued, was due to decades of poor economic growth, the impact of the Afghanistan war, and the enormous expense of attempting to shore up and maintain control over its allies. Mikhail Gorbachev's bid to save socialism by restructuring the Soviet economy and allowing a greater measure of political openness, in that context, effectively unleashed forces he could not control, resulting in the collapse of the system he desperately wanted to reform. Still other arguments stressed the vast comparative gap, between the Communist and Western worlds, in popular living standards and civil liberties. Once they had the chance, Soviet and Eastern European citizens played a crucial role by rebelling against a failed, corrupt, and repressive social order in favor of the far more affluent and attractive one they could see just over the Cold War's walls.[2]

At another level, well beyond the politics of the 1980s or the relative strengths and weaknesses of the Soviet and American societies, some analysts perceived a wider, far more powerful process at work. In these interpretations, the Soviet collapse represented a deeper historical phenomenon—the manifestation of an underlying global trend that had fundamentally shaped the past and would continue to transform the future. The most famous of these arguments appeared in a 1989 essay by Francis Fukuyama, then a little-known State Department official. Arriving as anti-Communist movements gained momentum in Eastern Europe, Gorbachev's reforms triggered upheavals in the Soviet Union, and a brief outpouring of democratic dissent took hold in China, Fukuyama's article seemed to capture the spirit of the times. Around the world, he argued, "an unabashed victory of economic and political liberalism" was taking hold. "What we may be witnessing," he declared, was not merely the end of the Cold War, but instead "the end of history as such: that is, the end point of mankind's ideological evolution and the universalization of Western liberal democracy as the final form of human government." Through two world wars and a long cold war, Fukuyama argued, the challenges of fascism and communism had been defeated, and liberal capitalism had emerged as the only remaining form of social order. As markets opened, and citizens across the globe pursued the benefits of thriving consumer culture, economic liberalism led to greater political liberalism, and freedom flourished. Drawing on Hegelian philosophy, Fukuyama insisted that the realization of a fundamental, universal ideal was now finally at hand.[3]

Fukuyama's assessment of a world converging on liberal, capitalist democracy was sensationally popular and immediately familiar. In essence, it recapitulated the same set of deeply rooted assumptions that had formed the base of Cold War visions of modernization. Like the modernization theorists of the 1960s, Fukuyama envisioned a universal process in which the world inexorably moved toward the kind of social and political order exemplified by the West and particularly by the United States. The United States, he asserted, represented an ideal end point, a "fundamentally egalitarian and moderately redistributionist" society with only a few remaining pockets of poverty and no intractable forms of economic injustice or class conflict. Forces of nationalism and religion, Fukuyama acknowledged, left the "vast bulk of the Third World" still "very much mired in history" and likely to remain a "terrain of conflict for many years to come." But eventually the postcolonial world would also be transformed by the inherent link between capitalist economics and liberal politics. Even in postrevolutionary Iran, he noted, "the omnipresent signs advertising the products of Sony, Hitachi, and JVC" conveyed a "virtually irresistible" appeal and "gave the lie to the regime's pretensions of restoring a state based on the rule of the *Shariah*." Though he professed personal unease with the materialism of the new order, and a wistful nostalgia for a "worldwide ideological struggle that called forth daring, courage, imagination, and idealism," Fukuyama's vision was ultimately a triumphant one. Liberal capitalism had vanquished its great adversary, and the field was now clear for the consolidation of its transformative global project.[4]

Though particularly sweeping in its claims, Fukuyama's argument was only one of many that defined the end of the Cold War as the start of an era of tremendous liberal promise. Beginning in the mid-1980s, the fall of many Latin American dictatorships, the erosion of authoritarian rule in parts of East and South Asia, the decline of one-party governments in some sub-Saharan African countries, and, finally, the momentous collapse of Soviet and Eastern European communism also inspired theories of a universal "democratic transition." Eager to define any movement *away* from dictatorial government as a step *toward* democratic progress, scholars and policymakers alike envisioned the unfolding of democracy through a common series of stages. In one case after another, they argued, insurgent popular protests led to divisions among ruling elites, the collapse of dictatorial regimes, and the emergence of democratic structures. Thomas Carothers critically observed that the concept of a natural "transition" implied that many varieties of political change all had a clear historical *direction*. It also obscured the degree to which many supposedly "democratizing" nations were still plagued by official corruption, low levels of political participation, lack of public trust in government, and the continued dominance of single parties, families, or leaders. Where they should have considered diverse and complex forms of political change, experts instead celebrated what former Secretary of State George Shultz defined as "the worldwide democratic revolution."[5]

These millennial interpretations also returned concepts of modernization to center stage. In the fall of 1990, Lucian Pye noted that the global "crisis of authoritarianism" vindicated the predictions that he and his colleagues had made decades before. The transformative forces of economic growth, global communications, technological innovation, and international trade had weakened dictatorial control, empowered individuals, and fostered pluralist movements, just as modernization theorists said they would. The only real mistake theorists had made, Pye argued, was to underestimate the "magnitude these factors of change would acquire in the decades ahead and the extent to which they would become part of closely knit international systems." Emphasizing a point he had made repeatedly in his long career, Pye stressed that political culture would frequently override economic factors. Markets alone would not produce democratization, as China's brutally repressive response to the Tiananmen protests of 1989 so clearly proved. But modernization would continue to advance, placing limits on the "free play of ideology," forcing authoritarian regimes to respond to demands for liberalization, and promoting the transition of the world's societies "from one state of equilibrium to another." Writing in 1991, political scientist Howard J. Wiarda acknowledged that scholars like Walt Rostow, Gabriel Almond, and Pye might have oversimplified matters thirty years ago, but they were clearly "correct in the long run." Although "there is no necessary, automatic, or exactly causative relationship between development and democracy—as some of the early development literature suggested—there are tendencies, correlations, and long-term relationships among these factors that cannot be ignored," Wiarda noted.[6]

Theories of a "democratic peace" reflected the moment's optimism as well. Political scientist Bruce Russett observed that the Soviets had surrendered "to the force of Western values of economic and especially political freedom." Moreover, noted Russett, the collapse of authoritarianism illuminated the "striking fact" that "in the modern international system, democracies have almost never fought each other." Because checks and balances restrained the quick resort to arms, and democratic leaders resolved disputes using the same patterns of conflict resolution that they used in domestic life, theorists argued, war among democracies was virtually unheard-of. Promoting democracy, therefore, should become an essential goal of the United States. "If history is imagined to be the history of wars and conquest," Russett contended, "then a democratic world might in that sense represent 'the end of history.'"[7]

Within a few years, celebratory accounts of "globalization" added a neoliberal, economic emphasis to the growing literature on democratization. As *New York Times* columnist Thomas Friedman declared in his immensely popular book *The Lexus and the Olive Tree* (1999), "the driving idea behind globalization is free-market capitalism—the more you let market forces rule and the more you open your economy to free trade and competition, the more efficient and flourishing your economy will be. Globalization means the spread of free-market capitalism to virtually every country in the world." In language that reprised older assumptions about the gap between tradition and modernity, Friedman acknowledged that some societies would certainly resist globalization as a threat to their culture, identity, and values, launching an angry backlash against what they perceived as hostile, external forces. On the whole, however, globalization would proceed from the bottom up, "from street level, from people's very souls and from their very deepest aspirations." Pushed forward by the "democratizations of finance, technology and information," globalization's irrepressible nature, Friedman explained, ultimately derived from "the basic human desire for a better life—a life with more freedom to choose how to prosper, what to eat, what to wear, where to live, where to travel, how to work, what to read, what to write and what to learn."[8]

This vision defined globalization as an inexorable force, driven by capitalism and the integration of nations and technologies, but deeply rooted in human nature. It also linked the expansion of markets with the ultimate spread of human liberty. Unlike laissez-faire conservatives, Friedman insisted that "globally integrated free market capitalism" had to proceed in tandem with at least minimal "social safety nets" to protect those that lacked the ability to adapt to globalization's potentially disruptive impact. Democracy, he also emphasized, was essential to enable individuals to become invested in the process and to shape its effects. Yet Friedman's work ultimately cast globalization as a powerfully benevolent process and defined the United States as its foremost exemplar. The United States, Friedman concluded, "not only can be, it must be, a beacon for the whole world." And he urged: "Let us not squander this precious legacy."[9]

Not all experts, of course, agreed with this shining vision of a world converging on liberal, democratic capitalism. Writing from the realist perspective, some warned that the essentially "anarchic nature of the international system" would only be exacerbated by the collapse of the Cold War's bipolar structure. Where the presence of two great alliance systems had at least provided for some element of stability, nations would now aggressively seek to ensure their survival by amplifying their military power. Given the risk of resurgent nationalism, the danger of devastating conflicts would only grow. Robert Kaplan expected that unresolved problems of overpopulation, environmental degradation, poverty, and disease would lead to civil and regional wars. Rather than moving toward an end point resembling the United States, much of the postcolonial world was coming to look like Sierra Leone, plagued by malaria, HIV, overcrowded cities, squalid living conditions, and rampant crime. Instead of embracing a utopian "end of history," Kaplan predicted, the "classificatory grid of nation-states" would soon be "replaced by a jagged-glass pattern of city-states, shanty-states, nebulous and anarchic regionalisms." Samuel P. Huntington, finally, continued his long crusade against the pretensions of liberal internationalism by predicting a "clash of civilizations." As the significance of ideology faded, he warned, the ancient elements of language, history, religion, and tradition would take on greater weight in international politics. Advances in communications and transportation would also sharpen perceptions of cultural difference and fuel growing resentment of Western attempts to promote "democracy and liberalism as universal values." Forecasting a Chinese and Islamic assault on the West, Huntington recommended that Americans and Europeans study foreign cultures, tighten their mutual alliance, and arm themselves to the teeth.[10]

On the whole, however, the more optimistic assessments carried the day. Like the modernization theories before them, the neoliberal arguments of the 1990s emphasized universal transformations. Celebrations of the global spread of "market democracy" made questions about the impact of specific historical and cultural forces on problems of development seem irrelevant. Markets, neoliberals insisted, would themselves provide the essential basis for the solution of all significant social problems. Like theories of modernization, finally, neoliberal arguments provided the people of the United States with a most appealing narrative about themselves and the world they lived in. To promote "market democracy," in this framework, was to reconcile self-interest with moral mission. It was to ensure U.S. security and economic prosperity while furthering the reach of the only system that truly served the cause of human freedom.[11]

Intervention and Nation Building in the 1990s

During the 1990s, the vision of market democracy's transformative potential also appeared repeatedly in the rhetoric of U.S. foreign policymakers. Once they realized that the Soviet Union was indeed on the way to dissolution, President George H. W. Bush and his advisers celebrated the global spread of liberal capitalism. Bush told the board of governors of the World Bank and the IMF in September 1990 that the "movement toward democratic rule" and the expansion of capitalist markets represented the fulfillment of a long human struggle. Such transformations were not always easy, he acknowledged, but "the jury is no longer out—history has decided." Defending the value of "setting individuals free...free to use their initiative and abilities in the marketplace," Bush pledged to promote development in the "newly emerging democracies of Latin America, Central and Eastern Europe, Africa and Asia."[12]

George H. W. Bush and his advisers also invoked the language of transformative mission to define their wider strategic goals. While the Iraqi invasion of Kuwait in 1990 threatened obvious U.S. interests regarding oil supplies, Middle Eastern stability, and the security of the United States' ally Israel, Bush framed the Gulf War as a struggle for a "new world order." The United States, of course, made little attempt to liberalize Kuwait, but the administration continued to define the spread of democracy as a policy imperative. As Secretary of State James Baker declared in February of 1992, "the Cold War has ended, and we now have a chance to forge a democratic peace, an enduring peace built on shared values—democracy and political and economic freedom."[13]

Even more dramatically, the administration of Bill Clinton framed the expansion of market capitalism and democratic government as a vital U.S. objective. Rejecting the realist tradition of balance-of-power politics, the president and his advisers embraced globalization as a benevolent transnational force. In February 1993, Clinton asserted that the elimination of government-imposed barriers to free trade would promote economic integration, allowing liberal values as well as goods to flow across international borders. "Our leadership," he argued, "is important for the world's new and emerging democracies. To grow and deepen their legitimacy, to foster a middle class and a civic culture, they need the ability to tap into a growing global economy.... If we could make a garden of democracy and prosperity and free enterprise in every part of this globe, the world would be a safer and a better and a more prosperous place for the United States and for all of you to raise your children in." Anthony Lake, Clinton's national security adviser, gave these ideas particularly forceful expression in September 1993: "Throughout the Cold War, we contained a global threat to market democracies; now we should seek to enlarge their reach, particularly in places of special significance to us." Making full use of the revolution in information technology produced by networks of computers, fiber optic cable, and satellites, the United States would spread liberal ideals that "are both American and universal." Since democracies "tend not to wage war on each other or sponsor terrorism," their proliferation would improve U.S. security.[14]

Lake also insisted that while liberal capitalism would ultimately transform the world, the United States could not simply wait for utopia to arrive. In some instances the United States would have to take direct action to fend off threats and quicken history's course. In an influential 1994 article, Lake identified Cuba, North Korea, Iran, Iraq, and Libya as "backlash states." Although their political systems varied, he explained, they shared a common "antipathy toward popular participation," and a "chronic inability to engage constructively with the outside world." Frightened by the prospect that the liberating forces of democratization and markets would undermine their authoritarian rule, a "siege mentality" led these states to sponsor terrorism and pursue weapons of mass destruction. Using diplomacy, economic pressure, and UN sanctions, the United States would contain and transform them. Iran and Iraq in particular, Lake warned, would learn "that there is a price to pay for their recalcitrant commitment to remain on the wrong side of history."[15]

Putting such principles into practice, however, was another matter altogether. While the administrations of George H. W. Bush and Bill Clinton enjoyed success in brokering the North American Free Trade Agreement with Canada and Mexico and maintained that expanded trade with Eastern Europe and China would ultimately liberalize areas long dominated by authoritarianism, many of their ambitions for the postcolonial world went unrealized. As with past attempts by the United States to promote modernization during the Cold War, interventions under the Bush and Clinton administrations in the name of development, democracy, and capitalism rarely went according to plan. In Panama, Somalia, and Haiti, in particular, U.S. objectives would prove far more difficult and costly than anticipated.

George H. W. Bush's reasons for invading Panama in December 1989 did not match his exalted rhetoric about the world's democratic destiny. Since the 1950s, U.S. intelligence agencies had viewed Manuel Noriega as an ideal anti-Communist ally, and the United States continued to support him after he seized power as the head of the Panamanian Defense Forces in 1983. By the mid-1980s, however, Noriega became a source of increasing embarrassment as his narcotics dealing, arms trading, and violations of the U.S. embargo against Cuba became the subject of congressional inquiry and extensive media coverage. After Noriega was indicted by U.S. federal grand juries on drug-trafficking, racketeering, and money-laundering charges in early 1988, the Reagan White House finally imposed economic sanctions on Panama. In May 1989, after Noriega's thuggish "Dignity Battalions" assaulted his political opponents, and he nullified the results of a national election, the Bush administration resolved to remove him from power. On December 17, Bush ordered Operation Just Cause, and three days later 27,000 U.S. troops invaded Panama. Under U.S. protection, the winners of the cancelled elections were then sworn into office.[16]

Given the degree to which U.S. officials had long supported Noriega's repressive rule, the Bush administration's insistence that the invasion was driven by a commitment to defend democracy lacked credibility. The need to eliminate a political liability as the U.S. government launched its own domestic antidrug campaign was a far more plausible motive. Yet once U.S. forces had removed the troublesome Panamanian from power, the problems of political reconstruction and "nation building" became difficult to avoid. Having declared that the invasion would support the construction of a successful democratic society, the Bush administration had little choice but to engage in that task. Civilian and military planners also approached it with a set of assumptions very similar to those that had shaped U.S. engagements with the postcolonial world during the Cold War. Panamanian society and culture, they expected, would be easily malleable, and reconstruction would be rapidly accomplished.

Operation Blind Logic, the appropriately named plan for the reconstruction of Panama, was extremely ambitious and deeply flawed. In the wake of the invasion U.S. Army officers were ordered to "conduct nation building operations to ensure that democracy, internationally recognized standards of justice, and professional public services are established and institutionalized in Panama." In addition to distributing food and fuel, ensuring water supplies, electricity, and communications, constructing a national police force, and publishing a newspaper, occupation forces were also charged with restructuring the Ministries of Justice, Planning and Finance, Industry and Commerce, Foreign Relations, Treasury, Presidency, Labor, Agriculture, Health, Education, Housing, and Public Works. All this, moreover, was expected to be done within a single year.[17]

The results were profoundly disappointing. As in the 2003 invasion of Iraq, planning for reconstruction was concentrated in the Pentagon, funding was woefully inadequate, and little effort was made to coordinate with the State Department, AID, and the Justice Department. As they would in Iraq, U.S. planners also assumed that once the head of the state was removed, the Panamanian government would continue to function efficiently, allowing for a rapid transition. U.S. forces, therefore, were totally unprepared to handle the realities of massive postinvasion looting, a bankrupt treasury, and the collapse of Panama's civilian agencies. General Maxwell Thurman, commander in chief of the U.S. Army's Southern Command and lead military planner, recounted: "Blind Logic was not suitable for the reconstruction of Panama because it did not accurately assess the dimensions of the task....It was based on the hope that life would quickly return to normal, people would go back to work, and schools would reopen. Unfortunately this was a faulty premise." Instead of simply facilitating and assisting the Panamanian authorities, Thurman lamented, "we ended up having to rebuild an entire government."[18]

More significantly, U.S. planners acted as if Panama's history, culture, and social structure were irrelevant, and their easy assumptions led to ill-defined and overly optimistic expectations. As frustrations mounted in the months after the invasion, planners finally acknowledged that the problem wasn't one of "restoring" democracy at all, because there really was "no history of democracy in Panama." As one analyst explained, platitudes about the ability to transform Panama obscured the hard questions about what the United States might realistically accomplish, questions such as the following: "What kind of democracy was possible in Panama? How long would it take to establish and secure? What were the major obstacles that had to be overcome? Would an operative civil government exist once the PDF [Panamanian Defense Force] was destroyed? What would replace the PDF? What was the state of the economic and social infrastructure?" The fact that Panama lacked civic and democratic traditions, and that there were few institutions through which democratic institutions could be constructed, never seemed to enter into the equation. The country's political economy, and the extent to which sharp inequalities of wealth and power would make democracy a difficult prospect, were also given little consideration.[19]

In his 1990 State of the Union address, President Bush declared that the invasion of Panama was part of the wider "Revolution of '89," a "chain reaction, changes so striking that it marks the beginning of a new era in the world's affairs." "One year ago—one year ago;" he proclaimed, "the people of Panama lived in fear, under the thumb of a dictator. Today democracy is restored; Panama is free." The reality, however, was more complex. Although an elected, civilian-led government was put in place, the overwhelming power of the executive branch prevented popular accountability, and endemic corruption continued to undermine the government's legitimacy. Through the mid-1990s Panama's gross domestic product also stagnated at preinvasion levels, and the country's income inequality remained among the highest in Latin America. When "nation building" in Panama turned out to be far more lengthy, costly, and uncertain than expected, the U.S. commitment to it quickly faded. Although Congress authorized $471 million in aid for Panama in 1990, and $395 million in 1991, making it the fifth largest recipient of U.S. economic aid in the world, assistance fell to less than $6 million by 1993 and remained at roughly that level through the end of the decade.[20]

U.S. motives for intervention in Somalia were radically different, yet assumptions that the United States could produce a rapid transformation contributed to disaster there as well. Created out of former British and Italian colonies in 1960, Somalia was governed under a military dictatorship from 1969 until 1991, when the country plunged into civil war. By the early 1990s, roughly a half-million Somalis had fled as refugees, another half-million were displaced internally, and an estimated 350,000 had perished due to a severe drought and famine. As regional warlords seized relief supplies and traded them for weapons, international humanitarian organizations found themselves unable to deliver food aid, and an already very weak state imploded. Under a Security Council resolution in April 1992, the United Nations deployed a small force to try to preserve a cease-fire and protect food delivery, but it soon became clear that a much larger commitment was necessary. In the fall of 1992, with public pressure for humanitarian action mounting, George Bush offered to bolster the UN operation with

U.S. troops serving under a separate American command. By the time Bill Clinton took office, 28,000 U.S. soldiers were deployed through Operation Restore Hope, a mission to secure ports and food distribution points, protect relief operations, and assist the UN and nongovernment organizations in providing humanitarian aid.[21]

Initially, Operation Restore Hope's purposes were narrowly defined, and with famine seemingly averted U.S. forces were reduced to 4,000 by June 1993. Before long, however, Clinton administration officials and UN authorities concluded that to prevent Somalia from reverting to anarchic warfare when peacekeeping forces left it would be essential to promote economic development and political reconstruction. This was a task that they embraced with enthusiasm. In March 1993, under Resolution 814, later nicknamed "the Mother of All Resolutions," the United States led the UN Security Council in calling for a program to "assist the people of Somalia to promote and advance political reconciliation, through broad participation by all sectors of Somali society, and the re-establishment of national and regional institutions and civil administration in the entire country." As U.S. ambassador to the United Nations Madeleine Albright declared, "we will embark on an unprecedented enterprise aimed at nothing less than the restoration of an entire country as a proud, functioning, and viable member of the community of nations." U.S. troops, she later added, would remain in Somalia "as long as needed to lift the country and its people from the category of a failed state into that of an emerging democracy."[22]

The essential problems of a country lacking any legitimate authority were not so easily overcome. Western governments, regional organizations, and Somali intellectuals promoted reconciliation efforts to stop the fighting, and conferences drafted plans for the formation of local administrative councils, a national police force, a health-care system, expanded primary education, and the delivery of water, food, and sanitation. In March 1993, a seventy-four member Transitional National Council, made up of representatives from across Somalia, also drafted a temporary charter for a new government. But while U.S. and UN forces helped alleviate the effects of a devastating, politically driven famine, Somali warlords refused to disarm, harassed relief agencies, and actively worked against the UN. In June 1993, troops under Mohamed Farah Aideed, one of the principal parties in the civil war, attacked Pakistani soldiers serving under UN authority, killing twenty-four. In retaliation, the UN command issued a bounty for Aideed's capture and launched a military offensive against him. On October 3, in the course of a firefight in Mogadishu, Aideed's forces downed two U.S. helicopters, killed eighteen American soldiers, wounded seventy-seven more, and dragged one of the dead through the streets. Extensive U.S. media coverage of the debacle stirred public and congressional anger as commentators sharply criticized the deployment of U.S. forces in a region where no immediate national interests could be discerned. Fearing a backlash that would damage his presidency, Bill Clinton quickly reversed course, promising to remove all U.S. troops by the following spring and insisting, in stark contrast to the UN resolution and his own administration's statements, that "the U.S. military mission is not now nor was it ever one of 'nation building.'"[23]

Following the debacle in Somalia, the Clinton administration also defined the purpose of its intervention in Haiti in narrower terms, closely linking the restoration of democracy to more traditional arguments about the United States' hemispheric interests. Since overthrowing the democratically elected, populist priest Jean-Bertrand Aristide in September 1991, the dictatorship of General Raoul Cedras had defied demands by the United States, the United Nations, and the Organization of American States that it restore the Haitian president to power. The Cedras regime also killed thousands of Haitians and forced tens of thousands more to flee the country, many of whom arrived in the United States as refugees. Under international pressure, Cedras finally agreed to step down, and 20,000 U.S. troops led a multinational UN force in an unopposed occupation, returning Aristide to office in September 1994. Backing away from broader arguments about the global "enlargement" of market democracies, Clinton opined: "The United States cannot, indeed, we should not, be the world's policemen.... But when brutality occurs close to our shores, it affects our national interests, and we have a responsibility to act." Clinton now stressed Haiti's proximity and a more specific responsibility in Latin America reminiscent of the Monroe Doctrine. "History," he reflected, "has taught us that preserving democracy in our own hemisphere strengthens America's security and prosperity."[24]

By the mid-1990s, the Clinton administration had retreated from its earlier ambitions. As critics attacked Clinton and his advisers for having "tried, and failed, to turn American foreign policy into a branch of social work," the erosion of domestic public support for policies intended to "rearrange the political and economic lives" of postcolonial nations became painfully clear. The United States put Aristide back in office, but as Haiti collapsed once more into turmoil, it rapidly decreased its commitment. Far from trying to impose democracy and development, the Clinton administration also refused to take any action at all to stop genocide in Rwanda in 1994. While AID continued to define the promotion of democracy as an essential goal, the administration increasingly spoke of globalization as a machine that would run on its own. In time, Clinton suggested, the universal solvent of open markets and integrated communications would inevitably produce democratic, liberalizing effects. In May 2000, Clinton declared that once more than 100 million of its people had Internet access, even China would find it "impossible to maintain a closed political and economic system."

Instead of trying to direct it, as modernizers had proposed, the United States could patiently wait for history to unfold.[25]

In other ways, however, the ambition to promote liberal, democratic trans-formations endured. UN Secretary-General Boutros Boutros-Ghali, for example, believed that the end of the Cold War invited greater international activism. "The nations and peoples of the United Nations," he asserted in 1992, "are fortunate in a way that those of the League of Nations were not. We have been given a second chance to create the world of our Charter that they were denied." That spirit, widely shared among many of the key delegations on the UN Security Council, led to increasing support for new forms of "expanded" peacekeeping, or "peace enforcement" missions. In traditional operations, impartial peacekeep-ers were expected to use a minimum of force to monitor an existing cease-fire with the consent of the conflicting parties. In "expanded" missions, mandates were far more ambitious, often involving combat operations and specifically in-tended to promote democratization and economic development in addition to conflict resolution. The results of these efforts, however, rarely met expectations. Transforming societies sharply polarized by ethnic, racial, religious, and ideolog-ical conflicts proved extremely difficult. Liberal internationalist hopes also ran aground on the fact that UN missions found it nearly impossible to impose de-mocracy when powerful local leaders and political movements had little interest in it, as in Somalia and Haiti. Nevertheless, expanded peacekeeping operations continued in the late 1990s, with deployments in some of the most complex, war-torn societies in the postcolonial world, including East Timor, Sierra Leone, and the Democratic Republic of the Congo (formerly Zaire).[26]

The link between development and security, one of the core assumptions of Cold War modernization theories, persisted through the century's end. Where modernizers once feared that poverty, unmet expectations, and a lack of devel-opment would make nonaligned, postcolonial states vulnerable to Communist subversion, the "failed states" of the 1990s were envisioned as possible sources for the spread of Islamic radicalism, terrorism, international crime, ethnic con-flict, and drug trafficking. The underlying assumption was a familiar one—failed transitions to modernity in the global South represented serious security threats to the economically advanced democracies of the West. After the terrorist attacks of September 11, 2001, that argument would take on much greater weight.[27]

Modernization and the Bush Worldview

In the 2000 election campaign, George W. Bush and his advisers rejected the idea of nation building. Interventions launched in the name of humanitarianism, they warned, had all too easily morphed into misguided attempts to restructure foreign societies with little strategic relevance. U.S. interests, they insisted, would be better served by a more modest policy grounded in the knowledge that markets would transform the world over time. As future National Security Advisor Condoleezza Rice argued in early 2000, "powerful secular trends are moving the world toward economic openness and—more unevenly—democracy and individual liberty. Some states have one foot on the train and the other off. Some still hope to find a way to decouple democracy and economic progress. Some hold on to old hatreds as diversions from the modernizing task at hand. But the United States and its allies are on the right side of history." In such a global environment, she suggested, the United States should focus primarily on its relationship with the world's great powers and seek to preserve the conditions in which capitalism would spread its universally applicable values. Countries like Saddam Hussein's Iraq, "left by the side of the road" in history's march, were indeed dangerous, but in general forceful intervention for the purposes of nation building was a serious mistake. In words that would soon take on an ironic ring, Rice warned: "[The U.S. military] is not a civilian police force. It is not a political referee. And it is most certainly not designed to build a civilian society."[28]

Those themes continued through the Bush administration's first several months in office. As the president himself asserted before Congress in February 2001, capitalism would ultimately drive the world in American directions. "Freedom," he declared, "is exported every day, as we ship goods and products that improve the lives of millions of people. Free trade brings greater political and personal freedom." While President Bush, Vice President Dick Cheney, and Secretary of Defense Donald Rumsfeld all believed that the United States should seek a position of global hegemony, supported by unparalleled military power and a willingness to take unilateral action, the administration also expected that the promotion of an increasingly liberal order would put time on the side of the United States.[29]

The terrorist attacks of September 11, 2001, triggered a reassessment of that optimistic vision. While the sudden realization of vulnerability created by the destruction of the World Trade Center and the strike on the Pentagon confirmed the administration's unilateralist preferences and reinforced a willingness to go it alone when international organizations failed to comply with U.S. demands, it also cast doubt on the idea that U.S. policymakers could wait for the expected unfolding of universal liberalism. Threats to U.S. security, they now believed, demanded far more immediate and forceful action. As one analyst put it, Bush and his advisers concluded that their faith in the ultimate, long-term triumph of the marketplace was "not nearly attentive enough to the levers of historical change." "History," the Bush administration decided, "needs deliberate organization,

patience no longer an option

leadership, and direction." To protect U.S. security from terrorist groups like Al Qaeda and "rogue states" like Iraq, the United States would have to *accelerate* history's course using the full range of tools available to it, including war.[30]

The sources of the Bush administration's approach to a "global war on terror" and the reasoning behind the invasions of Afghanistan and Iraq are varied and complex. With good reason, many accounts stress the role of prominent "neoconservatives." Figures like Deputy Secretary of Defense Paul Wolfowitz, National Security Council member Elliott Abrams, and Defense Policy Board member Richard Perle, these interpretations argue, pushed policies in dangerously moralistic and aggressive directions. Animated by a Manichaean vision of world politics, a moralistic focus on democracy, a disdain for diplomacy, and a reverence for military power, neoconservatives helped lead the charge for a sharp change of course. Uneasy with the bloodless vision of consumer capitalism's global march, they seized upon the attacks of September 11 as a means to revive a militant, moral crusade much like the one that animated Ronald Reagan's defiant stand against the Soviet "evil empire."[31]

To be sure, neoconservatives in public office and Washington think tanks had long pushed for a more aggressive, unilateralist, morally centered approach to the post–Cold War world. As early as 1992, working in the administration of George H. W. Bush, Paul Wolfowitz called for a massive military buildup to back unilateral interventions, enable preemptive strikes, and deter any other power from challenging the supremacy of the United States. During the mid-1990s, neoconservative editors and writers like William Kristol and Robert Kagan also pushed for a "neo-Reaganite foreign policy." Through journals like *The Weekly Standard* and *Commentary,* think tanks such as the American Enterprise Institute, and lobbying groups like the Project for a New American Century, neoconservatives consistently promoted doctrines based on unilateral action, military primacy, and the expansion of liberal democracy. Containment, moreover, was not enough. "When it comes to dealing with tyrannical regimes, especially those with the power to do us or our allies harm," Kagan and Kristol wrote in 2000, "the United States should not seek coexistence but transformation."[32]

After September 11, many of these ideas did indeed take center stage in Bush administration policymaking. But these principles also overlapped with other, broader patterns in American thinking. The drive for U.S. hegemony and the focus on military force, for example, recalled the Truman administration's pursuit of a "preponderance of power." The stress on preemption was certainly congruent with U.S. Cold War interventions in Iran, Guatemala, and the Dominican Republic. While preferring to build alliances, U.S. Cold War policymakers also were willing to go it alone (or with only a handful of allies) when they believed conditions demanded it, as in Vietnam. The expansion of liberal democracy, moreover, was at the core of Democratic thinking in the early 1990s, resonated with liberal internationalist ambitions present throughout the Cold War, and echoed the deeper strains of Wilsonian ideas as well. "The neoconservative appeal," historian Tony Smith noted, "could not have been as great as it was without finding resonance in older and varied sources of American culture and belief." What emerged in the wake of September 11, therefore, was less a revolutionary departure than a revival of older ways of thinking.[33]

Such an argument, of course, need not ignore the other immediate motives at hand. The destruction of Al Qaeda's training camps, the pursuit of Osama bin Laden, and the elimination of the Taliban regime, which sheltered him, obviously provided the immediate motives for the U.S. invasion of Afghanistan. Contrary to Vice President Dick Cheney's repeated assertions, no hard evidence ever emerged linking Iraq to the terrorist attacks. Yet the heightened sense of the United States' vulnerability after September 11 gave greater impetus to the claim that the mere possibility that Saddam Hussein might possess weapons of mass destruction (WMD) was an unacceptable risk. No longer willing to support the system of containment through UN weapons inspections, the Bush administration concluded with very little serious analysis or debate that its wish for Iraqi "regime change" had become a necessity. The largely unexamined assumptions that Saddam Hussein could not be deterred from acquiring WMD and that he might transfer them to terrorists, therefore, played vital roles in Bush administration planning. Iraq's geographic location, as well as its vast oil reserves, also gave that country enormous strategic significance.[34]

Yet these were certainly not the only forces at work. "Iraq's supposed cache of WMD," Paul Wolfowitz later acknowledged, "had never been the most compelling casus belli. It was simply one of several." Indeed, on another level, the invasions of Afghanistan and Iraq were defined as part of a much more sweeping, longer-term set of objectives. As the "war on terrorism" quickly expanded from a fight against Al Qaeda, to a mission to destroy the governments that sheltered terrorists, and then on to a campaign against hostile states suspected of producing WMD, the administration's ambitions expanded as well. Beyond eliminating immediate threats and controlling a strategically and economically vital region, the invasions were understood as part of a wider strategy to reshape the future of the Middle East.[35]

Those themes emerged with striking clarity in the two years after September 11. In June 2002, the president used his commencement address at West Point to outline the administration's overall approach. After reprising the argument that terrorist networks could not be deterred and that "unbalanced dictators" could not be contained, Bush went on to stress the wider contours of history, declaring that "the 20th century ended with a single surviving model of human progress," and promising to promote it globally. In the *National Security Strategy of the United States of America,* released in September 2002, the administration gave that transformative vision broader weight. "The events of September 11, 2001," it declared, "taught us that weak states, like Afghanistan, can pose as great a danger to our national interests as strong states. Poverty does not make poor people into terrorists and murderers. Yet poverty, weak institutions, and corruption can make weak states vulnerable to terrorist networks and drug cartels within their own borders." Here then was a vision of modernization reformulated to fit a new political era. As in the Cold War, security and development were firmly linked, yet now the danger of communism was replaced by the proliferation of terrorism. The solution shifted as well, from the export of New Deal institutions to a neoliberal emphasis on "free trade and free markets" as the forces that would "lift whole societies out of poverty" and serve as the primary catalysts of social change.[36]

As the United States launched the war in Iraq, the coupling of lethal force and reformist ambitions, another of modernization's hallmarks, became increasingly clear. In late February 2003, only a few weeks before going to war, Bush insisted that invading Iraq would accelerate vast changes throughout the entire Middle East. "A liberated Iraq," he declared, "can show the power of freedom to transform that vital region, by bringing hope and progress into the lives of millions." It would serve as a "dramatic and inspiring example," promote progressive trends "from Morocco to Bahrain and beyond," and encourage leaders to embrace a "new Arab charter that champions internal reform, greater politics participation [sic], economic openness, and free trade." In time, Bush predicted, it might even "begin a new stage for Middle Eastern peace, and set in motion progress towards a truly democratic Palestinian state." During the Cold War, Truman, Eisenhower, Kennedy, and Johnson had all warned that a failure to contain communism would only allow it to gather momentum and advance further. In the post–Cold War era, Bush and his advisers now embraced a "domino theory" of their own. This time, however, the pieces would fall in the U.S. direction. Invading Iraq would weaken tyrannical leaders, embolden reformist forces, and catalyze a universal process across the lines of culture, religion, and history.[37]

Over the next several months, the administration's emphasis on wider transformations continued. Speaking to the United Nations General Assembly in September 2003, six months after U.S. troops began their drive to Baghdad, Bush promised that a "transformed Middle East" would "benefit the entire world, by undermining the ideologies that export violence to other lands." A couple of months later, Bush again insisted that "as long as the Middle East remains a place where freedom does not flourish it will remain a place of stagnation, resentment, and violence ready for export." "Iraqi democracy," however, "will succeed—and that success will send the news, from Damascus to Tehran—that freedom can be the future of every nation. The establishment of a free Iraq at the heart of the Middle East will be a watershed event in the global democratic revolution." In these formulations, the war in Iraq was easily folded into the familiar framework of a struggle of modernity over tradition, a campaign to guide the development of that country and the rest of the region through a dangerous historical window.[38]

The public appeal of such formulations is obvious. By linking the pursuit of U.S. security objectives with the propagation of democracy and progress, Bush and his advisers reconciled U.S. interests with moral purpose. The neoliberal equation of capitalism with freedom and modernity, of course, also provided a framework through which U.S. economic interests might be defined in terms of progressive, global change. But it would be a mistake to treat such arguments as mere propaganda exercises, designed solely to deflect criticism of an intervention launched without UN approval and with only a thin layer of international support. While the Bush administration certainly recognized their value in that regard, such arguments were also the products of a deeper worldview that strongly influenced the conduct of policy. Ideologies, moreover, can be all the more damaging and destructive when they are sincerely held. As the U.S. experience in the occupation and reconstruction of Afghanistan and Iraq reveals, once these ideas were actually put into *practice* they led administration planners to rely on facile, unfounded assumptions of easy transformation and rapid conversion. Afghanistan and Iraq, it turned out, were not so malleable, and the "end of history" would soon appear very remote.

Imposing Modernity in Afghanistan and Iraq

In both Afghanistan and Iraq, the Bush administration expected that rapid, sweeping transformations would be possible. Where Bush administration strategists associated the term "nation building" with a difficult, costly, long-term commitment, they now envisioned a much lighter burden. Bolstered by a neoliberal vision, they imagined that once the oppressive Taliban regime and Saddam Hussein's brutal dictatorship were removed that grateful Afghans and Iraqis would eagerly embrace newfound opportunities to reorient their societies in democratic, capitalist directions. Because markets were a naturally occurring phenomenon, prolonged government intervention was unnecessary. Nations might need to be built, but markets only had to be liberated. Postwar reconstruction, therefore, would be smooth, rapid, and cheap, allowing U.S. forces to ensure security, transfer authority, establish stable, market-driven growth, and then quickly depart—all in a few short months. Reality, however, did not match those assumptions.

The initial war in Afghanistan exceeded even the Bush administration's high expectations. Relying on long-range, precision airpower, small special forces teams, and an alliance with Afghan warlords, an unconventional attack made rapid gains. By November 2001, only a month after the war started, the Taliban were driven from Kabul. Although U.S., coalition, and Afghan forces failed to prevent Al Qaeda and Taliban fighters from escaping into the mountains and across the Pakistani border, the Bush administration was delighted with the war's early progress.[39]

The reconstruction effort, by contrast, fared poorly as the administration confronted a serious fallacy in its thinking. Afghanistan, Bush and his advisers insisted, had become a dangerous threat precisely because it was a "failed state," a weak government presiding over a society so poor, divided, and backward that it had fallen prey to a radical Islamist movement willing to shelter transnational terrorists. Yet if modernization identified the absence of development as the ultimate source of danger, in its post–Cold War, neoliberal variant it also suggested that the necessary corrections could be made quickly and easily, and with a minimum of effort. That assumption helps explain the surprising fact that even as the administration constantly defined Afghanistan's destitution and instability as a security threat, its efforts at postwar reconstruction there were very poorly planned and consistently underfunded. The overwhelming emphasis on private, market forces as the essential engines behind Afghan reconstruction, moreover, undermined the possibility of building an effective, secure state and increased the prospects for the Taliban's resurgence.

During the run-up to the start of the Afghan war on October 7, 2001, the Bush administration paid little attention to questions of postwar planning. When the president finally raised the issue in a meeting with his primary advisers on October 4, he received few concrete answers. As political analysts Ivo Daalder and James Lindsay have emphasized, it "speaks volumes about the decisionmaking process that three full weeks into high-level planning for a war, no one had bothered to consider how the United States would win the peace." The question of Afghanistan's political future finally entered into administration discussions in mid-October, when the State Department began to work with the United Nations, different anti-Taliban factions, and neighboring countries to create a "broadly representative, multi-ethnic, governing structure." Talks under the direction of UN special representative Lakhdar Brahimi in Bonn, Germany, in late November 2001, finally established a nominal political framework as Hamid Karzai became the chair of an interim government and plans were made for *loya jirgas* (deliberative councils) of elected delegates to draft a constitution prior to national elections.[40]

As chair and then president, Karzai faced an enormous task in trying to build a productive economy, deliver public services, create a legal infrastructure, and resolve the deep disputes that divided Afghans along ethnic and political lines. U.S. policies, however, continued to focus on the United States' own immediate security objectives, often exacerbating the deeper problems of building a new state. Ties with local and regional warlords were vital to the U.S. military's strategy in the early stages of the war, and the United States and NATO forces continued to rely on them. Few of those actors, however, had any interest in surrendering their authority and arms to become part of a national democracy. With U.S. and international assistance, moreover, their continued power helped prevent Karzai's government from stretching its authority much beyond the Kabul city limits.[41]

At a more profound level, the attempt to engineer a market-driven Afghan transformation failed. Although the Bush administration continued to speak of the miracles of free trade and the entrepreneurial opportunities to be unleashed by the end of Taliban rule, Afghanistan simply lacked the essential elements for a wider market economy to function. Markets, of course, depend on a clear, unified legal framework to define property rights and enforce contracts, a missing element in Afghanistan's patchwork of conflicting state, civil, religious, and customary laws. As the World Bank pointed out in a 2005 report, without necessary public infrastructure, common legal standards, and highly educated individuals with managerial and technical backgrounds, Afghanistan was unlikely to experience an economic "take-off" anytime soon. Yet those essential ingredients, largely dependent on the creation of a viable state and its participation in national economic life, were precisely the elements that the neoliberal focus on free trade and investment tended to ignore.[42]

Patterns of international assistance, shaped by the neoliberal aversion to a strong state role in development, also weakened the prospects for an Afghan transformation. In rural Afghanistan, markets provided few incentives to meet the basic needs of a desperately poor population for nutrition, safe water, health care, and education, making these areas crucial for state intervention. After more than two decades of war, moreover, Afghanistan's life expectancy had fallen to forty-four, the adult literacy rate was only 28.7 percent, and child mortality rates were extremely high. International donors, however, largely ignored the Afghan state and provided funds through separate institutions directly accountable to their own authority. Because donors preferred to work through their own development agencies or in conjunction with private corporations and nongovernment organizations, in 2005 only 30 percent of international aid expenditures were incorporated into the Afghan national budget. Official corruption may have made that a shrewd approach, but such practices also drew the most talented national administrators and planners out of low-paying government employment and into international organizations, further weakening the foundations of the Afghan state. Unable to provide essential services or define a strategy for national development, the Afghan government's legitimacy and authority remained extremely weak.[43]

Even after eight years of U.S. and NATO occupation, U.S. claims about the victory of Afghan democracy were more form than reality. Presidential and parliamentary elections in 2004 and 2005 were contested with heavy voter turnout, and the drafting of a national constitution was a significant accomplishment. But emphasizing those facts alone obscures the degree to which Afghanistan continued to lack a functioning national government, a democratic political culture, or the de facto rule of law. U.S. and international funding for Afghan development also remained far short of public needs. In 2002, George W. Bush proclaimed that "true peace will only be achieved when we give the Afghan people the means to achieve their own inspirations," but by 2004 the White House included no funding for Afghanistan in its budget. In 2006, the Afghan government's National Development Strategy estimated that it would require more than $14 billion beyond its expected revenue over the next five years, yet international donors committed only $10.5 billion. As Human Rights Watch pointed out, on a per capita basis, the reconstruction budgets for the 1990s interventions in Kosovo, Bosnia, and East Timor were up to fifty times larger. As most Afghans continued to survive on less than one dollar per day, the country's opium economy increasingly expanded, making up 35 percent of the country's gross domestic product and supplying 92 percent of the world's heroin in 2005. Finally, from 2006 through 2009, the Taliban mounted a serious resurgence, making steady gains in the southern and eastern provinces of the country and demonstrating that even the United States' immediate security goals remained unmet.[44]

The expectation that the United States could engineer a rapid, sweeping, and modernizing transition in Iraq also proved disastrous. Here too the Bush administration imagined that ending a brutal, tyrannical regime would prepare the ground for the swift, natural emergence of market-driven, capitalist democracy, sweeping away any historical or cultural barriers to the construction of a new social order. Vice President Dick Cheney told a television audience three days before the war started: "The read we get on the people of Iraq is there is no question but they want to get rid of Saddam Hussein and they will welcome as liberators the United States when we come to that." U.S. policymakers, journalist Anthony Shadid explained, viewed Iraq through a "simple, two-dimensional" frame. They imagined a country "trapped in a relationship of submission and victimization; its people were voiceless, deprived of the power to determine their own destiny. Once the dictator was removed, by force if need be, Iraq would be free, a tabula rasa on which to build a new and different state." While no doubt correct in interpreting a broad level of alienation regarding Saddam Hussein's vicious dictatorship, the ideal of rapid liberation suggested that the specific Iraqi context really did not matter. Instead of a country with no experience in democratic governance, deeply divided along religious and ethnic lines, and economically devastated by years of war and sanctions, the Bush administration and U.S. occupation officials perceived Iraq as an empty vessel, an infinitely malleable society awaiting U.S. instruction and direction.[45]

That assessment reinforced the dominant conviction that serious, long-term planning for a difficult, costly, and complex occupation would be unnecessary. Expecting that the "shock and awe" of precision bombing and a lightning-fast drive to Baghdad would overwhelm the Iraqi resistance, Bush administration officials assumed that they could avoid the problems of "nation building" and focus instead on merely "enabling" the work of liberated Iraqis. "The concept," Condoleeza Rice later explained, "was that we would defeat the army, but the institutions would hold, everything from ministries to police forces." The United States, in effect, would lop off the head of the Iraqi state, and then redirect the still functioning, eagerly cooperative body toward the construction of a new liberal order. Instead of the chaos and violence encountered in Somalia during the 1990s, policymakers anticipated a transformative moment akin to the successful occupations of Germany and Japan at the close of World War II. Setting aside all consideration of Iraqi conditions, they ignored the crucial distinction that in Germany and Japan the occupation forces enjoyed a high degree of political legitimacy among the citizens of the defeated nations. Those occupations aimed to reconstruct countries with essentially homogenous populations and a strong, enduring sense of national identity, factors absent in Iraq.[46]

With its ideological assumptions about the ease with which Iraqi society might be reprogrammed firmly in place, Bush administration policymakers rejected serious assessments that challenged their convictions. In early 2002, more than a year before the March 2003 invasion, the State Department started its "Future of Iraq" project, an ambitious attempt to anticipate what postwar Iraq would be like and to make recommendations for the occupation. Drawing on the efforts of seventeen different working groups made up of Iraqi exiles, country specialists, intelligence personnel, and Middle East experts, the project eventually produced a thirteen-volume report running some 2,500 pages. To be sure, the study was not flawless. Some issues were thinly treated, it provided only general recommendations, and some exiles viewed the project as a way to promote themselves for future Iraqi leadership. But with sections on the rebuilding of Iraqi infrastructure, the country's legal framework, the removal of Baath Party influence, public finance, agriculture, and the oil industry, the study raised many problems that should have merited serious consideration. In the wake of the invasion, contributors advised, it would be crucial to restore electricity and water supplies immediately in order to temper the likely Iraqi resentment of a foreign occupying army. The removal of Saddam Hussein's regime, a section on civil society argued, would create a "power vacuum" generating "popular anxieties about the viability of all Iraqi institutions" and making looting and violent retribution likely. In a similar fashion, studies by the Central Intelligence Agency emphasized the deep divisions within Iraqi society, the fact that years of dictatorship provided a weak foundation for the construction of a democratic political culture, and the potential for violence to prevent a rapid transfer of sovereignty and an easy U.S. exit. At weekly meetings with AID staff, representatives from NGOs and relief organizations drew on their experience in the 1990s in countries like Panama, Haiti, Somalia, and Lebanon to warn that nation building in Iraq would be extremely difficult.[47]

With the benefit of hindsight, such arguments appear more than a little prescient. What is most striking, however, is the degree to which the Bush administration policymakers in charge of the war and its aftermath did everything they could to rule such objections out of court. The president gave the responsibility for postwar Iraq to the Defense Department, and although the Pentagon and the army's Central Command had carried out intensive planning for an invasion since the fall of 2001, Donald Rumsfeld and his aides did not create a postwar planning office until late January 2003, less than two months before the war began. Jay Garner, the retired general in charge of the new Office of Reconstruction and Humanitarian Assistance (ORHA), found himself hamstrung by the Pentagon's determination to conceal any evidence that might challenge the reigning assumptions. When he asked for all government studies on the problems of postwar Iraq, Pentagon officials told Garner that none existed, despite the fact that postwar planning assessments had been carried out by the State Department, the CIA, and the National Defense University. Garner finally learned of the State Department research at an interagency conference in late February, but when he added the director of the "Future of Iraq" project to his staff, Rumsfeld ordered that he be removed. In testimony before the House Budget Committee, Paul Wolfowitz also aggressively attacked General Eric Shinseki's call for a much larger U.S. force as "wildly off the mark," declaring: "It's hard to conceive that it would take more forces to provide stability in post-Saddam Iraq than it would take to conduct the war itself and to secure the surrender of Saddam's security forces and his army. Hard to imagine."[48]

As one four-star general later recalled, a firmly held ideology was at work. The White House and the senior Defense Department leadership "*knew* that postwar Iraq would be easy and would be a catalyst for change in the Middle East. They were making simplistic assumptions and refused to put them to the test....They did it because they already had the answer, and they wouldn't subject their hypothesis to examination." For these officials the reassurances provided by figures like Ahmad Chalabi were far more appealing. The leader of the Iraqi National Congress, a prominent exile organization, Chalabi was a London banker and mathematician trained at MIT and the University of Chicago. He was just the sort of Western-educated, "native elite" that modernization theorists of the 1960s and 1970s had envisioned as the ideal leader—ready to provide technical knowledge, secure bureaucratic order, and build the foundation for enlightened democratization. Pleased with Chalabi's rosy prediction that Iraqis would welcome U.S. invaders, Defense Department figures like Donald Rumsfeld, Paul Wolfowitz, and Douglas Feith saw Chalabi as an ideal lever for the country's transformation, disregarding the problem that after forty years in exile his support within the country was uncertain at best.[49]

Bush administration planners also expected that the transformation of Iraq would be a relatively inexpensive proposition. Speaking before the House Appropriations Committee on March 27, 2003, just over a week after the war started, Wolfowitz assured Congress: "There's a lot of money to pay for this. It doesn't have to be U.S. taxpayer money." Andrew Natsios, the head of AID, gave that claim a concrete figure, suggesting that the price tag for the entire U.S. contribution to Iraqi reconstruction would not exceed $1.7 billion. While the modernizers of the 1960s had expected that the United States might engineer stunning transformations in the postcolonial world, they had at least recognized that their ambitions to promote a global New Deal would be expensive, requesting ever larger amounts of foreign aid and multiyear authorizations. In the Bush administration's neoliberal variation, however, history could be accelerated at bargain basement prices.[50]

As in Afghanistan, the initial course of the war in Iraq was a smashing success. After a day of bombing, the ground attack began on March 20, 2003. With a total force of only 145,000 troops, U.S. and British commanders raced across Iraq. By April 7, U.S. forces took control of Baghdad's airport and Saddam Hussein's palace complex, and two days later they helped Iraqis tear down a massive statue of the dictator in the city's center, an image endlessly reproduced in the U.S. media. On May 1, wearing a flight suit and riding in the copilot seat of a U.S. Navy fighter, George W. Bush triumphantly landed aboard the U.S.S. Abraham Lincoln. Standing on the aircraft carrier's deck before a massive banner reading "Mission Accomplished," the president then proclaimed: "Major combat operations in Iraq have ended. In the battle of Iraq, the United States and our allies have prevailed."[51]

The facts on the ground, of course, soon belied that assessment. As U.S. troops entered Baghdad and the Iraqi army dispersed, widespread looting of government offices, private businesses, museums, and weapons storage depots began. Undermanned and unprepared for the growing chaos, U.S. forces lacked the resources to secure Iraq's borders, allowing foreign jihadists to enter the country. While persistent blackouts, growing street violence, increasing crime, and the lack of safe water and sanitation embittered Iraqi civilians, U.S. military commanders discovered that there were no real reconstruction plans and scrambled to come up with their own. With Iraqi ministries destroyed, the military absent, police stations vacant, and communications systems paralyzed, Jay Garner's ORHA was quickly and totally overwhelmed. To make matters worse, by early May a Sunni insurgency including former Baath Party officials, soldiers, and intelligence officers emerged in the towns to the west of the capital.[52]

U.S. officials were slow to react to the fact that their ideological assumptions were wrong. Convinced by their own rhetoric of liberation, they were caught off guard by the insurgency, and their initial attempts to respond to the situation only made matters worse. On May 12, the White House replaced Garner and ORHA with the new Coalition Provisional Authority (CPA) under L. Paul "Jerry" Bremer III. Bremer's subsequent decision to fire all Baath Party members through the first three management levels in all government ministries, state-owned corporations, universities, and hospitals then forced roughly 85,000 former officials into unemployment. His decision to dissolve the Iraqi army, national police, and security forces compounded that problem, depriving hundreds of thousands of increasingly alienated, well-armed men from the income needed to support their families, and providing additional recruits for the growing Sunni insurgency, Shiite militias, and a long, bloody, anti-American guerrilla war.[53]

Over the next year, expectations that the United States could easily create and control a government that would win broad legitimacy left occupation officials ill prepared to deal with the complexity of post-Saddam politics. In the early stages of the occupation, Bremer appointed a twenty-five-member Iraqi Governing Council, a body with representation across the country's ethnic and religious groups including exiles like Chalabi as well as internal opponents of Saddam Hussein's regime. He then prepared a multiyear plan for the council to draft a constitution that would be ratified by a national referendum and followed by an election to establish a new government. Only then would a transfer of sovereignty take place. Rejecting calls for early elections out of fear that Baathists or religious radicals might win, Bremer also ignored powerful Shiite leader Grand Ayatollah al-Sistani's fatwa that any Iraqi constitution had to be drafted by elected representatives. Bremer soon discovered, however, that he could not govern by fiat. While he expected the council to follow his instructions, the Iraqi leaders instead decided to respect al-Sistani's position. In September 2003, when they charged that the U.S. occupation was fueling the insurgency, and demanded a more rapid transfer of power, Bremer faced an impasse. Worried that the growing insurgency would damage Republican prospects in the 2004 U.S. elections, the Bush administration finally reversed course, agreeing that sovereignty should be transferred by mid-2004, and accepting a proposal that UN envoy Lakhdar Brahimi would select the members of the interim government in consultation with Iraqi leaders, the Governing Council, and the CPA. Where Defense Department officials originally hoped that they could simply put Chalabi and other favorites into power, they found that Iraqi resistance demanded another course of action. In the end, the transfer of sovereignty and the creation of a government of at least minimum legitimacy among a divided Iraqi people required the intervention of the United Nations, the same body that the Bush administration officials had rebuffed in launching a unilateral, preemptive invasion.[54]

As in Afghanistan, the administration's neoliberal approach to reconstruction fared poorly. Under Saddam Hussein, Iraq's economy was driven by a large number of state-owned factories and enterprises. Through the 1970s and early 1980s, salaries were low, but government employment and state subsidies made consumer necessities affordable. State control of the oil industry and rising petroleum prices also helped fund free education and health care. The devastating war with Iran in the 1980s, however, created a massive national debt, while a decade of sanctions after the 1991 Gulf War cut Iraq off from the world's economy and sharply eroded Iraqi living standards. As the U.S. occupation began, therefore, the problems of repairing the war's damage were magnified by a long-term trend of economic decline.[55]

Bush administration and CPA officials, however, were determined to push forward a rapid, neoliberal transformation, immediately placing the country on a free-market footing. While the economy did indeed need serious restructuring, U.S. policymakers rejected the idea that conditions might demand careful, gradual change. Instead they tried to drive their program through with little regard for its effects on the Iraqi population and without consulting the interim Iraqi government. Drafted by AID and the Treasury Department, a classified plan titled "Moving the Iraqi Economy from Recovery to Sustainable Growth" proposed that the occupation create "the groundwork for a market-oriented private sector recovery" by selling state-owned enterprises, building a "world-class" stock exchange, and creating a new income tax system. Bremer and his economic advisers firmly shared that view, convinced that the abolition of subsidies and the swift creation of markets would be essential for Iraqi democracy to take root. Under privatization, they believed, the rigors of the competitive marketplace would naturally purge the Iraqi economy of its unproductive elements, eliminating dead wood and allowing profitable ventures to thrive.[56]

Plans for a swift economic transformation soon went awry. Few of the business executives working in the CPA's Office of Private Sector Development had any experience in transitional economies, but they were all convinced that the immediate need in Iraq was to "remove barriers." By abolishing import duties, the CPA allowed a wave of luxury products, including televisions, cars, electronics, and air conditioners, to flood into major cities, where wealthy Iraqis, many of them with salaries funded by the CPA itself, eagerly bought them up. While CPA officials proclaimed that the imported consumer goods were evidence of capitalism's irresistible momentum, the trade was hardly a solid foundation for longer-term economic growth and investment. The CPA plans to sell off state-owned enterprises were also opposed by the Iraqi Governing Council, which warned that such a move would deprive millions of Iraqi workers of their paychecks, increasing unemployment at the very moment that the security situation threatened to spiral out of control. Finally faced with the fact that the vast majority of the country's state-owned firms were damaged, insolvent, or running on obsolete equipment, the CPA abandoned the plan. Instead of repairing Iraqi companies that could meet the large domestic demand for cement, fertilizer, clothing, and food, the CPA free marketeers allowed them to collapse, limiting the possibility of future economic growth and making the country all the more dependent on external sources of support. Neoliberal policies slashing social welfare spending also alienated the Iraqi public.[57]

From 2004 through 2006, U.S. forces found themselves fighting on multiple fronts. A growing Sunni insurgency to the north and west of Baghdad and a multifaceted Shiite rebellion in parts of the capital and the south of the country worsened security and imperiled reconstruction plans. Although sovereignty was transferred, and Iraqi citizens turned out for elections in astonishing numbers, political conflict among Shiites, Sunnis, and Kurds also continued to threaten a fragile Iraqi government. Through it all, however, the Bush administration continued to stand by its original, upbeat assumptions. The president declared in a May 2005 address that even the United States had gotten off to a rocky start in the "years of chaos" following the American Revolution. The first American form of government, the Articles of Confederation, moreover, had "failed miserably." Yet Iraq too would ultimately move down the universal path toward capitalist democracy. Initiatives like the cheerfully named Operation Adam Smith, a program in which the U.S. Army's First Cavalry Division set up "local chambers of commerce, providing Iraqi entrepreneurs with small business loans, and teaching them important skills like accounting, marketing, and writing small business plans," would ultimately unleash the neoliberal miracle in Iraq as well.[58]

The future of Iraq, of course, remains unclear. Yet several years of war and occupation there demonstrated the extent to which the assumptions that shaped the U.S. intervention were deeply flawed. Beyond the fact that there were no weapons of mass destruction to be found, the ideology of rapid, neoliberal transformation led to a long, costly, and brutal war. As Iraqi institutions collapsed, the

Bush administration was forced to confront the very "nation-building" problems that it had initially eschewed, making a speedy U.S. withdrawal impossible. Instead of welcoming their liberators, large sections of Iraqi society also went to war against a foreign occupation. Nor did the Iraqi economy enjoy a rapid, free-market resurgence under U.S. guidance. Elections to seat a national assembly, ratify a constitution, and select a new government were important steps forward, but prospects for the legal institutions and political culture needed to foster strong democracy remained uncertain. In contrast to the optimistic assessments put forward by its advocates, the war and occupation proved staggeringly expensive in both human and material terms, costing roughly $600 billion, taking the lives of nearly 4,000 U.S. servicemen and women, and contributing to the violent deaths of approximately 93,000 Iraqi civilians in its first five years. After mid-2007 the security situation improved as Washington deployed additional troops, the rebellious Shiite militias lost ground, and the prospect of steady, paid employment led many former Sunni insurgents to work alongside coalition forces. In 2009, however, even that gain remained fragile.[59]

Toward a Reckoning

History certainly did not end in 1989, but the central assumptions of modernization survived the close of the Cold War and continued to exert a strong pull on U.S. approaches to the postcolonial world. In its revised, neoliberal framework, modernization still provided a compelling narrative, reassuring Americans that the ongoing project of development would ultimately lead the world to converge on liberal, capitalist democracy, and suggesting that the United States could direct and accelerate that universal process. The failures and reversals of the Bush administration in Afghanistan and Iraq demonstrated that foreign societies and cultures were not so pliable, and that the United States could not easily impose its own vision of modernity at the point of a gun. Given the appeal of such a deeply rooted ideology, however, modernization and its promise that accelerated development will help ensure security seem likely to endure.

The broader history of modernization, however, clearly suggests the need for a reassessment. In both its 1960s form and its later neoliberal variant, modernization promised that development would be easy and fast. Social scientists of the Cold War period emphasized that a concentrated "big push" of directed investment and foreign aid would allow postcolonial societies to reach the crucial "take-off" point, after which they would enter the period of "self-sustaining growth," ready and able to enjoy a global New Deal without recourse to external help. From the 1980s onward, neoliberals presented their own panaceas. Just get the state out of the way and let markets do their work, they insisted, and the rising tide of prosperity would lift all boats. But markets, of course, have no automatic mechanisms to encourage steps to address inequality, poverty, hunger, or disease. The neoliberal hostility to government-directed social welfare policy has also left most of the world's poor to suffer on their own. History, moreover, appears to have accelerated in the wrong direction. By 2008, claims about the miracles of markets were overshadowed by a deep global recession—and it is worth remembering that this crisis started in the "modern" world and spread outward, doing enormous damage to the "developing" regions. While international lending institutions demand "structural adjustments," impoverished nations find the thin lines of Western charity eroding amid the broad economic downturn.

Seen from this perspective, the burst of creative dissent and constructive energy unleashed by modernization's critics merits another look. During the interregnum of the 1970s, as the liberal version of modernization came under fire and before the neoliberal one seized the throne, critics and commentators had dared to step outside the dominant narrative. Instead of worshipping at the altar of economic growth, they had turned their eyes to questions of inequality and basic needs. Instead of assuming that technologies could be readily inserted without attention to local context, they had raised hard questions about suitability and likely effects, often suggesting alternatives. Instead of assuming that the mass-consumption economies of advanced industrialized nations could continue to grow and be replicated without limit, they had warned of their environmental and gendered effects. The complexity of their critique, of course, also left them vulnerable. By making development appear a difficult, multifaceted, and enduring problem, they framed an appeal that was politically far less powerful than the simple rhetoric of rapid acceleration. Their warnings of crisis also proved unable to compete with the more palatable claim that history was still on the side of the United States.

But by trying to rescue development from modernization they had taken an important step in the right direction. If the United States truly intends to improve the lives of the world's most vulnerable people, it should ally itself with the international and nongovernmental organizations that have followed those insights, emphasizing the problems of poverty, inequality, and environment, and combining them with a renewed focus on an expanded conception of human rights and social justice. Drafted in 1948, and honored since then mostly in the breach, the United Nations Universal Declaration of Human Rights still sets a compelling standard, holding that all are entitled to education, employment, adequate living standards, health care, social security, and civil liberties. The UN's Millennium Development Goals, focused on problems of hunger, education, health care, environmental stability, and women's rights, are an especially worthwhile project, reflecting a commitment to address the poverty-centered issues raised by the dissenters more than thirty years ago.

As liberals, the modernizers of the 1960s shared many of those progressive values, yet their Cold War obsessions betrayed their own principles, and their ambivalence about popular democracy facilitated authoritarian outcomes. An effective campaign for progress will need to overcome that legacy and pursue forms of development far more committed to empowering the poor themselves. As many development experts have argued, the best approaches are often locally centered and promoted through institutions led by and directly accountable to the people they assist. The process will be a long and difficult one, marked less by "take-offs" than by incremental gains and periodic setbacks. It certainly will not lead to "the end of history," nor will it necessarily ensure, as economists W. W. Rostow and Max Millikan put it, "the evolution of a world in which threats to our security and, more broadly, to our way of life are less likely to arise." But it can help improve what Nobel laureate Amartya Sen has referred to as the "life chances" of those in the world's poorest regions, expanding their "human capability to lead more worthwhile and more free lives." That objective is certainly one to strive for.[60]

NOTES

1. Ronald Steel, *Temptations of a Superpower* (Cambridge, MA: Harvard University Press, 1995), 1.

2. Ellen Schrecker, "Introduction: Cold War Triumphalism and the Real Cold War," in *Cold War Triumphalism: The Misuse of History after the Fall of Communism,* ed. Ellen Schrecker (New York: New Press, 2004), 4.

3. Francis Fukuyama, "The End of History?" *The National Interest* 16 (Summer 1989): 3–18.

4. Ibid.

5. Thomas Carothers, "The End of the Transition Paradigm," *Journal of Democracy* 13 (January 2002): 5–21.

6. Lucian Pye, "Political Science and the Crisis of Authoritarianism," *American Political Science Review* 84, no. 1 (1990): 7, 12, 14; Howard J. Wiarda, "Toward the Future: Old and New Directions in Comparative Politics," in *New Directions in Comparative Politics,* ed. Howard J. Wiarda (Boulder, CO: Westview, 1991), 238–39, 241.

7. Bruce Russett, *Grasping the Democratic Peace: Principles for a Post–Cold War World* (Princeton, NJ: Princeton University Press, 1993), 4, 35, 40, 138.

8. Thomas L. Friedman, *The Lexus and the Olive Tree: Understanding Globalization* (New York: Random House, 2000), 9, 348; Mark T. Berger, The *Battle for Asia: From Decolonization to Globalization* (London: RoutledgeCurzon, 2004), 130–31.

9. Friedman, *Lexus and the Olive Tree,* 434–51, 475.

10. John J. Mearsheimer, "Back to the Future: Instability in Europe after the Cold War," *International Security* 15, no. 1 (1990): 5–56; Robert D. Kaplan, "The Coming Anarchy," *Atlantic Monthly* 273, no. 2 (1994): 72; Samuel P. Huntington, "The Clash of Civilizations?" *Foreign Affairs* 72 (Summer 1993): 22–49.

11. John Brohman, "Universalism, Eurocentrism, and Ideological Bias in Development Studies: From Modernisation to Neoliberalism," *Third World Quarterly* 16 (March 1995): 121–40; Nelson Lichtenstein, "Market Triumphalism and Wishful Liberals," in Schrecker, *Cold War Triumphalism,* 103, 105–6.

12. George H. W. Bush, Remarks at the Annual Meeting of the Board of Governors of the IMF and World Bank, September 25, 1990, George H. W. Bush Library, http://bushlibrary.tamu.edu/research/public_papers.php?id=2255&year=1990&month=9.

13. William G. Hyland, *Clinton's World: Remaking American Foreign Policy* (Westport, CT: Praeger, 1999), 4–5; George Bush, State of the Union Address, January 29, 1991, George H. W. Bush Library, http://bushlibrary.tamu.edu/research/public_papers.php?id=26596&year=1991&month=1; Russett, *Grasping the Democratic Peace*, 128–29.

14. Bill Clinton, Speech at American University, February 26, 1993, and Anthony Lake, Speech at Johns Hopkins University School of Advanced International Studies, September 21, 1993, in *The Clinton Foreign Policy Reader: Presidential Speeches and Commentary,* ed. Alvin Z. Rubinstein, Albina Shayevich, and Boris Zlotnikov (Armonk, NY: M. E. Sharpe, 2000), 11–12, 20–22.

15. Lake, Speech at Johns Hopkins, in Rubinstein et al., *Clinton Foreign Policy Reader,* 22, 25; Anthony Lake, "Confronting Backlash States," *Foreign Affairs* 73, no. 2 (1994): 45–46, 55.

16. Karin von Hippel, *Democracy by Force: US Military Intervention in the Post–Cold War World* (Cambridge: Cambridge University Press, 2000), 26–34.

17. Ibid., 35–39.

18. Richard H. Shultz, Jr., *In the Aftermath of War: US Support for Reconstruction and Nation-Building in Panama Following Just Cause* (Maxwell Air Force Base, AL: Air University Press, 1993), 18.

19. Ibid., 17, 23; von Hippel, *Democracy by Force,* 45.

20. George H. W. Bush, State of the Union Address, January 31, 1990, George H. W. Bush Library, http://bushlibrary.tamu.edu/research/public_papers.php?id=1492&year=1990&month=1; von Hippel, *Democracy by Force,* 40–42, 50–51; Orlando J. Pérez, "Democratization and Economic Development: Challenges and Opportunities for the Next Century," in *Post-Invasion Panama: The Challenges of Democratization in the New World Order,* ed. Orlando J. Pérez (Lanham, MD: Lexington Books, 2000), 152; William L. Furlong, "Panama, a Nation Apart: Its Foreign Policy and Its Challenges," in Pérez, *Post-Invasion Panama,* 47.

21. Von Hippel, *Democracy by Force,* 58–60, 62–63; Hyland, *Clinton's World,* 51–53; Warren I. Cohen, *America's Failing Empire: U.S. Foreign Relations since the Cold War* (Malden, MA: Blackwell, 2005), 60.

22. Von Hippel, *Democracy by Force,* 63–64, 73; Hyland, *Clinton's World,* 55–56.

23. Von Hippel, *Democracy by Force,* 65–69; Bill Clinton, Message regarding Somalia to Congress, October 13, 1993, in Rubinstein et al., *Clinton Foreign Policy,* 147.

24. Bill Clinton, Address to the Nation on Haiti, September 15, 1994, in Rubinstein et al., *Clinton Foreign Policy,* 150.

25. Michael Mandelbaum, "Foreign Policy as Social Work," *Foreign Affairs* 75, no. 1 (1996): 18–19; Hyland, *Clinton's World,* 197, 200; Andrew Bacevich, *American Empire: The Realities and Consequences of U.S. Diplomacy* (Cambridge, MA: Harvard University Press, 2002), 106.

26. James Mayall, "Introduction," in *United Nations Interventionism, 1991–2004,* ed. Mats Berdal and Spyros Economides (Cambridge: Cambridge University Press, 2007), 1, 18, 28–30; Frederick H. Fleitz, Jr., *Peacekeeping Fiascoes of the 1990s: Causes, Solutions, and U.S. Interests* (Westport, CT: Praeger, 2002), 11, 51–64, 164–70.

27. Mark Duffield, *Global Governance and the New Wars: The Merging of Development and Security* (London: Zed, 2001).

28. Condoleezza Rice, "Promoting the National Interest," *Foreign Affairs* 79, no. 1 (2000): 46, 53.

29. George W. Bush, Address to Congress, February 27, 2001, American Presidency Project, http://www.presidency.ucsb.edu/ws/print.php?pid=29643.

30. Ken Jowitt, "Rage, Hubris, and Regime Change," *Policy Review* 118 (April/May 2003): 37–38.

31. Stefan Harper and Jonathan Clarke, *America Alone: The Neo-Conservatives and the Global Order* (Cambridge: Cambridge University Press, 2004), 10; Francis Fukuyama, *America at the Crossroads: Democracy, Power, and the Neoconservative Legacy* (New Haven, CT: Yale University Press, 2006); Corey Robin, "Remembrance of Empire's Past: 9/11 and the End of the Cold War," in Shrecker, *Cold War Triumphalism,* 274–97.

32. Stanley Hoffman, *Chaos and Violence: What Globalization, Failed States, and Terrorism Mean for U.S. Foreign Policy* (Lanham, MD: Rowman and Littlefield, 2006), 118; William Kristol and Robert Kagan, "Toward a Neo-Reaganite Foreign Policy," *Foreign Affairs* 75, no. 4 (1996): 21–23, 28–31; Kristol and Kagan, "The Present Danger," *The National Interest* 59 (Spring 2000): 66.

33. Tony Smith, *A Pact with the Devil: Washington's Bid for World Supremacy and the Betrayal of the American Promise* (New York: Routledge, 2007), 44; Melvyn P. Leffler, "9/11 and American Foreign Policy," *Diplomatic History* 29 (June 2005): 395–413.

34. Robert S. Litwak, *Regime Change: U.S. Strategy through the Prism of 9/11* (Washington, DC: Woodrow Wilson Center Press, 2007).

35. Smith, *Pact with the Devil*, 39; Hoffman, *Chaos and Violence*, 122–23.

36. George W. Bush, Graduation Speech at West Point, June 1, 2002, American Presidency Project, http://www.presidency.ucsb.edu/ws/index.php?pid=62730&st=&st1=; *National Security Strategy of the United States of America*, September 17, 2002, White House Archive, http://georgewbush whitehouse.archives.gov/nsc/nss/2002/.

37. George W. Bush, Speech to the American Enterprise Institute, February 26, 2003, American Presidency Project, http://www.presidency.ucsb.edu/ws/index.php?pid=62953&st=&st1=.

38. George W. Bush, Address to the UN General Assembly, September 23, 2003, American Presidency Project, http://www.presidency.ucsb.edu/ws/index.php?pid=58801&st=&st1=; George W. Bush, Speech to the National Endowment for Democracy, November 6, 2003, American Presidency Project, http://www.presidency.ucsb.edu/ws/index.php?pid=844&st=&st1=.

39. Fred Kaplan, *Daydream Believers: How a Few Grand Ideas Wrecked American Power* (Hoboken, NJ: Wiley, 2008), 32–39.

40. Ivo H. Daadler and James M. Lindsay, *America Unbound: The Bush Revolution in Foreign Policy* (Washington, DC: Brookings Institution Press, 2005), 111.

41. Robert I. Rotberg, *Building a New Afghanistan* (Cambridge, MA: World Peace Foundation; Washington, DC: Brookings Institution Press, 2007), 82–83; Barnett R. Rubin, "Peace Building and State-Building in Afghanistan: Constructing Sovereignty for Whose Security?" *Third World Quarterly* 27, no. 1 (2006): 179.

42. William Maley, *Rescuing Afghanistan* (Sydney: University of New South Wales Press, 2006), 80, 88–89; World Bank, *Afghanistan—State Building, Sustaining Growth, and Reducing Poverty* (Washington, DC: World Bank, 2005), xviii–xix.

43. Rubin, "Peace Building," 182; Maley, *Rescuing Afghanistan*, 53–54.

44. Daadler and Lindsay, *America Unbound*, 111–12; Maley, *Rescuing Afghanistan*, 131–32, 136–37; Rotberg, *Building a New Afghanistan*, 6–7.

45. James Fallows, "Blind into Baghdad," *Atlantic Monthly* 293, no. 1 (2004): 65; Anthony Shadid, *Night Draws Near: Iraq's People in the Shadow of America's War* (New York: Henry Holt, 2005), 7–8.

46. Michael R. Gordon and Bernard E. Trainor, *Cobra II: The Inside Story of the Invasion and Occupation of Iraq* (New York: Pantheon, 2006), 142; John W. Dower, "Occupation: A Warning from History," in *The New American Empire: A 21st-Century Teach-in on U.S. Foreign Policy*, ed. Lloyd C. Gardner and Marilyn B. Young (New York: New Press, 2005), 182–97; Daadler and Lindsay, *America Unbound*, 173.

47. Fallows, "Blind into Baghdad," 56–58, 62, 71–72; Gordon and Trainor, *Cobra II*, 158–59; Thomas E. Ricks, *Fiasco: The American Military Adventure in Iraq* (New York: Penguin, 2006), 64–5.

48. Rajiv Chandrasekaran, *Imperial Life in the Emerald City: Inside Iraq's Green Zone* (New York: Knopf, 2006), 31; Ricks, *Fiasco*, 102–3; Fallows, "Blind into Baghdad," 71–73.

49. Ricks, *Fiasco*, 99, emphasis in original; Kaplan, *Daydream Believers*, 154–56; Harry Harootunian, *The Empire's New Clothes: Paradigm Lost, and Regained* (Chicago: Prickly Paradigm Press, 2004), 59–60.

50. Harper and Clarke, *America Alone*, 223; Ricks, *Fiasco*, 109.

51. Ricks, *Fiasco*, 117, 145; George W. Bush, Address from the USS Abraham Lincoln, May 1, 2003, American Presidency Project, http://www.presidency.ucsb.edu/ws/index.php?pid=68675&st=&st1=.

52. Gordon and Trainor, *Cobra II*, 466–68; Ricks, *Fiasco*, 138–42, 150–51.

53. Ricks, *Fiasco*, 159–65.

54. Chandrasekaran, *Imperial Life*, 163–64, 186–96, 244–48.

55. Ibid., 110–14.

56. Ibid., 115–20; Robert Looney, "The Neoliberal Model's Planned Role in Iraq's Economic Transition," *Strategic Insight* 2 (August 2003), www.ccc.nps.navy.mil/si/aug03/middleeast.asp.

57. Chandrasekaran, *Imperial Life*, 123–24; Anne Ellen Henderson, "The Coalition Provisional Authority's Experience with Economic Reconstruction in Iraq: Lessons Identified," United States Institute of Peace, *Special Report no. 138*, April 2005, www.usip.org/pubs/specialreports/sr138.html.

58. Richard W. Stevenson, "Bush Says Patience Is Needed to Build a Democracy," *New York Times*, May 19, 2005, A12.

59. David M. Herszenhorn, "Estimates of Iraq War Cost Were Not Close to Ballpark," *New York Times*, March 19, 2008, www.nytimes.com/2008/03/19/washington/19cost.html; Iraq Body Count Project, www.iraqbodycount.org/database/.

60. Millikan and Rostow, *Proposal*, 3; Amartya Sen, *Development as Freedom* (New York: Random House, 1999), 295.

Bibliography

Abernethy, David B. *The Dynamics of Global Dominance: European Overseas Empires, 1415–1980.* New Haven, CT: Yale University Press, 2000.

Abrahamian, Ervand. *Iran: Between Two Revolutions.* Princeton, NJ: Princeton University Press, 1982.

Adamson, Michael R. "'The Most Important Single Aspect of Our Foreign Policy?' The Eisenhower Administration, Foreign Aid, and the Third World." In *The Eisenhower Administration, the Third World, and the Globalization of the Cold War,* edited by Kathryn C. Statler and Andrew L. Johns, 47–72. Lanham, MD: Rowman and Littlefield, 2006.

Adas, Michael. *Dominance by Design: Technological Imperatives and America's Civilizing Mission.* Cambridge, MA: Harvard University Press, 2006.

Afkhami, Gholam Reza. *The Life and Times of the Shah.* Berkeley: University of California Press, 2009.

Alexander, Jeffrey. *Twenty Lectures: Sociological Theory since World War II.* New York: Columbia University Press, 1987.

Allison, Roy. *The Soviet Union and the Strategy of Non-Alignment in the Third World.* Cambridge: Cambridge University Press, 1988.

Almond, Gabriel A. *The American People and Foreign Policy.* New York: Praeger, 1960.

——. *The Appeals of Communism.* Princeton, NJ: Princeton University Press, 1954.

——. "A Functional Approach to Comparative Politics." In *The Politics of Developing Areas,* edited by Gabriel A. Almond and James S. Coleman, 3–8. Princeton, NJ: Princeton University Press, 1960.

——. "The Seminar on Comparative Politics, June 1956." *Social Science Research Council Items* 10, no. 4 (1956): 45–48.

Anderson, Robert S., Edwin Levy, and Barrie M. Morrison. *Rice Science and Development Politics: Research Strategies and IRRI's Technologies Confront Asian Diversity, 1950–1980.* Oxford: Oxford University Press, 1991.

Ansari, Ali M. "The Myth of the White Revolution: Mohammad Reza Shah, 'Modernization,' and the Consolidation of Power." *Middle Eastern Studies* 37, no. 3 (2001): 1–24.

Arias, Arturo. "Changing Indian Identity: Guatemala's Violent Transition to Modernity." In *Guatemalan Indians and the State, 1540 to 1988,* edited by Carol A. Smith. Austin: University of Texas Press, 1990.

Arndt, H. W. *Economic Development: The History of an Idea.* Chicago: University of Chicago Press, 1987.

Ayres, Robert L. *Banking on the Poor: The World Bank and World Poverty.* Cambridge, MA: MIT Press, 1983.

Bacevich, Andrew J. *American Empire: The Realities and Consequences of U.S. Diplomacy.* Cambridge, MA: Harvard University Press, 2002.

Badeau, John S. *The American Approach to the Arab World.* New York: Harper and Row, 1968.

Baran, Paul. *The Political Economy of Growth.* New York: Monthly Review, 1957.

Barkan, Elazar. *The Retreat of Scientific Racism: Changing Concepts of Race in Britain and the United States between the World Wars.* Cambridge: Cambridge University Press, 1992.

Bauer, P. T. *Dissent on Development: Studies and Debates in Development Economics.* Cambridge, MA: Harvard University Press, 1972.

——. "Remembrance of Studies Past: Retracing First Steps." In *Pioneers in Development,* edited by Gerald M. Meier and Dudley Seers, 25–43. New York: Oxford University Press, 1984.

Behrens, Susan Fitzpatrick. "From Symbols of the Sacred to Symbols of Subversion to Simply Obscure: Maryknoll Women Religious in Guatemala, 1953–1967." *The Americas* 61, no. 2 (2004): 189–216.

Bell, Daniel, ed. *The Radical Right: The New American Right.* Garden City, NY: Doubleday, 1963.

Berelson, Bernard. "Beyond Family Planning." *Science* 163, no. 3867 (1969): 533–43.

Berger, Mark T. *The Battle for Asia: From Decolonization to Globalization.* London: RoutledgeCurzon, 2004.

Berman, William C. *America's Right Turn: From Nixon to Bush.* Baltimore: Johns Hopkins University Press, 1994.

Bill, James A. *The Eagle and the Lion: The Tragedy of American-Iranian Relations.* New Haven, CT: Yale University Press, 1988.

Blackmer, Donald L. M. *The MIT Center for International Studies: The Founding Years, 1951–1969.* Cambridge, MA: MIT Center for International Studies, 2002.

Borgwardt, Elizabeth. *A New Deal for the World: America's Vision for Human Rights.* Cambridge, MA: Harvard University Press, 2005.

Borlaug, Norman E. "The Green Revolution: For Bread and Peace." *Bulletin of the Atomic Scientists* 27, no. 6 (1971): 6–9, 42–48.

Borstelmann, Thomas. *The Cold War and the Color Line: American Race Relations in the Global Arena.* Cambridge, MA: Harvard University Press, 2001.

Boserup, Ester. *Woman's Role in Economic Development.* London: Allen and Unwin, 1970.

Bradley, Mark Philip. "Franklin Roosevelt, Trusteeship, and US Exceptionalism: Reconsidering the American Vision of Postcolonial Vietnam." In *A Companion to the Vietnam War,* edited by Marilyn Young and Robert Buzzanco, 130–45. Malden, MA: Blackwell, 2002.

——. *Imagining Vietnam and America: The Making of Postcolonial Vietnam, 1919–1950.* Chapel Hill: University of North Carolina Press, 2000.

Brands, H. W. *Bound to Empire: The United States and the Philippines.* New York: Oxford, 1992.

Brazinsky, Gregg. *Nation Building in South Korea: Koreans, Americans, and the Making of a Democracy.* Chapel Hill: University of North Carolina Press, 2007.

Brick, Howard. *Age of Contradiction: American Thought and Culture in the 1960s.* New York: Twayne, 1998.

——. *Transcending Capitalism: Visions of a New Society in Modern American Thought.* Ithaca, NY: Cornell University Press, 2006.

Briggs, Laura. *Reproducing Empire: Race, Sex, Science, and U.S. Imperialism in Puerto Rico.* Berkeley: University of California Press, 2002.

Brockett, Charles D. *Political Movements and Violence in Central America.* Cambridge: Cambridge University Press, 2005.

Brohman, John. "Universalism, Eurocentrism, and Ideological Bias in Development Studies: From Modernisation to Neoliberalism." *Third World Quarterly* 16, no. 1 (1995): 121–40.

Brown, David S. *Richard Hofstadter: An Intellectual Biography.* Chicago: University of Chicago Press, 2006.

Brown, Judith M. *Nehru: A Political Life.* New Haven, CT: Yale University Press, 2003.

Brown, Lester R. "The Agricultural Revolution in Asia." *Foreign Affairs* 46, no. 4 (1968): 688–98.

——. *Building a Sustainable Society.* New York: Norton, 1981.

Brown, Seyom. *The Faces of Power: Constancy and Change in United States Foreign Policy from Truman to Clinton.* New York: Columbia University Press, 1994.

Burns, William J. *Economic Aid and American Policy toward Egypt, 1955–1981.* Albany: State University of New York Press, 1985.

Byrne, Malcolm. "The Road to Intervention: Factors Influencing U.S. Policy toward Iran, 1945–1953." In *Mohammad Mossadeq and the 1953 Coup in Iran,* edited by Mark J. Gasiorowski and Malcolm Byrne, 201–26. Syracuse, NY: Syracuse University Press, 2004.

Candar, Céngiz, and David Pryce-Jones. "Ataturk's Ambiguous Legacy." *Wilson Quarterly* 24 (2000): 88–96.

Carothers, Thomas. "The End of the Transition Paradigm." *Journal of Democracy* 13 (January 2002): 5–21.

Carter, James M. *Inventing Vietnam: The United States and State Building, 1954–1968.* Cambridge: Cambridge University Press, 2008.

Catton, Philip E. "Parallel Agendas: The Ngo Dinh Diem Regime, the United States, and the Strategic Hamlet Program, 1961–1963." PhD diss., Ohio University, 1998.

Chambers, William Nisbet. *Political Parties in a New Nation: The American Experience, 1776–1809.* New York: Oxford University Press, 1963.

Chandler, Robert F. *An Adventure in Applied Science: A History of the International Rice Research Institute.* Manila: International Rice Research Institute, 1982.

Chandrasekaran, Rajiv. *Imperial Life in the Emerald City: Inside Iraq's Green Zone.* New York: Knopf, 2006.

Chenery, Hollis, Montek S. Ahluwalia, C. L. G. Bell, John H. Duloy, and Richard Jolly. *Redistribution with Growth: Policies to Improve Income Distribution in Developing Countries in the Context of Economic Growth.* New York: Oxford University Press, 1974.

Chomsky, Noam. *American Power and the New Mandarins.* New York: Pantheon, 1969.

Citino, Nathan J. "The Ottoman Legacy in Cold War Modernization." *International Journal of Middle East Studies* 40 (November 2008): 579–97.

Coale, Ansley J., and Edgar M. Hoover. *Population Growth and Economic Development in Low-Income Countries: A Case Study of India's Prospects.* Princeton, NJ: Princeton University Press, 1958.

Cohen, Eliot A. "World War IV: Let's Call This Conflict What It Is." *Wall Street Journal,* November 20, 2001.

Cohen, Warren I. *America in the Age of Soviet Power, 1945–1991.* Cambridge: Cambridge University Press, 1993.

——. *America's Failing Empire: U.S. Foreign Relations since the Cold War.* Malden, MA: Blackwell, 2005.

Coleman, James S. "The Political Systems of Developing Areas." In *The Politics of Developing Areas,* edited by Gabriel A. Almond and James S. Coleman, 532–38. Princeton, NJ: Princeton University Press, 1960.

Collins, Robert M. *More: The Politics of Economic Growth in Postwar America.* New York: Oxford University Press, 2000.

Connelly, Matthew. *A Diplomatic Revolution: Algeria's Fight for Independence and the Origins of the Post–Cold War Era.* Oxford: Oxford University Press, 2002.

———. *Fatal Misconception: The Struggle to Control World Population.* Cambridge, MA: Harvard University Press, 2008.

———. "Taking Off the Cold War Lens: Visions of North-South Conflict during the Algerian War for Independence." *American Historical Review* 105, no. 3 (2000): 739–69.

Cullather, Nick. "The Foreign Policy of the Calorie." *American Historical Review* 112 (April 2007): 337–64.

———. "'Fuel for the Good Dragon': The United States and Industrial Policy in Taiwan, 1950–1965." In *Empire and Revolution: The United States and the Third World since 1945,* edited by Peter L. Hahn and Mary Ann Heiss, 242–68. Columbus: Ohio State University Press, 1996.

———. "Miracles of Modernization: The Green Revolution and the Apotheosis of Technology." *Diplomatic History* 28, no. 2 (2004): 227–54.

Daadler, Ivo H., and James M. Lindsay. *America Unbound: The Bush Revolution in Foreign Policy.* Washington, DC: Brookings Institution Press, 2005.

Dalrymple, Dana G. "The Adoption of High-Yielding Grain Varieties in Developing Nations." *Agricultural History* 53, no. 4 (1979): 704–26.

Davis, Kingsley. "The Political Impact of New Population Trends." *Foreign Affairs* 36, no. 2 (1958): 293–301.

———. "Population and the Further Spread of Industrial Society." *Proceedings of the American Philosophical Society* 95, no. 1 (1951): 8–19.

———. "Population Policy: Will Current Programs Succeed?" *Science* 158, no. 802 (1967): 730–39.

———. "The World Demographic Transition." *Annals of the American Academy of Political and Social Science* 237 (January 1945): 1–11.

Demeny, Paul. "On the End of the Population Explosion." *Population and Development Review* 5, no. 1 (1979): 141–62.

———. "Social Science and Population Policy." *Population and Development Review* 14, no. 3 (1988): 451–79.

Deutsch, Karl W., ed. *Ecosocial Systems and Ecopolitics: A Reader on Human and Social Implications of Environmental Management in Developing Countries.* Paris: UNESCO, 1977.

Diamond, Sigmund. *Compromised Campus: The Collaboration of Universities with the Intelligence Community, 1945–1955.* New York: Oxford University Press, 1992.

Donaldson, Peter J. *Nature against Us: The United States and the World Population Crisis, 1965–1980.* Chapel Hill: University of North Carolina Press, 1990.

Donnell, John C., and Gerald C. Hickey. *The Vietnamese "Strategic Hamlets": A Preliminary Report, Memorandum RM-3208-ARPA.* Santa Monica: Rand Corporation, 1962.

Dower, John W. *Embracing Defeat: Japan in the Wake of World War II.* New York: Norton, 1999.

———. "Occupation: A Warning from History." In *The New American Empire: A 21st-Century Teach-in on U.S. Foreign Policy,* edited by Lloyd C. Gardner and Marilyn B. Young, 182–97. New York: New Press, 2005.

Dudziak, Mary L. *Cold War Civil Rights: Race and the Image of American Democracy.* Princeton, NJ: Princeton University Press, 2000.

Duffield, Mark. *Global Governance and the New Wars: The Merging of Development and Security.* London: Zed, 2001.

"Editorial Foreword." *Comparative Studies in Society and History* 20, no. 2 (1978): 175–76.

Ehrman, John. *The Rise of Neoconservatism: Intellectuals and Foreign Affairs, 1945–1994.* New Haven, CT: Yale University Press, 1995.

Ekbladh, David. *The Great American Mission: Modernization and the Construction of an American World Order.* Princeton, NJ: Princeton University Press, 2010.

——. "'Mr. TVA': Grass-Roots Development, David Lilienthal, and the Rise and Fall of the Tennessee Valley Authority as a Symbol for U.S. Overseas Development, 1933–1973." *Diplomatic History* 26, no. 3 (2002): 335–74.

El-Ghonemy, M. Riad. "An Assessment of Egypt's Development Strategy, 1952–1970." In *Rethinking Nasserism: Revolution and Historical Memory in Modern Egypt,* edited by Elie Podeh and Onn Winckler, 253–63. Gainesville: University of Florida Press, 2004.

Engerman, David C. "American Knowledge and Global Power." *Diplomatic History* 31, no. 4 (2007): 599–622.

——. *Modernization from the Other Shore: American Intellectuals and the Romance of Russian Development.* Cambridge, MA: Harvard University Press, 2003.

——. "The Romance of Economic Development and New Histories of the Cold War." *Diplomatic History* 28, no. 1 (2004): 23–54.

——. "West Meets East: The Center for International Studies and Indian Economic Development." In *Staging Growth: Modernization, Development, and the Global Cold War,* edited by Nils Gilman, David Engerman, Mark Haefele, and Michael Latham, 199–223. Amherst: University of Massachusetts Press, 2003.

Engerman, David C., and Corinna R. Unger. "Introduction: Toward a Global History of Modernization." *Diplomatic History* 33, no. 3 (2009): 375–85.

Fall, Bernard. *The Two Viet-Nams: A Political and Military Analysis.* New York: Praeger, 1963.

Fallows, James. "Blind into Baghdad." *Atlantic Monthly* 293, no. 1 (2004): 52–74.

Farazmand, Ali. *The State, Bureaucracy, and Revolution in Modern Iran: Agrarian Reforms and Regime Politics.* New York: Praeger, 1989.

Farber, David. *The Age of Great Dreams: America in the 1960s.* New York: Hill and Wang, 1994.

Farmer, B. H. "Perspectives on the 'Green Revolution' in South Asia." *Modern Asian Studies* 20, no. 1 (1986): 175–99.

Ferris, Jesse. "Soviet Support for Egypt's Intervention in Yemen, 1962–1963." *Journal of Cold War Studies* 10 (Fall 2008): 5–36.

Finnemore, Martha. "Redefining Development at the World Bank." In *International Development and the Social Sciences,* edited by Frederick Cooper and Randall Packard, 203–27. Berkeley: University of California Press, 1997.

Fishel, Wesley R. "Problems of Democratic Growth in Free Vietnam." In *Problems of Freedom: South Vietnam since Independence,* edited by Wesley R. Fishel, 9–28. New York: Free Press, 1961.

Fisher, Christopher T. "The Illusion of Progress: CORDS and the Crisis of Modernization in South Vietnam, 1965–1968." *Pacific Historical Review* 75, no. 1 (1996): 25–51.

Fisher, James T. *Dr. America: The Lives of Thomas A. Dooley, 1927–1961.* Amherst: University of Massachusetts Press, 1997.

Fleitz, Frederick H., Jr. *Peacekeeping Fiascoes of the 1990s: Causes, Solutions, and U.S. Interests.* Westport, CT: Praeger, 2002.

Frank, Andre Gunder. *Latin America: Underdevelopment or Revolution: Essays on the Development of Underdevelopment and the Immediate Enemy.* New York: Monthly Review Press, 1969.

Frank, Charles R., and Mary Baird. "Foreign Aid: Its Speckled Past and Future Prospects." *International Organization* 29, no. 1 (1975): 133–68.

Frankel, Francine R. *India's Political Economy, 1947–1977: The Gradual Revolution.* Princeton, NJ: Princeton University Press, 1978.

Friedman, Milton. *Capitalism and Freedom.* Chicago: University of Chicago Press, 1962.

Friedman, Thomas L. *The Lexus and the Olive Tree: Understanding Globalization.* New York: Random House, 2000.

——. "World War III." Foreign Affairs, *New York Times,* September 13, 2001.

Fukuyama, Francis. *America at the Crossroads: Democracy, Power, and the Neoconservative Legacy.* New Haven, CT: Yale University Press, 2006.

——. "The End of History?" *The National Interest* 16 (Summer 1989): 3–18.

Furlong, William L. "Panama, a Nation Apart: Its Foreign Policy and Its Challenges." In *Post-Invasion Panama: The Challenges of Democratization in the New World Order,* edited by Orlando J. Pérez, 29–56. Lanham, MD: Lexington Books, 2000.

Gasiorowski, Mark J. *U.S. Foreign Policy and the Shah: Building a Client State in Iran.* Ithaca, NY: Cornell University Press, 1991.

Gasiorowski, Mark J., and Malcolm Byrne, eds. *Mohammad Mosaddeq and the 1953 Coup in Iran.* Syracuse, NY: Syracuse University Press, 2004.

Geiger, Roger L. *Research and Relevant Knowledge: American Research Universities since World War II.* New York: Oxford University Press, 1993.

Gendzier, Irene L. *Managing Political Change: Social Scientists and the Third World.* Boulder, CO: Westview, 1985.

Gerhardt, Uta. *Talcott Parsons: An Intellectual Biography.* Cambridge: Cambridge University Press, 2002.

Gerschenkron, Alexander. *Economic Backwardness in Historical Perspective.* Cambridge, MA: Harvard University Press, 1966.

Gilman, Nils. *Mandarins of the Future: Modernization Theory in Cold War America.* Baltimore: Johns Hopkins University Press, 2003.

Go, Julian. "The Chains of Empire: State Building and 'Political Education' in Puerto Rico and the Philippines." In *The American Colonial State in the Philippines: Global Perspectives,* edited by Julian Go and Anne L. Foster, 182–216. Durham, NC: Duke University Press, 2003.

Gocking, Roger S. *The History of Ghana.* Westport, CT: Greenwood Press, 2005.

Goldman, Eric F. *The Crucial Decade: America, 1945–1955.* Westport, CT: Greenwood Press, 1956.

Goode, James F. *The United States and Iran: In the Shadow of Mussadiq.* New York: St. Martin's Press, 1997.

Goodell, Grace. "Conservatism and Foreign Aid." *Policy Review* 19 (Winter 1982): 111–12, 118.

Gopal, S., and Uma Iyengar, eds. *The Essential Writings of Jawaharlal Nehru.* Vol. 2. Oxford: Oxford University Press, 2003.

Gordon, Michael R., and Bernard E. Trainor. *Cobra II: The Inside Story of the Invasion and Occupation of Iraq.* New York: Pantheon, 2006.

Greenhalgh, Susan. "The Social Construction of Population Science: An Intellectual, Institutional, and Political History of Twentieth-Century Demography." *Comparative Studies in Society and History* 38, no. 1 (1996): 26–66.

Guha, Ramachandra. *India after Gandhi: The History of the World's Largest Democracy.* New York: Ecco, 2007.

Gusfield, Joseph R. "Tradition and Modernity: Misplaced Polarities in the Study of Social Change." *American Journal of Sociology* 72 (January 1967): 351–62.

Gwatkin, Davidson R. "Political Will and Family Planning: The Implications of India's Emergency Experience." *Population and Development Review* 5, no. 1 (1979): 29–59.

Halliday, Fred. *Iran: Dictatorship and Development.* 2nd ed. New York: Penguin, 1979.

Halpern, Manfred. *The Politics of Social Change in the Middle East and North Africa.* Princeton, NJ: Princeton University Press, 1963.

Handy, Jim. *Gift of the Devil: A History of Guatemala.* Boston: South End Press, 1984.

Hanhimäki, Jussi, and Odd Arne Westad, eds. *The Cold War: A History in Documents and Eyewitness Accounts.* Oxford: Oxford University Press, 2003.

Haq, Mahbub ul. *The Poverty Curtain: Choices for the Third World.* New York: Columbia University Press, 1976.

Harkavy, Oscar. *Curbing Population Growth: An Insider's Perspective on the Population Movement.* New York: Plenum Press, 1995.

Harootunian, Harry. *The Empire's New Clothes: Paradigm Lost, and Regained.* Chicago: Prickly Paradigm Press, 2004.

Harper, Stefan, and Jonathan Clarke. *America Alone: The Neo-Conservatives and the Global Order.* Cambridge: Cambridge University Press, 2004.

Harrison, James P. *The Endless War: Vietnam's Struggle for Independence.* New York: Columbia University Press, 1989.

Hazell, Peter B. R., and C. Ramasamy. *The Green Revolution Reconsidered: The Impact of High-Yielding Rice Varieties in South India.* Baltimore: Johns Hopkins University Press, 1991.

Henderson, Anne Ellen. "The Coalition Provisional Authority's Experience with Economic Reconstruction in Iraq: Lessons Identified." United States Institute of Peace, *Special Report no. 138,* April 2005, www.usip.org/pubs/specialreports/sr138.html.

Herring, George C. *America's Longest War: The United States and Vietnam, 1950–1975.* 3rd ed. New York: McGraw-Hill, 1996.

Herszenhorn, David M. "Estimates of Iraq War Cost Were Not Close to Ballpark." *New York Times,* March 19, 2008, www.nytimes.com/2008/03/19/washington/19cost.html.

Hettne, Bjorn. *Development Theory and the Three Worlds.* Essex, England: Longman, 1990.

Higham, John. "Beyond Consensus: The Historian as Moral Critic." *American Historical Review* 67, no. 3 (1962): 609–25.

Hippel, Karin von. *Democracy by Force: US Military Intervention in the Post–Cold War World.* Cambridge: Cambridge University Press, 2000.

Hirschman, Albert O. "How the Keynesian Revolution Was Exported from the United States, and Other Comments." In *The Political Power of Economic Ideas: Keynesianism across Nations,* edited by Peter A. Hall. Princeton, NJ: Princeton University Press, 1989.

Hodgson, Dennis. "Demography as Social Science and Policy Science." *Population and Development Review* 9, no. 1 (1983): 1–34.

Hoffman, Stanley. *Chaos and Violence: What Globalization, Failed States, and Terrorism Mean for U.S. Foreign Policy.* Lanham, MD: Rowman and Littlefield, 2006.

Hofstadter, Richard. *The Age of Reform: From Bryan to FDR.* New York: Knopf, 1955.

Hogan, Michael. *The Marshall Plan: America, Britain, and the Reconstruction of Western Europe, 1947–1952.* Cambridge: Cambridge University Press, 1987.

Hollinger, David A. "Cultural Relativism." In *The Cambridge History of Science,* vol. 7, *The Modern Social Sciences,* edited by Theodore Porter and Dorothy Ross, 708–20. Cambridge: Cambridge University Press, 2003.

Hooglund, Eric J. *Land and Revolution in Iran, 1960–1980.* Austin: University of Texas Press, 1982.

Horsman, Reginald. *Race and Manifest Destiny: The Origins of American Racial Anglo-Saxonism.* Cambridge, MA: Harvard University Press, 1981.

Hoselitz, Bert F. *Sociological Aspects of Economic Growth.* New York: Free Press, 1960.

Hunt, Michael. *The American Ascendancy: How the United States Gained and Wielded Global Dominance.* Chapel Hill: University of North Carolina Press, 2007.

Huntington, Samuel P. "The Clash of Civilizations?" *Foreign Affairs* 72 (Summer 1993): 22–49.

———. "Political Development and Political Decay." *World Politics* 17, no. 2 (1965): 386–430.

———. *Political Order in Changing Societies.* New Haven, CT: Yale University Press, 1968.

Hyland, William G. *Clinton's World: Remaking American Foreign Policy.* Westport, CT: Praeger, 1999.

Jacobs, Seth. *America's Miracle Man in Vietnam: Ngo Dinh Diem, Religion, Race, and U.S. Intervention in Southeast Asia, 1950–1957.* Durham, NC: Duke University Press, 2004.

Jaquette, Jane S. "Women and Modernization Theory: A Decade of Feminist Criticism." *World Politics* 34, no. 2 (1982): 267–84.

Jian, Chen. *Mao's China and the Cold War.* Chapel Hill: University of North Carolina Press, 2001.

Jolly, Richard, Louis Emmerij, Dharam Ghai, and Frédéric Lapeyre. *UN Contributions to Development Thinking and Practice.* Bloomington: Indiana University Press, 2004.

Jowitt, Ken. "Rage, Hubris, and Regime Change." *Policy Review* 118 (April/May 2003): 33–42.

Kahin, George McT., Guy J. Pauker, and Lucian W. Pye. "Comparative Politics of Non-Western Countries." *American Political Science Review* 49 (December 1955): 1022–41.

Kaplan, Fred. *Daydream Believers: How a Few Grand Ideas Wrecked American Power.* Hoboken, NJ: Wiley, 2008.

Kaplan, Robert D. "The Coming Anarchy." *Atlantic Monthly* 273, no. 2 (1994): 44–77.

Kaufman, Burton I. *The Arab Middle East and the United States: Inter-Arab Rivalry and Superpower Diplomacy.* New York: Twayne, 1996.

———. *Trade and Aid: Eisenhower's Foreign Economic Policy, 1953–1961.* Baltimore: Johns Hopkins University Press, 1982.

Kaysen, Carl. "The Computer That Printed Out W*O*L*F." *Foreign Affairs* 50 (July 1972): 660–68.

Keddie, Nikki R. *Roots of Revolution: An Interpretive History of Modern Iran.* New Haven, CT: Yale University Press, 1981.

Kennan, George F. "To Prevent a World Wasteland." *Foreign Affairs* 48, no. 3 (1970): 401–13.

Kennedy, John F. *The Strategy of Peace.* New York: Harper and Brothers, 1960.

Killian, James R., Jr. *The Education of a College President.* Cambridge, MA: MIT Press, 1985.

Killick, Tony. *Development Economics in Action: A Study of Economic Policies in Ghana.* London: Heinemann, 1978.

Kinzer, Stephen. *All the Shah's Men: An American Coup and the Roots of Middle East Terror.* Hoboken, NJ: Wiley, 2003.

Kirk, Dudley. "Population Changes in the Postwar World." *American Sociological Review* 9, no. 1 (1944): 28–35.

Kirkpatrick, Jeanne. "Dictatorships and Double Standards." *Commentary* 68 (November 1979): 34–45.

Klein, Christina. *Cold War Orientalism: Asia in the Middlebrow Imagination, 1945–1961.* Berkeley: University of California Press, 2003.

Kloppenberg, Jack Ralph, Jr. *First the Seed: The Political Economy of Plant Biotechnology, 1492–2000.* Cambridge: Cambridge University Press, 1988.

Knock, Thomas J. *To End All Wars: Woodrow Wilson and the Quest for a New World Order.* Princeton, NJ: Princeton University Press, 1992.

Kothari, Rajni. *Politics in India.* Boston: Little, Brown, 1970.

Kramer, Paul A. *The Blood of Government: Race, Empire, the United States, and the Philippines.* Chapel Hill: University of North Carolina Press, 2006.

Kristol, William, and Robert Kagan. "The Present Danger." *The National Interest* 59 (Spring 2000): 57–69.

——. "Toward a Neo-Reaganite Foreign Policy." *Foreign Affairs* 75, no. 4 (1996): 18–32.

Kunz, Diane. *Butter and Guns: America's Cold War Economic Diplomacy.* New York: Free Press, 1997.

Kuzmarov, Jeremy. "Modernizing Repression: Police Training, Political Violence, and Nation-Building in the 'American Century.'" *Diplomatic History* 33 (April 2009): 191–221.

LaFeber, Walter. *Inevitable Revolutions: The United States in Central America.* New York: Norton, 1984.

Lake, Anthony. "Confronting Backlash States." *Foreign Affairs* 73, no. 2 (1994): 45–55.

Lang, James. *Feeding a Hungry Planet: Rice, Research, and Development in Asia and Latin America.* Chapel Hill: University of North Carolina Press, 1996.

Lasswell, Harold D. "The Policy Orientation." In *The Policy Sciences,* edited by Daniel Lerner and Harold D. Lasswell, 3–15. Stanford, CA: Stanford University Press, 1951.

——. *World Politics and Personal Insecurity.* New York: McGraw-Hill, 1935.

Latham, Michael E. *Modernization as Ideology: American Social Science and "Nation Building" in the Kennedy Era.* Chapel Hill: University of North Carolina Press, 2000.

——. "Redirecting the Revolution? The USA and the Failure of Nation-Building in South Vietnam." *Third World Quarterly* 27, no. 1 (2006): 27–41.

——. "W. Arthur Lewis." In *The American National Biography,* edited by John A. Garraty and Marc C. Carnes, 13: 609–11. New York: Oxford University Press, 1999.

Lawrence, Mark Atwood. *Assuming the Burden: Europe and the American Commitment to War in Vietnam.* Berkeley: University of California Press, 2005.

Leaf, Murray J. "The Green Revolution and Cultural Change in a Punjab Village, 1965–1978." *Economic Development and Cultural Change* 31, no. 2 (1983): 227–70.

——. *Man, Mind, and Science: A History of Anthropology.* New York: Columbia University Press, 1979.

Leffler, Melvyn. "9/11 and American Foreign Policy." *Diplomatic History* 29 (June 2005): 395–413.

Lerner, Daniel. *The Passing of Traditional Society: Modernizing the Middle East.* 1958. New York: Free Press, 1964.

Lerner, Max. *America as a Civilization: Life and Thought in the United States Today.* New York: Simon and Schuster, 1957.

Levinson, Jerome, and Juan de Onís. *The Alliance That Lost Its Way.* Chicago: Quadrangle Books, 1970.

Lewis, W. Arthur. "Economic Development with Unlimited Supplies of Labor." *Manchester School* 22 (May 1954): 139–91.

Lichtenstein, Nelson. "Market Triumphalism and Wishful Liberals." In *Cold War Triumphalism: The Misuse of History after the Fall of Communism,* edited by Ellen Schrecker, 103–25. New York: Free Press, 2004.

Lipset, Seymour Martin. *The First New Nation: The United States in Historical and Comparative Perspective.* New York: Basic Books, 1963.

Little, Douglas. *American Orientalism: The United States and the Middle East since 1945.* Chapel Hill: University of North Carolina Press, 2002.

———. "From Even-Handed to Empty-Handed: Seeking Order in the Middle East." In *Kennedy's Quest for Victory: American Foreign Policy, 1961–1963,* edited by Thomas G. Paterson, 156–77. New York: Oxford University Press, 1989.

———. "The New Frontier on the Nile: JFK, Nasser, and Arab Nationalism." *Journal of American History* 75, no. 2 (1998): 501–27.

Little, Ian M. D. *Economic Development: Theory, Policy, and International Relations.* New York: Basic Books, 1982.

Litwak, Robert S. *Regime Change: U.S. Strategy through the Prism of 9/11.* Washington, DC: Woodrow Wilson Center Press, 2007.

Looney, Robert. "The Neoliberal Model's Planned Role in Iraq's Economic Transition." *Strategic Insight* 2 (August 2003), www.ccc.nps.navy.mil/si/aug03/middleeast.asp.

Louis, William Roger, and Ronald Robinson. "The Imperialism of Decolonization." *Journal of Imperial and Commonwealth History* 22, no. 3 (1994): 462–511.

Luce, Henry R. *The American Century.* New York: Farrar and Rinehardt, 1941.

Mahoney, Richard D. *JFK: Ordeal in Africa.* New York: Oxford University Press, 1983.

Maley, William. *Rescuing Afghanistan.* Sydney: University of New South Wales Press, 2006.

Mamdani, Mahmood. *The Myth of Population Control: Family, Caste, and Class in an Indian Village.* New York: Monthly Review Press, 1972.

Mandelbaum, Michael. "Foreign Policy as Social Work." *Foreign Affairs* 75, no. 1 (1996): 16–32.

Matusow, Allen J. *The Unraveling of America: A History of Liberalism in the 1960s.* New York: Harper and Row, 1984.

May, Ernest R., ed. *American Cold War Strategy: Interpreting NSC-68.* New York: Beford Books, 1993.

May, Glenn Anthony. *Social Engineering in the Philippines: The Aims, Execution, and Impact of American Colonial Policy, 1900–1913.* Westport, CT: Greenwood Press, 1980.

May, Rachel. *Terror in the Countryside: Campesino Responses to Political Violence in Guatemala, 1954–1985.* Athens, OH: Ohio University Center for International Studies, 2001.

Mayall, James. "Introduction." In *United Nations Interventionism, 1991–2004,* edited by Mats Berdal and Spyros Economides, 1–31. Cambridge: Cambridge University Press, 2007.

Mayer, Albert, and associates, in collaboration w/ McKim Marriott and Richard L. Park. *Pilot Project, India: The Story of Rural Development at Etawah, Uttar Pradesh.* Berkeley: University of California Press, 1958.

Mazrui, Ali A. "From Social Darwinism to Current Theories of Modernization: A Tradition of Analysis." *World Politics* 21 (October 1968): 69–83.

McClintock, Michael. *The American Connection.* Vol. 2, *State Terror and Popular Resistance in Guatemala.* London: Zed, 1985.

McMahon, Robert J. *The Cold War on the Periphery: The United States, India, and Pakistan.* New York: Columbia University Press, 1994.

———. "Eisenhower and Third World Nationalism: A Critique of the Revisionists." *Political Science Quarterly* 101, no. 3 (1986): 453–73.

———. *Major Problems in the History of the Vietnam War.* 3rd ed. Boston: Houghton Mifflin, 2003.

McNamara, Robert S. *The McNamara Years at the World Bank: Major Policy Addresses of Robert S. McNamara, 1968–1981.* Baltimore: Johns Hopkins University Press, 1981.

McNeill, J. R. *Something New under the Sun: An Environmental History of the Twentieth-Century World.* New York: Norton, 2000.

Meadows, Donella H., Dennis L. Meadows, Jorgen Randers, and William W. Behrens III. *The Limits to Growth: A Report for the Club of Rome's Project on the Predicament of Mankind.* New York: Universe Books, 1972.

Mearsheimer, John J. "Back to the Future: Instability in Europe after the Cold War." *International Security* 15, no. 1 (1990): 5–56.

Meier, Gerald M. "The Formative Period." In *Pioneers of Development,* edited by Gerald M. Meier and Dudley Seers, 1–26. New York: Oxford University Press, 1984.

Meriwether, James. "'A Torrent Running over Everything': Africa and the Eisenhower Administration." In *The Eisenhower Administration, the Third World, and the Globalization of the Cold War,* edited by Kathryn C. Statler and Andrew L. Johns, 175–96. Lanham, MD: Rowman and Littlefield, 2006.

Merrill, Dennis. *Bread and the Ballot: The United States and India's Economic Development, 1947–1963.* Chapel Hill: University of North Carolina Press, 1990.

Millikan, Max, and W. W. Rostow. *A Proposal: Key to an Effective Foreign Policy.* New York: Harper and Brothers, 1957.

Mills, C. Wright. *The Sociological Imagination.* New York: Oxford University Press, 1959.

Mitchell, Timothy. *Rule of Experts: Egypt, Techno-Politics, Modernity.* Berkeley: University of California Press, 2002.

Mufti, Malik. "The United States and Nasserist Pan-Arabism." In *The Middle East and the United States: A Historical and Political Reassessment,* edited by David W. Lesch, 141–60. Boulder, CO: Westview, 2007.

Muravchik, Joshua. "Losing the Peace." *Commentary* 94, no. 1 (1992): 37–42.

Nasser, Gamal Abdel. "The Egyptian Revolution." *Foreign Affairs* 33, no. 2 (1955): 199–211.

———. *The Philosophy of the Revolution.* Translated by Dar Al-Maaref. Buffalo: Economica Books, 1959.

Needell, Allan A. "'Truth Is Our Weapon': Project TROY, Political Warfare, and Government-Academic Relations in the National Security State." *Diplomatic History* 17 (Summer 1993): 399–420.

Nehru, Jawaharlal. *The Discovery of India.* New York: John Day, 1946.

Niazi, Tarique. "Rural Poverty and the Green Revolution: The Lessons from Pakistan." *Journal of Peasant Studies* 31, no. 2 (2004): 242–60.

Nighswonger, William A. *Rural Pacification in Vietnam.* New York: Praeger, 1966.

Ninkovich, Frank. *Modernity and Power: A History of the Domino Theory in the Twentieth Century.* Chicago: University of Chicago Press, 1994.

———. "The Rockefeller Foundation, China, and Cultural Change." *Journal of American History* 70, no. 4 (1984): 799–820.

———. *The United States and Imperialism.* Malden, MA: Blackwell, 2001.

———. *The Wilsonian Century: U.S. Foreign Policy since 1900.* Chicago: University of Chicago Press, 1999.

Nisbet, Robert A. *Social Change and History: Aspects of the Western Theory of Development.* New York: Oxford University Press, 1969.

Nkrumah, Kwame. "African Prospect." *Foreign Affairs* 37, no. 1 (1958): 45–53.

———. *Ghana: The Autobiography of Kwame Nkrumah.* New York: International Publishers, 1957.

Noer, Thomas J. "The New Frontier and African Neutralism: Kennedy, Nkrumah, and the Volta River Project." *Diplomatic History* 8, no. 1 (1984): 61–79.

Notestein, Frank W. "Population—The Long View." In *Food for the World,* edited by Theodore W. Schultz, 36–57. Chicago: University of Chicago Press, 1945.

——. "The Reduction of Human Fertility as an Aid to Programs of Economic Development in Densely Settled Agrarian Regions." In *Modernization Programs in Relation to Human Resources and Population Problems,* edited by Milbank Memorial Fund, 89–100. New York: Milbank Memorial Fund, 1950.

Nwaubani, Ebere. "Eisenhower, Nkrumah, and the Congo Crisis." *Journal of Contemporary History* 36, no. 4 (2001): 599–622.

——. *The United States and Decolonization in West Africa, 1950–1960.* Rochester, NY: University of Rochester Press, 2001.

O'Connor, Alice. *Poverty Knowledge: Social Science, Social Policy, and the Poor in Twentieth-Century U.S. History.* Princeton, NJ: Princeton University Press, 2001.

Olson, James S., and Randy Roberts. *Where the Domino Fell: America and Vietnam, 1945–1990.* New York: St. Martin's Press, 1991.

Oren, Ido. *Our Enemies and US: America's Rivalries and the Making of Political Science.* Ithaca, NY: Cornell University Press, 2003.

Osei, Akwasi P. *Ghana: Recurrence and Change in a Post-Independence African State.* New York: Peter Lang, 1999.

Paine, Thomas. *Common Sense.* Mineola, NY: Dover, 1997.

Palmer, Ingrid. "Rural Women and the Basic Needs Approach to Development." *International Labour Review* 115, no. 1 (1977): 97–107.

Parayil, Govindan. "The Green Revolution in India: A Case Study of Technological Change." *Technology and Culture* 33, no. 4 (1992): 737–56.

Parker, Jason C. "Small Victory, Missed Chance: The Eisenhower Administration, the Bandung Conference, and the Turning Point of the Cold War." In *The Eisenhower Administration, the Third World, and the Globalization of the Cold War,* edited by Kathryn C. Statler and Andrew L. Johns, 153–74. Lanham, MD: Rowman and Littlefield, 2006.

Parsons, Talcott. "Democracy and Social Structure in Pre-Nazi Germany." In *Essays in Sociological Theory,* edited by Talcott Parsons, 104–23. New York: Free Press, 1964.

——. *Structure and Process in Modern Societies.* New York: Free Press, 1960.

Parsons, Talcott, and Edward Shils. *Towards a General Theory of Action.* Cambridge, MA: Harvard University Press, 1951.

Paterson, Thomas G. "Foreign Aid under Wraps: The Point Four Program." *Wisconsin Magazine of History* 56, no. 2 (1972): 122–25.

Pearce, Kimber Charles. *Rostow, Kennedy, and the Rhetoric of Foreign Aid.* East Lansing: Michigan State University Press, 2001.

Pérez, Louis A., Jr. *Cuba under the Platt Amendment, 1902–1934.* Pittsburgh: University of Pittsburgh Press, 1986.

Pérez, Orlando J. "Democratization and Economic Development: Challenges and Opportunities for the Next Century." In *Post-Invasion Panama: The Challenges of Democratization in the New World Order,* edited by Orlando J. Pérez, 147–54. Lanham, MD: Lexington Books, 2000.

Perkins, John H. *Geopolitics and the Green Revolution: Wheat, Genes, and the Cold War.* New York: Oxford University Press, 1997.

Piotrow, Phyllis Tilson. *World Population Crisis: The United States Response.* New York: Praeger, 1973.

Popp, Roland. "An Application of Modernization Theory during the Cold War? The Case of Pahlavi Iran." *International History Review* 30, no. 1 (2008): 76–98.

——. "Benign Intervention? The Kennedy Administration's Push for Reform in Iran." In *John F. Kennedy and the "Thousand Days,"* edited by Manfred Berg and Andreas Etges, 197–219. Heidelberg: Universitätsverlag Winter, 2007.

Potter, David M. *People of Plenty: Economic Abundance and the American Character.* Chicago: University of Chicago Press, 1954.

Prakash, Gyan. *Another Reason: Science and the Imagination of Modern India.* Princeton, NJ: Princeton University Press, 1999.

Prebisch, Raúl. "Five Stages in My Thinking on Development." In *Pioneers in Development,* edited by Gerald M. Meier and Dudley Seers, 173–91. New York: Oxford University Press, 1984.

Purcell, Edward A., Jr. *The Crisis of Democratic Theory: Scientific Naturalism and the Problem of Value.* Lexington: University Press of Kentucky, 1973.

Pye, Lucian. *Aspects of Political Development.* Boston: Little, Brown, 1966.

——. *Guerrilla Communism in Malaya: Its Social and Political Meaning.* Princeton, NJ: Princeton University Press, 1956.

——. "Political Modernization and Research on the Process of Political Socialization." *Social Science Research Council Items* 13, no. 3 (1959): 25–28.

——. "Political Science and the Crisis of Authoritarianism." *American Political Science Review* 84, no. 1 (1990): 3–19.

Rabe, Stephen G. *Eisenhower and Latin America: The Foreign Policy of Anticommunism.* Chapel Hill: University of North Carolina Press, 1988.

——. *The Most Dangerous Area in the World: John F. Kennedy Confronts Communist Revolution in Latin America.* Chapel Hill: University of North Carolina Press, 1999.

Race, Jeffrey. *War Comes to Long An: Revolutionary Conflict in a Vietnamese Province.* Berkeley: University of California Press, 1972.

Rafael, Vicente L. "White Love: Surveillance and Nationalist Resistance in the U.S. Colonization of the Philippines." In *Cultures of United States Imperialism,* edited by Amy Kaplan and Donald Pease, 185–218. Durham, NC: Duke University Press, 1993.

Rao, K. Raghavendra. *Society, Culture, and Population Policy in India.* Delhi: Ajanta, 1989.

Ravenholt, R. T. "The A.I.D. Population and Family Planning Program—Goals, Scope, and Progress." *Demography* 5, no. 2 (1968): 561–73.

Reed, James. *From Private Vice to Public Virtue: The Birth Control Movement and American Society since 1830.* New York: Basic Books, 1978.

Renda, Mary A. *Taking Haiti: Military Occupation and the Culture of U.S. Imperialism, 1915–1940.* Chapel Hill: University of North Carolina Press, 2001.

Rice, Condoleezza. "Promoting the National Interest." *Foreign Affairs* 79, no. 1 (2000): 45–62.

Ricks, Thomas E. *Fiasco: The American Military Adventure in Iraq.* New York: Penguin, 2006.

Rist, Gilbert. *The History of Development: From Western Origins to Global Faith.* London: Zed, 1997.

Rogin, Michael. *The Intellectuals and McCarthy: The Radical Specter.* Cambridge, MA: MIT Press, 1967.

Rooney, David. *Kwame Nkrumah: The Political Kingdom in the Third World.* New York: St. Martin's Press, 1988.

Rosen, George. *Western Economists and Eastern Societies: Agents of Change in South Asia, 1950–1970.* Baltimore: Johns Hopkins University Press, 1985.

Rosenberg, Emily. *Financial Missionaries to the World: The Politics and Culture of Dollar Diplomacy, 1900–1930.* Durham, NC: Duke University Press, 2003.

Rosenstein-Rodan, Paul N. "Natura Facit Saltum: Analysis of the Disequilibrium Growth Process." In *Pioneers of Development*, edited by Gerald M. Meier and Dudley Seers, 207–21. New York: Oxford University Press, 1984.

Rostow, W. W. "Countering Guerrilla Attack." In *Modern Guerrilla Warfare: Fighting Communist Guerrilla Movements, 1941–1961*, edited by Franklin Mark Osanka, 464–71. New York: Free Press, 1962.

———. "Development: The Political Economy of the Marshallian Long Period." In *Pioneers of Development*, edited by Gerald M. Meier and Dudley Seers, 229–61. New York: Oxford University Press, 1984.

———. *The Diffusion of Power: An Essay in Recent History.* New York: Macmillan, 1972.

———. "Marx Was a City Boy, or Why Communism May Fail." *Harper's Magazine* 210 (February 1955): 25–30.

———. *The Stages of Economic Growth: A Non-Communist Manifesto.* Cambridge: Cambridge University Press, 1960.

Rotberg, Robert I. *Building a New Afghanistan.* Cambridge, MA: World Peace Foundation; Washington, DC: Brookings Institution Press, 2007.

Rotter, Andrew J. *Comrades at Odds: The United States and India, 1947–1964.* Ithaca, NY: Cornell University Press, 2000.

Rubin, Barnett R. "Peace Building and State-Building in Afghanistan: Constructing Sovereignty for Whose Security?" *Third World Quarterly* 27, no. 1 (2006): 175–85.

Rubin, Barry. *Paved with Good Intentions: The American Experience in Iran.* New York: Oxford University Press, 1980.

Rubinstein, Alvin Z., Albina Shayevich, and Boris Zlotnikov, eds. *The Clinton Foreign Policy Reader: Presidential Speeches with Commentary.* Armonk, NY: M. E. Sharpe, 2000.

Russett, Bruce. *Grasping the Democratic Peace: Principles for a Post–Cold War World.* Princeton, NJ: Princeton University Press, 1993.

Sackley, Nicole. "Passage to Modernity: American Social Scientists, India, and the Pursuit of Development, 1945–1961." PhD diss., Princeton University, 2004.

Schlesinger, Arthur M., Jr. *The Vital Center.* Boston: Houghton Mifflin, 1949.

Schmitz, David F. *The United States and Right-Wing Dictatorships.* Cambridge: Cambridge University Press, 2006.

Schrecker, Ellen. "Introduction: Cold War Triumphalism and the Real Cold War." In *Cold War Triumphalism: The Misuse of History after the Fall of Communism*, edited by Ellen Schrecker, 1–26. New York: New Press, 2004.

Schulman, Bruce J., ed. *Lyndon B. Johnson and American Liberalism: A Brief Biography with Documents.* Boston: Bedford, 1995.

Schultz, Theodore W. *Transforming Traditional Agriculture.* New Haven, CT: Yale University Press, 1964.

Schulzinger, Robert D. *A Time for War: The United States and Vietnam, 1941–1975.* New York: Oxford University Press, 1997.

Schumacher, E. F. *Small Is Beautiful: Economics as If People Mattered.* New York: Harper and Row, 1973.

Schusky, Ernest L. *Culture and Agriculture: An Ecological Introduction to Traditional and Modern Farming Systems.* New York: Bergin and Garvey, 1989.

Schuster, Ilsa. "Recent Research on Women in Development: Review Article." *Journal of Development Studies* 18, no. 4 (1982): 511–35.

Scott, Catherine V. *Gender and Development: Rethinking Modernization and Dependency Theory.* Boulder, CO: Lynne Rienner, 1995.

Seers, Dudley. "What Are We Trying to Measure?" *Journal of Development Studies* 8, no. 3 (1972): 21–36.

Sela, Avraham. "Abd al-Nasser's Regional Politics: A Reassessment." In *Rethinking Nasserism: Revolution and Historical Memory in Modern Egypt*, edited by Elie Podeh and Onn Winckler, 179–204. Gainesville: University Press of Florida, 2004.

Sen, Amartya. *Development as Freedom*. New York: Random House, 1999.

Shadid, Anthony. *Night Draws Near: Iraq's People in the Shadow of America's War*. New York: Henry Holt, 2005.

Shapley, Deborah. *Promise and Power: The Life and Times of Robert McNamara*. Boston: Little, Brown, 1993.

Sharpless, John. "Population Science, Private Foundations, and Development Aid: The Transformation of Demographic Knowledge in the United States, 1945–1965." In *International Development and the Social Sciences: Essays on the History and Politics of Knowledge*, edited by Frederick Cooper and Randall Packard, 176–200. Berkeley: University of California Press, 1997.

Sherry, Michael S. *In the Shadow of War: The United States since the 1930s*. New Haven, CT: Yale University Press, 1995.

Shils, Edward. "The Military in the Political Development of the New States." In *The Role of the Military in Underdeveloped Countries*, edited by John J. Johnson, 7–67. Princeton, NJ: Princeton University Press, 1962.

——. "On the Comparative Study of the New States." In *Old Societies and New States: The Quest for Modernity in Africa and Asia*, edited by Clifford Geertz, 1–26. New York: Free Press, 1963.

Shiva, Vandana. *The Violence of the Green Revolution: Third World Agriculture, Ecology, and Politics*. London: Zed Books, 1991.

Shultz, Richard H., Jr. *In the Aftermath of War: US Support for Reconstruction and Nation-Building in Panama Following Just Cause*. Maxwell Air Force Base, AL: Air University Press, 1993.

Siekmeier, James F. "'The Most Generous Assistance': U.S. Economic Aid to Guatemala and Bolivia, 1944–1959." *Journal of American and Canadian Studies* 11 (1993): 1–47.

Simpson, Bradley R. *Economists with Guns: Authoritarian Development and U.S.-Indonesian Relations, 1960–1968*. Stanford, CA: Stanford University Press, 2008.

Simpson, Christopher. *Science of Coercion: Communication Research and Psychological Warfare, 1945–1960*. New York: Oxford University Press, 1994.

——, ed. *Universities and Empire: Money and Politics in the Social Sciences during the Cold War*. New York: Free Press, 1998.

Smith, Peter H. *Talons of the Eagle: Dynamics of U.S.-Latin American Relations*. New York: Oxford University Press, 1996.

Smith, Tony. *A Pact with the Devil: Washington's Bid for World Supremacy and the Betrayal of the American Promise*. New York: Routledge, 2007.

Solomon, Robert. *The Transformation of the World Economy*. 2nd ed. New York: St. Martin's, 1999.

Sorensen, Theodore, ed. *"Let the Word Go Forth": The Speeches, Statements, and Writings of John F. Kennedy, 1947–1963*. New York: Laurel, 1988.

"A Special Place." *The Economist*, July 18, 1987, 12.

Springhall, John. *Decolonization since 1945: The Collapse of European Overseas Empires*. Houndmills, UK: Palgrave, 2001.

Srinivas, M. N. *Social Change in Modern India*. Berkeley: University of California Press, 1966.

Staples, Amy L. S. *The Birth of Development: How the World Bank, Food and Agriculture Organization, and the World Health Organization Changed the World, 1945–1965*. Kent, OH: Kent State University Press, 2006.

Steel, Ronald. *Temptations of a Superpower.* Cambridge, MA: Harvard University Press, 1995.

Stevenson, Richard W. "Bush Says Patience Is Needed to Build a Democracy." *New York Times,* May 19, 2005.

Streeter, Stephen M. "The Failure of 'Liberal Developmentalism': The United States's Anti-Communist Showcase in Guatemala, 1954–1960." *International History Review* 21, no. 2 (1999): 386–413.

———. *Managing the Counterrevolution: The United States and Guatemala, 1954–1961.* Athens, OH: Ohio University Center for International Studies, 2000.

———. "Nation-Building in the Land of Eternal Counterinsurgency: Guatemala and the Contradictions of the Alliance for Progress." *Third World Quarterly* 27, no. 1 (2006): 57–68.

Sun, Yat-Sen. *The International Development of China.* 2nd ed. Chungking: China Publishing, 1941.

Szreter, Simon. "The Idea of Demographic Transition and the Study of Fertility Change: A Critical Intellectual History." *Population and Development Review* 19, no. 4 (1993): 659–701.

Thompson, Robert. *Defeating Communist Insurgency: Experiences from Malaya and Vietnam.* London: Chatto and Windus, 1966.

Thompson, W. Scott. *Ghana's Foreign Policy, 1957–1966: Diplomacy, Ideology, and the New State.* Princeton, NJ: Princeton University Press, 1969.

Tipps, Dean C. "Modernization Theory and the Comparative Study of Societies: A Critical Perspective." *Comparative Studies in Society and History* 15 (March 1973): 199–226.

Tomes, Robert R. *Apocalypse Then: American Intellectuals and the Vietnam War, 1954–1975.* New York: New York University Press, 1998.

Toye, John. *Dilemmas of Development: Reflections on the Counter-Revolution in Development Theory and Policy.* Oxford: Blackwell, 1987.

U.S. Congress, House, Committee on Foreign Affairs. *Regional and Other Documents concerning United States Relations with Latin America.* Washington, DC: U.S. Government Printing Office, 1962.

U.S. Department of State. *Foreign Relations of the United States.* Washington, DC: Government Printing Office, 1949–2000.

"The U.S. Recovery Has Four Asian Nations Roaring Back." *Business Week,* June 25, 1984, 42.

Wahba, Mourad Magdi. *The Role of the State in the Egyptian Economy, 1945–1981.* Reading, UK: Ithaca Press, 1994.

Wall, Irwin M. *France, the United States, and the Algerian War.* Berkeley: University of California Press, 2001.

Wallerstein, Immanuel. "Modernization: Requiescat in Pace." In *The Capitalist World Economy,* edited by Immanuel Wallerstein, 132–37. Cambridge: Cambridge University Press, 1979.

———. "The Rise and Demise of the Capitalist World System: Concepts for Comparative Analysis." In *The Essential Wallerstein,* edited by Immanuel Wallerstein, 71–105. New York: New Press, 2000.

Ward, Barbara, J. D. Runnalls, and Lenore D'Anjou, eds. *The Widening Gap: Development in the 1970s.* New York: Columbia University Press, 1971.

Warwick, Donald P. *Bitter Pills: Population Policies and Their Implementation in Eight Developing Countries.* Cambridge: Cambridge University Press, 1982.

Westad, Odd Arne. *The Global Cold War: Third World Interventions and the Making of Our Times.* Cambridge: Cambridge University Press, 2005.

"Where Reds May Take Over Next in Latin America." *U.S. News and World Report,* March 18, 1963, 50.

Whitaker, C. S., Jr. "A Dysrhythmic Process of Political Change." *World Politics* 19, no. 2 (1967): 190–217.

Wiarda, Howard J. "Toward the Future: Old and New Directions in Comparative Politics." In *New Directions in Comparative Politics,* edited by Howard J. Wiarda, 221–50. Boulder, CO: Westview, 1991.

Wiegersma, Nancy. *Vietnam: Peasant Land, Peasant Revolution.* New York: St. Martin's Press, 1988.

Wood, Robert C. "The Future of Modernization." In *Modernization: The Dynamics of Growth,* edited by Myron Weiner, 40–52. New York: Basic Books, 1966.

World Bank. *Afghanistan—State Building, Sustaining Growth, and Reducing Poverty.* Washington, DC: World Bank, 2005.

——. *The East Asian Miracle: Economic Growth and Public Policy.* New York: Oxford University Press, 1993.

——. *Population Planning Sector Working Paper.* New York: World Bank, 1972.

World Commission on Environment and Development. *Our Common Future.* Oxford: Oxford University Press, 1987.

Wyon, John B., and John E. Gordon. *The Khanna Study: Population Problems in the Rural Punjab.* Cambridge, MA: Harvard University Press, 1971.

Yaqub, Salim. *Containing Arab Nationalism: The Eisenhower Doctrine and the Middle East.* Chapel Hill: University of North Carolina Press, 2004.

Yergin, Daniel, and Joseph Stanislaw. *The Commanding Heights: The Battle between Government and the Marketplace That Is Remaking the Modern World.* New York: Simon and Schuster, 1998.

— "modernizing" developing
world has been for self-interest
instead of claimed altruism (p. 123)

— US foreign policy naturally protected
"interests"
  guised under "modernization" and
  development

— contradictory — @ same time as
Civil Rights Movement in U.S.A.

— development must come
  from within — ownership

Index